for Martha
& Ernie
from Charlie
& John

HARMONICS
OF
HISTORY

HARMONICS
OF
HISTORY

by

John P. Sedgwick, Jr.

Philosophical Library
New York

Library of Congress Cataloging in Publication Data

Sedgwick, John P.
   Harmonics of History.

   1. Astrology.   2. Symbolism of numbers.   3. History—
Miscellanea.   I. Title.
BF1729.H57S43   1985   133.5'89   83-24309
ISBN 0-8022-2455-5

Copyright 1985, by Philosophical Library, Inc.
200 West 57th Street, New York, N.Y. 10019
All rights reserved.
Manufactured in the United States of America.

For my Father and Mother

Preface

What follows is a study of certain configurations demonstrable in cultural history. Such configurations are of interest in themselves, and may also be of value in estimating the potential character of coming developments. But it must further be asked whether these configurations have meaning or value as entities. An answer lies in the correlation between their functions and the traditional values of astrological or numerological entities.

It must be made clear at the start that this study is not the application of astrology or numerology to history: rather it is the search for principles underlying various aspects of history. Such principles appear, however, to be remarkably similar to certain relationships found in the operation of planets, signs, and numbers. That is to say, rather than finding that astrological or numerological principles apply to history, it is found that certain principles of order and organization are detectable in history, and that these principles may be expressed in astrological or numerological terms for the sake of elucidation and comparison.

The principles themselves are greater and more basic than the astrological signs, planetary correlations, or numerological qualities. Since they touch upon the absolute, we may never know them in their

viii   HARMONICS OF HISTORY

[margin: hint of abs. real. — harm., propor — etc. style in art — evidence]

intrinsic identities. (But aspects of these principles are revealed in ratios and harmonies, proportions and equations, each of which gives a hint, at least, of absolute reality.) As in art and in science, so in history, wherever harmonic principles are manifested they may be taken to reveal something of the inner process of creation.

The evidence presented in this study is taken from various fields of cultural activity—political, religious, social, philosophical, scientific, literary—depending in considerable part on the character of a given period. Particular emphasis, however, has been placed on style in the visual arts, which have the advantage of providing very concrete evidence. Flinders Petrie (an archeologist) noted that styles in art are the most sensitive indicator of the profiles and stages of civilizations; and Rushton Coulborn (a prehistorian) found that the "style of human societies is worked up most dramatically in their fine arts—the finer, the more dramatic, the more powerful in effect."

[margin: prehistorian - before ?]

Contents

Preface — vii

Introduction — xiii

Acknowledgments — xix

I. The Structure of a Major Culture — 1

    A. The Overall Span — 1
    B. Dating of the Evolutionary Centuries — 9
    C. The Centuries by Astrological Sign — 29

II. The Major Cultures by Sign — 57

    A. The African Culture — 62
    B. The Indus Valley Culture — 64
    C. The Babylonian Culture — 66
    D. The Egyptian Culture — 69
    E. The Chinese Culture — 73

	F. The Indian Culture	76
	G. The Classical Culture	79
	H. The Levantine Culture	95
	I. The Ancient American Culture	102
	J. The Western Culture	106
	K. The Russian Culture	118
III.	Dating of the Russian Culture	123
	A. Inaugurations	130
	1. The Ten-century Germinative	130
	2. The 640-year Inauguration	133
	B. Anticipations	135
	1. The 110-year Anticipation	135
	2. The Quarter Century Marks	140
	3. The Quarter Marks in Russia	152
	C. Overlaps	156
	1. The Four-century Overlap	156
	2. The Two-century Overlap	164
	D. The Meaning of Numbers	170
IV.	The Astrological Month	174
	Bibliography	201
	Index	209

List of Plates

		page
I.	Degas. *La Toilette*.	27
II.	Degas. *Le Tub*.	28
III.	Greek classical torso.	86
IV.	The "Canopus," at Hadrian's Villa.	87
V.	Winchester Crucifixion.	111
VI.	Joseph, from Adoration group.	112
VII.	Painting attributed to Li Ch'eng	185

history as process not causation

Introduction

This is a study of history as process. It is not concerned with historical causation. If agreement cannot be reached on the causes of human behavior, how can we expect to agree on the causes of historical behavior? But it is not necessary to know the causes of things in order to observe how they function. We do not know the cause of electricity or of organic life, yet we observe with increasing accuracy how they behave.

The study of historical process is a relatively new field. It has emerged during an age given widely to the scientific analysis of all manner of things, yet whether a given historical approach should be called "scientific" or not depends entirely on definition. Often the emulation of science in other fields is limited to supposedly scientific techniques and has little to do with either spirit or substance. It seems more useful to call science that which systematically studies the natural world. Thus we can say: Scientists study nature, somebody studies history. But history as studied is of at least two kinds. One is, in essence, biography, for it entertains the role of human decision within the course of history. Another deals with history as process. Here the laws of periodic development are no less legal than the laws of physical structure.

history as process xiii vs. hist. as biography

A philosophical error is made when these two studies are confused. Clearly human decision plays its role in the particular turns and forms made possible by historical process. But clearly this process in itself has never been subject to human volition. Recurring historical phenomena such as Renaissance and Baroque, or Classical and Romantic, will obtain no matter what men may wish and try. And so the work of Raphael, while it bears the stamp of his personality and creative genius, and while it could not have been produced by someone else, is necessarily Renaissance Italian.

Analogies are limited but can help. Consider the image of history as a river. This is appropriate in the context of terms such as the "flow" of events, the "course" of civilization, the "stream" of developments. The image of a river entails strict limitations. The river does not run haphazardly; it follows a certain course. It is contained by its banks, it has a certain contour, and runs in a given direction. Of itself, however, the river consists of various kinds of movement, operating at different levels. Playing its surface are froth and spume. This may be likened to the play of fashions in history, fashions which seem to be ruled only by vagaries, by the whim of the moment. Even here, however, it should be cautioned that fashions, at a deeper level, reveal certain regularities of flow, as the studies of dress modes by Alfred Kroeber with Jane Richardson have shown.

At another level, the river is subject to eddies and swirls. These may be likened to those historical movements which turn back upon themselves, as from High Renaissance to Mannerism to Baroque, or Classicism to Romanticism to Realism. At still another level the river is subject to long, sweeping drifts which occupy parts of it but do not affect the rest. To these may be likened the role of institutions in history, forms which emerge from slow beginnings, gather momentum in long, broad sweeps, and gradually dissolve. Examples include creeds or cults, feudalisms or parliaments, even the coinage of money.

Under the froth, the eddies, and the drifts, run deeper and more meaningful activities. These are the underlying currents of the river, and their movements are rhythmic and periodic. They are not simple in their operation, for there are currents and cross-currents, making new patterns withal. But they can be deciphered, and it is here, among the periodic currents of history, that we search for evidence of history's laws.

This is not to say that history is more durable or more real than biography. What could be more real than the decisions of the human soul, or more durable than its evolution? But it is important to distinguish biography from periodic history. In the analogy of the river, man's fate is like the boat that moves upon it, and man's will is the navigator. Exercising his will, man the navigator in history can make certain choices. Thus the boat can be started or halted; it can move to the left or to the right. But it cannot go against the current, at least not effectively nor for long. It must stay within the river's banks at all times and, in order to gain optimum power and sureness, its navigator must know and use the currents.

In such an image, man is in no way deprived of his free will. He remains in complete charge of his own craft, but he can operate it only within solid banks or limits, and in relation to the force and direction of the currents. Urged on by the river's new vistas and purged by her torrents, man directs his evolution within the context of historical processes which he does not direct.

The history of history may be summarized roughly as follows. First is history as chronicle or account; it is reportage—narration for record or for celebration. Then there is the attempt to restore the past, to picture what it was like, to aim at what Niebuhr called "reviving former times." Next there is the study of tendencies in history: the investigation of movements and their sequence. Sometimes attached to these studies are attempts to explain history—for example, to explain intellectual history by social history, or the cultural by the economic. These often amount to what have been called explanations that do not explain. And then there is the rather recent study known as "historiology"—which means the study of history as legal process, or the study of those aspects of history which operate according to law.

Such aspects are represented by the deeper and more insistent currents of the river of history, unaffected by wind and spray on the surface, and unaffected by man's boat, which can make brief eddies of superficial scope, but which cannot affect the underlying rhythms and directions of the stream.

It is to certain of these underlying currents that the present study is addressed. To certain aspects only, for there is evidence of much more: We are only beginning to probe the depths of this wondrous stream. It is not necessary to accept the image of history as a stream; we might prefer to picture the "climate" of history, which at a given time and place encourages certain growths and discourages others. Accordingly, human culture may appear as a multifoliate plant, rich with branches and buds in many directions, luxurious and seemingly infinite in its manifestations, yet all operating according to inner impulses of periodic character, reflecting the tickings of internal clocks. Whether history is looked upon as plant, as river, or in some other image, there remains the tacit acknowledgment that history is organic process. That is to say, for all its clockwork history is not mechanical. The periodic laws underlying historical tendencies may be absolute, but the actual manifestations are variable. These manifestations—these blossoms of human culture—represent individual variations upon the historical norm. For this norm, as Ernest McClain has put it, admits "the approximation or exception characteristic of organic life."

Still, the underlying laws are laws, and as such they have an absolute identity. This kind of law does not mean statute, it means formula. After pleading that scientific speculation be directed by facts but not by sense impressions alone, Galileo stressed that the laws of the universe "must also be sought through mathematical models—formulas and equations." In our day, when human creativity is widely attributed to social condition or circumstance, it is appropriate to recall the finding of Alfred Kroeber, that "no amount or type of external influence will produce a burst of cultural productivity unless the internal situation is ripe."

But ripening involves rhythm, and rhythm means regularity and periodicity. Investigators like Spengler and Kroeber did not often admit—at any rate not publicly—of regularity in history. But their studies continue to prove valuable to historiology, not only for the observation of clusters and directions but for the latent implication of underlying periodicities. In Kroeber's writings we find certain evidence of symmetries and oscillations; and Friedell observed of Spengler that he was "certainly no believer in astrology. All the same, his theory of the culture-cycles can only be interpreted astrologically."

In the chapters that follow, astrological correlations are sometimes made to historical configurations. This does not mean that history is governed by astrology. It means simply that there is a co-relation,

Co-relation

The twelve astrological signs, the four elements, the three qualities, and comparable factors all stand for certain cosmic principles, which are reflected in numerous other concepts, from the mythical to the mathematical. The correlations between historical and astrological or numerological configurations show that the law operates in all, and that the law has meaning. Observing some of these correlations, we may be struck by the marvelous powers of organization that lie behind the evolution of cultural form, and we may feel as Newton did, that we are children playing on the shore, while the vast ocean of truth lies undiscovered before us.

Since history, astrology, and numerology reflect higher orders of creation, no one of them proceeds from another. Each is the manifestation of a higher principle; but when they reflect the same principle, then one may shed light on another. For example, the fact that the Egyptian civilization was Cancerian helps us to understand the inner purpose of this civilization; but at the same time the study of the Egyptian character may help us further to grasp the nature of the Cancerian principle.

The study of harmonics in history opens windows on the beauty of creation. It sharpens the essential correspondence between number and form. It strengthens our grasp of the logical order of evolution, and advances our intimations of the relationship between human will and historical principle. For man's choices do indeed affect the particular forms of historical expression, even though there is no justification for assuming that they change the course of history. Man's creative imagination and practical application give form to the possibilities tossed up by the river of history.

In the end there is no problem of determination versus free will; there is only the appearance of such a problem, arising from the limitations of our grasp of the relation between historical process and man's role within it. Historical process operates according to strict law, to which there are no exceptions and from which there is no appeal. History produces changing possibilities, within which man is given room to operate. Surely man is responsible for the creation of particular social and artistic forms—but this should not lead him to suppose he can create whatever he fancies. Michelangelo could create sculpture undreamt of by anyone else, but he could not have created worthwhile sculpture in Romanesque or Egyptian style.

xviii HARMONICS OF HISTORY

The individual forms of history are not pre-ordained, but its direction and purposes are. We live in a lawful universe: Why should historical process be exempt when physical or natural process is not? But man, having free will, is given a certain choice within these lawful operations: He is allowed to employ his imagination and reason within the range of opportunities available at the given stage of historical development. So the operation of human genius does determine the particular forms and meanings whose chronicle we recount under the name of history. Human genius is a function of the human spirit, and can choose—not any way it likes, but at least between this way and that way. Fritz Novotny nicely summed the situation in saying, "Naturally, I am not thinking of a 'blind' law of development, and I shall avoid saying that it had to come. For being a matter of the history of spirit, it could surely have been different. But since it took place as it did, we must note that a highly consistent process is visible here."

Acknowledgments:

The author gratefully acknowledges kind permission to quote from the following sources:

From Paul Frankl, *Gothic Architecture* (The Pelican History of Art, 1962). Copyright © Paul Frankl, 1962. Reprinted by permission of Penguin Books, Ltd. Pages 28, 79, 81, 93, and 223.

From *An Encyclopedia of World History.* William L. Langer, ed. Copyright © 1940, 1948, 1952 and 1968. 1972 by Houghton Mifflin Company. Reprinted by permission of Houghton Mifflin Company.

From Nikolaus Pevsner, *An Outline of European Architecture* (Pelican Books, Revised Edition, 1970). Copyright © Nikolaus Pevsner, 1943. Reprinted by permission of Penguin Books, Ltd. Pages 32, 57, 61, 64, 79, 116, 128, 131, 201, and 368.

From Stuart Piggot, *Prehistoric India to 1000 BC* (Penguin Books, 1952). Copyright 1950 by Stuart Piggott. Reprinted by permission of Penguin Books, Ltd. Pages 104, 144, 184.

From Laurence Sickman and Alexander Soper, *The Art & Architec-*

ture of China (Pelican History of Art, First integrated edition, 1971). Copyright © Laurence Sickman and Alexander Soper, 1956, 1960, 1968, 1971. Reprinted by permission of Penguin Books, Ltd. Pages 78, 106, 123, 129, 201.

From George Vernadsky, *A History of Russia* (New Haven: Yale University Press, 1944).

From Philippe Wolff, *The Cultural Awakening*, translated by Anne Carter (New York: Alfred A. Knopf, Inc., 1968).

HARMONICS OF HISTORY

Handwritten notes at top:
I. 3960 - span of a major culture
A. Germinative - 1st 10 centuries
B. Evolutionary - 3 four-cent. epicycles of (ethos-pathos) logical growth
C. Redundant - final 18 cent.

I

The Structure of a Major Culture

A. THE OVERALL SPAN

The major culture is an historical entity as exemplified by ancient Egypt or China or India; it is the primary unit of civilization as we know it. The major culture holds a unique site in the world's geography, for while at a given time a part of its area may overlap that of another culture, its core area is never the same as another's.

The time span of all major cultures is forty centuries, or just under four thousand years. All historically functioning centuries (as opposed to calendar centuries) are 99 years long, so that the actual span of the major culture is 3960 years. These forty centuries are divided into three successive epochs, which will be called the Germinative, the Evolutionary, and the Redundant epochs.

The Germinative epoch continues for ten centuries following the identifiable beginning of the major culture's span. In the Western culture, the Germinative occupied approximately the first ten centuries AD; in the Russian culture, the Germinative lasted from the later 9th to the later 19th century.

2 HARMONICS OF HISTORY

The Evolutionary epoch is the definitive as well as the central part of the major culture's span. It is the period during which there is a strict, unbroken development; its "evolution" contains no gaps and no redundancies. It is composed of twelve centuries which alternate according to an *ethos/pathos* principle, and which are divisible into three four-century periods called epicycles.

The Redundant epoch comprises the final eighteen centuries of the span of the major culture. The Classical Redundant ended around 1900, the Levantine Redundant began in the 12th century. During this long epoch, many forms of the major culture may be perpetuated, sometimes brilliantly. But nothing essentially new appears. Borrowings are made from other cultures as well as from the native past, and there is no sense of an inevitable and directed development of cultural forms. Such measured development is found only in the Evolutionary epoch, that period during which the sense of time is most acutely felt, and when impatience—or at least a sense of paced activity—may be contrasted with the more patient passivity of the Germinative and the Redundant periods.

During the Evolutionary, the leading forms at any given time are found in a process of directed and measurable development. For example, a good piece of Gothic, or even of classical Greek, sculpture can ordinarily be dated within a few years on style alone. During the Evolutionary there is a sense of the ordered march of time. The important things appear to be developing as they should, without baseless novelty and, at the same time, careless of that which belonged to an earlier generation. Thus the builders of the new Parthenon, or of new Gothic cathedrals where the older ones had burned, showed a healthy lack of respect for recent remains.

The Evolutionary epoch is the period of sequential and organic development. Forms grow logically, styles develop according to a natural rhythm and process. Always, in the leading areas, there is a sense that people are doing things to continuous purpose, that forms are evolving in a necessary direction. "Historians," wrote Max Friedländer, "have learnt to reckon with the possibility of change, but not with its necessity." In the Evolutionary, change is necessary because there is a process that needs to be fulfilled.

In the Redundant epoch, changes of style occur in accord with changes in taste; they evince no sustained progression, or sense of inevitable unfolding. In the Germinative, change tends to be experimental, abortive, sometimes misdirected—though often serving sound purpose in preparing the soil. The condition of the pre-Evolutionary is expressed in L. Wiener's description of Russia before the time of Peter and his successors. There was, in those early times, no hope for maturity, "for one century was like another, and there were no new factors growing up from within to change the condition of Russian society." Throughout the Germinative, one century is very like another.

The Germinative epochs of most of the major cultures are still dim in outline, although some—including the Levantine, the Western and the Russian—provide us with considerable information (see Chapter III). The Redundant epochs are more abundant in their evidence. The earliest Redundant we can date with usefulness is that of the Babylonian culture. The Babylonian Redundant was scheduled to end around 200 AD. The Chaldeans infiltrated Babylon around 900; their empire was defeated in 539 by Cyrus the Persian (that is, of the young Levantine culture). The last visible manifestation of the Babylonian culture was Carthage, traditionally founded by Phoenicians from Tyre in the 9th century, thereby continuing the ancient Babylonian tradition. Carthage was destroyed by the Romans in 146 BC, but as this was not a natural death it is at least conceivable that Carthage might have lived out the full span of the Babylonian Redundant epoch. Carthage died less from senility than from excessive zeal.

In Rome herself, Baal (from the Babylonian Bel) was venerated as late as the time of Elagabalus (218-222) who tried at least to spread some worship of this god. At Baalbek (mid-2nd century) Baal was honored in Lebanon, the home area of the Phoenicians. After 64 BC Phoenicia had been incorporated in the Roman province of Syria, and Phoenician language and institutions gradually became extinct even though Sidon, Tyre, and some other cities were allowed to preserve self-governance. At the same time Greek influence appeared on coins and inscriptions; nevertheless, Phoenician legends "do not entirely vanish till the 2nd century AD" (*Encyclopedia Britannica*).

The Redundant epoch of the Egyptian culture ran from roughly 1400 BC to 400 AD. Coptic art is the art of Christian Egypt: in both expression and form it belongs to the Levantine culture. According to Herbert Read, it is not until the Coptic period, "beginning at the end of the 4th century AD, that we finally get rid of the hieratic principle in the art of Egypt." The hieratic had been as persistently identifiable with the ancient Egyptian culture as the hieroglyph or the hierophant. The old Egyptian traditions, which had been alive so long that to Classical man they seemed interminable, eventually gave out. The millennial art, as G.M.A. Hanfmann puts it, "which had survived the Greek onslaught, finally died in Roman times."

The Redundant epoch of the Chinese culture came to an end soon after 1700 AD. The poetry and drama had died earlier, but (according to Kroeber) the novel continued to flourish until the early 18th century. The imperial kilns enjoyed a brilliant period in the late 17th century (William Watson), but after 1726 European styles were introduced into pottery. Many encyclopedias and dictionaries (some extraordinarily voluminous) were produced through the early 18th century; the period was distinguished also by private scholars such as the mathematician Mei Wen-ting, who died in 1721.

An outstanding development of the Chinese Redundant epoch was the art of painting. These late painting styles (T'ang, Sung) did not show continuous evolution but they did enjoy recurrent periods of brilliance throughout a number of centuries, down through the 17th. Why Chinese painting was not revitalized "in the 18th century would be an interesting subject for speculation" (Laurence Sickman). Kroeber cites Wang Hui "as probably the best Ch'ing painter"; he was apparently also the last of any real significance, and he died in 1717. The painters of the 18th and 19th centuries, according to the current view, "represent a genuine decline in artistic creativity"; there were lots of them, but they painted "by the book" (C.O. Hucker).

In social and economic life the decline was contemporary. Probably "as late as the 16th century if not later, the Chinese economy was sophisticated and productive beyond comparison with any other region and gave the Chinese a higher standard of living than any other people in the world. But by 1800...domestic economic problems were turning China into a powder keg waiting to be exploded" (*ibid*.). It was the 18th century that witnessed the degeneration of Chinese civilization. Hucker dates a "real decline and stagnation in many aspects of Chinese life between the 17th and 19th centuries" and notes that by the 19th century the "vitality of traditional Chinese civilization in all its aspects was at a low ebb." For this reason, the Opium

War and the Taiping Rebellion "precipitated an almost total collapse, not merely of the Ch'ing dynasty, but of the whole cultural tradition."

Japanese civilization, as we know it, is a latter-day derivative of the Chinese. In Japan a cultural renaissance culminated in the Genroka calendrical era (1688-1704); after this time there were no major institutional developments (Garraty and Gay) and things moved slowly and sluggishly until Japan was opened to Western culture. Although by the end of the 18th century the Japanese were leading the East in painting (Peter Swann), it remains generally true that after 1700 Japanese art is imitative of that of China and inferior to Japanese painting before that time. Sculpture degenerated or disappeared, except in miniatures, whose workmanship astonished the West. Ceramics and porcelain remained strong and inventive until perhaps the mid-18th century; subsequently they, like the famous block prints, were reduced to a folk art. The only science that the Japanese ever developed, a remarkable algebra that carried on the forgotten one of China, culminated around 1675-1700 (Kroeber). Thus the end of the Chinese Redundant epoch, as seen reflected in its Japanese offshoot, may likewise be dated from the 18th century.

The end of the Redundant epoch of the Indian culture came a little before 1800. During the 18th century, the Mahrattas and Sikhs weakened the empire, while the French and British carved colonies out of it. In the 18th century there was a "gradual decline of industry, education, and cultural progress except as maintained by some Moslem and Hindu poets and scholars" (Langer). Neo-Indic literature ran its course from around 1150 down to 1800 or a little after (Lallu Ji Lal flourished about 1804). The latest phases of Chola architecture belong to the 17th and 18th centuries. Mughal painting may be dated about 1600-1800.

During the course of the 18th century, it would seem that the spirit simply went out of the ancient Indic civilization; its morale departed. At Plassey (1757) the Indians fought not for India, but for power and booty— "the ultimate triumph of the British was preordained" (de Reincourt). The momentous resuscitation of the ancient Indian texts during the 19th century was done by Europeans.

The next major culture, the Classical, ended its Redundant epoch about 1900. The Roman state withered in the 5th century AD, and

Classical Latin literature shortly after. Buildings, paintings, and liturgies expressive of the young Levantine culture occupied much of the old empire's soil, and by the 9th century representatives of the new Western culture occupied most of the remainder. Yet through all this time a Classical spirit continued, now here and now there, to give evidence that it had not died out.

We are accustomed to the notion that the Classical tradition expired or fell into a deep slumber, from which it revived on rare occasions called renaissances (such as those of the Carolingian, of the 12th century, of the 15th century). But in fact the Classical spirit did not die with Constantine, nor with Boethius. Lacking its original homeland, it spurted up when some phase of another major culture was propitious to it, and where the area was originally a part of the Classical domain. From the 13th to the 16th centuries this meant Italy, and from the 17th through the 19th, France.

But the period between the decay of ancient Rome and the 12th century "Renaissance" in Western Europe was not devoid of a Classical tradition. From the 5th through the 11th century it made significant reappearances within the Byzantine culture, centered in formerly Greek lands. "The educated man in the East had his mind steeped in Greek literature. He could quote from the classics of Greek poetry and drama. He was familiar with the scientific knowledge and philosophic concepts of Plato and Aristotle" (W.O. Ault). Thence Greek philosophy and science were transmitted to the West by Arab Islam.

The rediscovery of Latin classics by the 14th century Italians was not a radical discovery. Medieval scholars had been familiar with the main body of classical literature; what the Humanists did was to gather such works and make them available (W.K. Ferguson). The culture of Greece and Rome "which, from the 14th century, obtained so powerful a hold on Italian life as the source and basis of culture, as the object and ideal of existence...had long been exerting an occasional influence on medieval Europe, even beyond the boundaries of Italy" (Burckhardt). A Classical spirit emerged from time to time not only in Italy and southern France, where Classical form had long been tilled into the very soil, but also in northern France, in Austria and Germany, even in Holland and Britain. The Spanish, Dutch, and

English transported something of this Classical residue into portions of the New World.

The Classical "renascences" of Charlemagne, of the 12th century, of the Renaissance, or of the 18th century, can all be interpreted in terms of Western phases of development. Yet the fact that it was specifically Greek and Roman themes and forms that were revived cannot be put aside. These themes and forms carried a certain residual meaning to modern Europeans and Americans down through the 19th century.

Latin and Greek were taught as an essential part of the curriculum of institutions of higher learning until the early 20th century; through this time they were considered, at least by the many people who practiced them, to be living languages; today they are considered "dead". Liturgies in Latin have in our century given way to liturgies in local tongues.

The prevalence of Classical themes and forms in all the arts during the Neoclassical period of the 18th century was counteracted during the Romantic and subsequent periods. Nevertheless modern art has had Classical aspects right up to the 20th century. Greek Revival and Neoclassicism in architecture continued until the middle of the 19th century. Roman forms, though but whited sepulchers, reappeared in the Chicago World's Fair of 1893. The Pennsylvania Station in New York, a veritable Roman Bath, was built in 1906-10, but was torn down in the 1960s. The Lincoln Memorial in Washington (1914-21) may be "the last truly monumental Neoclassic structure in this country" (G.H. Hamilton). Until the 20th century, the primary burden of the architect's training was to master the classical Orders and their proportions. The most classic of automobiles, the Rolls-Royce, adopted a classical pediment with pilasters for its radiator facade in 1904.

In France, seat of the major developments of Western painting and sculpture from the late 17th to the mid-20th century, Classical themes and forms have been especially strong. It is not surprising to find them in the Neoclassicism of the 18th century, but it is impressive to recognize that they persist throughout the romantic and revolutionary 19th century as well. With the end of the 19th and the beginning of the 20th century, these Classical predilections came to an end, at least

8   HARMONICS OF HISTORY

in the most vital art forms. The end may be marked by the painting of Puvis de Chavannes (d. 1898) or Renoir (*Judgment of Paris*, 1914), in the sculpture of Renoir (*Venus Victorious*, 1913) or the early Maillol, whose *Mediterranean* of 1912-15 looks all the way back to the Temple of Zeus of Olympia.

The Classical "tradition" had moved from Greece to Etruria to Rome (before the Slavic invasions, the Balkans provided a natural bridge). When Rome foundered, it emerged at Trier, and later surfaced in Aachen. In the 12th century it appeared in Paris, and in the 13th it reappeared in Sicily and South Italy. In the 14th century it removed from Pisa to Florence, in the 16th from Florence to Rome, in the 17th from Rome to France, where, shortly after 1900, it finally gave up the last true forms of the Redundant.

The Levantine Redundant began around 1200 AD and is scheduled to continue until nearly 3000. In our own time, the reestablishment of Israel and the resurgence of the Arab states testify to the vitality, along with the lack of continuity, that typify the Redundant epoch.

The chronology of the Ancient American culture follows that of the Levantine by around three-quarters of a century. It is usually supposed that the Ancient American culture was demolished by the Spanish in the 16th century. Spengler described it as "murdered in the full glory of its unfolding." Applied to the outward manifestations of this ancient civilization, Spengler's remark is not only poetic but accurate. Yet a reservation must be made. Had not Montezuma taken Cortez for the god Quetzalcoatl, whose arrival had been designated for the very day Cortez arrived—in other words, had the Spanish been taken for invaders—they would not "have remained alive for long" (S. Linné).

The maintenance of a culture's outward trappings during the Redundant depends in great degree upon the impingements of other cultures, especially those enjoying the force of their own Evolutionary epoch. Thus Chinese remoteness helped to preserve her external forms, whereas the remains of the Roman empire were taken over first by the Levantine, then by the Western culture.

Sooner or later the European and modern American polities must have overrun the Ancient American. The point is that this civilization, though long destroyed in its outward forms, has not yet completed its inner course. This is indicated by the force of Mexican painting or of Latin American writing. "It is even arguable that the American civilizations were not destroyed by Cortez and Pizarro," writes Matthew Melko. "These civilizations can be seen as continuing under a new set of governors." The last two major cultures, the Western and the Russian, are still in their Evolutionary epochs.

B. Dating of the Evolutionary Centuries

The arrival of an Evolutionary epoch is signalled by a burst of creative activity unprecedented in the major culture. The areas of activity are those germane (1) to the native genius of the culture, and (2) to the first century, and especially the first epicycle (or four-century group) of the Evolutionary.

The first epicycle of the Western Evolutionary is contained under the stylistic concepts Romanesque and Gothic. Since the Western is a Capricornian culture (cf. Chapter II) it is particularly strong in architecture; and since the first epicycle is strongly religious in orientation, we should be justified in looking for the emergence of the Western Evolutionary in a burst of new religious architecture. The first century of the Western evolutionary ran from 995 to 1094. Henceforth we shall call it the "11th century," since, while not identical to, it is close enough to the calendric century for convenience.

The Evolutionary centuries for the West so far may now be given as follows:

Eleventh	995 - 1094
Twelfth	1094 - 1193
Thirteenth	1193 - 1292
Fourteenth	1292 - 1391
Fifteenth	1391 - 1490
Sixteenth	1490 - 1589
Seventeenth	1589 - 1688
Eighteenth	1688 - 1787
Nineteenth	1787 - 1886
Twentieth	1886 - 1985

The beginning of the Evolutionary epoch, scheduled for 995, required that the soil be prepared, and it was in the 10th and 11th centuries that European forests were cleared, swamps drained, cities built in large numbers, and that there grew some fixity in the distribution and density of population (C. Kluckhohn).

Cluny The 11th Century

The pre-eminent religious center of the entire Romanesque period, the abbey of Cluny, acquired the right of sanctuary in 994, and was supplemented with further privileges granted by Gregory V in 997 or 998. A systematic rebuilding of the monastery was undergone between 981 and 1010. Here lay the beginning of the extraordinary rule and role of Cluny.

Raoul Glaber, a French monk and chronicler of the early 11th century, made a famous remark which apparently is no great exaggeration: "It was as if the world renewed itself, spreading a glittering robe of churches over everything." Jean Hubert notes that the fever of building described by Glaber is attested by many other texts, and that it began, in fact, "during the last years of the 10th century." Since architecture is the leading creative form in this period, the inception of this building activity is of particular importance in dating the Evolutionary. The 9th century "was the darkest of the centuries," said H.J. Randall, and it could be added that, until close to its end, the 10th century had been one of the darkest of the West. Panofsky refers to the years from around 880 to around 970 as only a "period of incubation," adding that it is not until the last third of the 10th century "that we can observe a general resurgence of artistic competence and discipline." This is manifested in painting and sculpture too, but is of chief importance in architecture.

In their style, early Romanesque motifs can be traced singly, as Pevsner notes, back to Carolingian architecture; but they combine (that is, to form a Romanesque "style") only in the late 10th century. A key event was the rebuilding of St. Martin of Tours after the fire of 997. Of the rebuilt church, Conant says that the "ambulatory and radiating chapels...were undoubtedly of mature form and proportions." The plan with ambulatory and radiating chapels was to be crucial to Romanesque architecture; Pevsner finds that the radiating plan "can perhaps be traced back to the church of S. Martin."

The Structure of a Major Culture 11

The 12th Century

The second Evolutionary century—the "12th" century—began in 1094. In social history it is distinguished by the Crusades. While the first Crusade actually got under way in 1096, it should be dated from Pope Urban's exhortation of 1095; in the same year Count Raymond of Toulouse took the cross.

In architectural history, 12th century style is marked by stone-vaulting of the entire building. St. Etienne at Nevers was rebuilt and vaulted between 1083 and 1097. At the end of the 11th century the wooden ceiling of St. Hilaire of Poitiers was replaced by a stone vault.

As Pevsner puts it, "Just before 1100...the pioneer work was done in architecture; Early Romanesque was transformed into High Romanesque. Durham is the crucial monument in England, begun in 1093." Pevsner considers that the "earliest vault seems to be the groin vault over the chancel of the Trinité at Caen of the last years of the 11th century."

The 13th Century

The "13th" century began in 1193. The style of the 13th century is Gothic. While many anticipations of Gothic form may be dated well back into the 12th century, the full or High Gothic appears in Chartres Cathedral as rebuilt from 1194. According to Frankl, "the master who rebuilt the cathedral at Chartres after the fire of 10 June 1194 was the first man to draw the logical consequences from the construction of flying buttresses. He eliminated the galleries.... The exterior and the interior, governed by a few principles, form a unity...in which the principles which were inherent in the first rib-vaults have been transferred to the whole. It is the achievement of this organic blending of the interior and exterior which gives the cathedral at Chartres its position of historical significance as the birthplace of the High Gothic style.... Chartres represents the first step beyond the Early Gothic style, but not the last." Chartres was followed immediately by Bourges (begun before 1200), Soissons (begun about 1200), Reims (begun 1210), Le Mans (begun 1217), Amiens (begun 1220). Here is a classic instance of a major style emerging in a series of quickly succeeding stages.

The 14th Century

The 14th century began in 1292. The difference between the style of the 13th century and that of the 14th is best seen in the distinction between High and Late Gothic, even though these terms are used variously by different writers. Just as the 18th century represents a late and decorative stage of the Baroque, so does the 14th of the Gothic. Pevsner observes of the Late Gothic style that "it might be wise to approach it from the point of view of decoration first," and emphasizes its delight in the decorative rather than the strictly architectural. He dates the Late Gothic from the time of the chapter-house at York, around 1290, and of Bristol cathedral, from 1298, noting such elements of "surprise and ambiguity" as may once again remind us of the 18th century.

Grodecki sees at York Minster (c. 1291-1300) a curvilinear style and "the first Flamboyant forms such as ogee arches, spirals and prismatic mouldings." Frankl sees in the chapter-house at Wells the multiplication of tiercerons which he calls "the first definite step towards the Late Gothic style" because "the structural function of the rib is ignored." He dates the Wells chapter-house at c. 1293-c. 1300.

The 15th Century

The Early Renaissance is usually associated with the Quattrocento, that is, the 15th century in Italy. But as some students have observed, the Renaissance in the North was not only just as rich (when all the arts are taken into account), but came just as early as it did in Italy. Thus Panofsky matches Netherlandish developments in music, painting, and sculpture against Italian developments in architecture, sculpture and painting during the early part of the 15th century; and Michael Levey warns that the "discussion of the origins of the Early Renaissance need not restrict itself to Italy."

The period around 1400 was a time when sculpture was the most advanced of the visual arts. It seems logical, then, to look for the first Renaissance expression in sculpture, assuming it is still available or at least known about. It would be tempting to identify the Competition reliefs of Brunelleschi and Ghiberti in 1401 as the first Renaissance sculpture, but this would limit us to Italy, and in fact the first effectively Renaissance work known today was created in the north, a full decade earlier.

In 1391 Claus Sluter installed his Virgin and Child on the trumeau at Dijon; the Duchess was installed two years later. The completed portal presents in embryo the new independence of the arts, and the dramatic stage which was to occupy the entire Renaissance and Baroque era. In this portal Gothic drapery has become transformed into personal expression. The Virgin advances, as Focillon felicitously observed, in a tumult of draperies, which "are complete dramatic compositions in their own right." The Virgin protects the Child (from instruments of the Passion above) with dramatic psychological involvement, physical movement, and emotional focus. The drapery, like the body, is used for physical gesture and is realized in three-dimensional form, and these forms occupy a three-dimensional space.

The figures are free-standing—entirely detached from the architecture. They are monumental in a new sense: "Sluter cut right across the fashionable delicate style of his day in favor of monumental figures, highly charged with emotion" (Peter Kidson). This combination of monumentality and independence renders sculpture free of architecture for the first time, and signifies that independence of the art forms which was characteristic of the Renaissance. The figures actually overpower the architecture and reach out into surrounding space (H.W. Janson), thus anticipating Donatello's progression from the St. Mark to the Gattamelata.

Another result was that Sluter emancipated (as Panofsky put it) "the donors—and, by implication, the patron saints and the Madonna—from the architectural context...the statues became free agents enacting a scene...the portal itself became a stage." This is the first recognizable stage in Western art, and the vehicle of the first Renaissance drama; for the drama (Panofsky reminds us), "as we know it, did not exist in the Middle Ages."

The donors are actual portraits; their figures are full-sized for the first time—that is, they are commensurate in scale with the sacred figures, whose space they are now permitted to share; they are detached as from a backdrop, while the space over their heads further frees them from the architecture. Spatially, the Virgin and Child are no longer contained within the silhouette of the trumeau, as in true Gothic sculpture.

In these figures, surface texture is newly exploited at the expense of Gothic line, and we tend to probe the form rather than following a surface rhythm. Originally all the figures were painted in naturalistic colors, and constituted a tableau of tangible reality. Sluter "conceives sculpture like a great painter and an epic poet" (Focillon), and he "contains potentially both Michelangelo and Bernini" (Panofsky).

In content, then, this portal establishes the beginning of Renaissance individualism, and of the independent stance of architecture, sculpture, or painting. In form, the portal is dominated by horizontal axes—especially but not only the one which maintains the "stage"; this horizontality is the crucial significance in that it was the basic orientation of all Renaissance art down to Tintoretto. Also notable in Sluter's Madonna is its "impressive gravity" (A. Martindale) and an originality which seems to have impressed every observer.

But even the originality of Sluter's genius did not stand entirely alone. In Jacques de Baerze's altarpiece at Dijon (completed 1391) the most important figures are carved in the round and are so readily detachable that the Crucifix was stolen in the mid-19th century. Furthermore, the sculptor has achieved "the transformation of volumetric relief space into pictorial stage space" (Panofsky), very like the transformation in Sluter's portal, and done at the same time.

But Italy played its part as well in the origins of Renaissance style. Altichiero's fresco in Sta Anastasia seems to have been done at the very end of his life (c. 1395). It revives Giottesque formal solidity, but introduces a naturalism of the kind later notable in Pisanello; furthermore, as Focillon put it, Altichiero sought "to suggest by the gyratory rhythm of his compositions that the hollow of space was spherical"— a Renaissance concept. His contemporary, Avanzo, "gives us a foretaste of the great period of Venetian art" (E. Arslan). About 1390 Cennino Cennini wrote his treatise on painting, one that describes late medieval practices, but sets the stage for Renaissance concepts in holding that nature is the best master—what we would call the mimetic approach.

Back in the north, between 1390 and 1395, Jacquemart de Hesdin directed and painted in the *Brussels Hours*. The first dedication page of this manuscript is "a remarkable achievement. Apparently for the first time, no difference is made in scale and prominence between the sacred personnages and the donor, whose status approaches that which he was to enjoy in the works of Claus Sluter and Jan van Eyck. The Madonna is the earliest known instance of an iconography that was to spread, in all conceivable media, as far as Hildesheim in Germany and Perugia in Italy." Panofsky adds another point of enormous importance; referring to the frame, he notes that what "had been a decorative fringe becomes a quasi-functional 'picture frame'." And the picture frame is a Renaissance-Baroque concept. Before this era, the picture belongs to wall, book, or furniture, and in the 19th century the frame—as an object setting off the picture's view—dwindles or changes its function.

Meanwhile, at the newly flowering cultural center of Dijon, Melchior Broederlam in 1394 began his panels of the Annunciation and the Presentation (on the back of the altarpiece carved by Jacques de Baerze). While much of the style of these paintings is Gothic, certain aspects are new; for example, the figure of S. Joseph has a new solidity and reality of posture, and "points the way towards the new developments to come" (Margaret Whinney). Furthermore, these panels are distinct examples of what Panofsky calls disguised symbolism, a pictorial or literary kind of symbolism or allegory which in the early Renaissance replaced the more purely symbolic language of the Middle Ages. If this is the first substantial example of disguised symbolism, then we may identify another Renaissance feature in the early 1390s.

But Florence too began to take steps toward the introduction of the Renaissance before 1400. For it was in Florence (as Charles Avery notes) during the 1390s that the patronage we think of as Renaissance patronage began.

The 16th Century

As the 15th century—in the stylistic sense—is identified with the Early Renaissance, so the 16th century (whether early or throughout) is identified with the High Renaissance. If we can locate the first productive examples of High Renaissance style, we should then be able to locate the beginning of the 16th century as a stylistic entity. By "productive" is meant that the new style flows more or less without interruption from that time. Michael Levey finds Leonardo's early *Virgin of the Rocks* (c. 1483) a "seminal High Renaissance object," but warns that "its creation did not create the High Renaissance" in the sense of producing a "tide of victorious new style." Possibly no single work does all that, but we can locate historical works from whose date new styles develop continuously—at least in the most advanced centers, which are all that matter so far as new styles are concerned.

Thus Leonardo's *Adoration* (1481-2) anticipates but does not establish High Renaissance composition. With his *Last Supper*, all would agree that the High Renaissance is under way. This is variously dated from 1493 to 1498. The turning point then must lie somewhere in between 1483 and 1495. As early as 1480-5, in the Villa Medici at Poggio, Sangallo shows a "delight in manipulating pristine volumes to form a building in which each part will appear to belong to a larger, single whole" (Bates Lowry). The principle of subordination is basic to the High Renaissance, but this building does not comply fully with the new style, for it remains lacking in overall organization, and still emphasizes the plane.

In general usage the Cinquecento begins with Leonardo, even though he was born in 1452 and was making art in the early 1470s. And at a certain point this usage becomes correct. There are drawings by Leonardo showing plans and elevations or perspective views of domed churches; these are usually dated in the late 1480s or about 1490. They show a type of central plan which constitutes "as against the central schemes worked out by Renaissance architects before Leonardo not a major contrasted with a number of radiating minor members, but a system of these grades each subordinate to the one above" (Pevsner). For the first time, it would seem, the High Renaissance principles of centrality, cohesiveness, subordination, and comprehensibility are fully worked out. For the result is "something entirely new. The building is no longer a juxtaposition of flat planes as in Brunelleschi or an inert mass as in Alberti, but a living organism radiating outward from a central core" (F. Hartt). Furthermore, what Leonardo "discovered—and this is certainly the basis of High Renaissance composition in any artistic field—is a total organization that is the product of the dynamic interrelationship of its moving components" (Hartt).

Around 1490 Leonardo began the drawings for the Sforza monument, the model for which (24 feet high) was exhibited in 1493. It was twice the size of the *Gattamelata*, and far beyond the scale of realism; its scale could only be called heroic. Leonardo was a student of Verrocchio, whose *Colleone* represented a later example of the early Renaissance tradition out of which Leonardo's Sforza horse sprang. After the *Colleone* "the vital Quattro Cento spark was extinguished" (Adrian Stokes); since the statue was incomplete at Verrocchio's death in 1488, we have a sort of working terminal. The Sforza drawings show "a colossal statue in the round" (Hartt). Moreover, Leonardo "established for the animal, which was second only to man in importance and 'nobility', a canon of perfection" (Kenneth Clark). All these qualities—the heroic, the colossal, nobility, and a canon or ideal—are High Renaissance desiderata, when compared with the love of the modest, the minute, and the proliferation of detail which prevailed in Early Renaissance style.

Out of Leonardo's architecture drawings came Bramante's High Renaissance buildings; out of the Sforza monument drawings came Dürer's *Knight, Death, and the Devil,* and who knows how many equestrian monuments. And both groups of drawings were followed directly by the inception of the *Last Supper.* Therefore these drawings, unlike some Leonardo paintings of the early 1480s, have a direct progeny; they cannot be regarded as other than the beginning of the High Renaissance. And since the High Renaissance is identified with the beginning of 16th century style, we must date this right about 1490.

The 17th Century

With the 17th century begins the Baroque. The opera is a signal Baroque invention, and is considered to date from Peri's lost opera *Daphne* of 1597. However William Byrd's *Psalms, Sonnets and Songs of Sadness and Piety* seem to introduce an emotional emphasis indicative of the forthcoming century; these are dated 1588. M.F. Bukofzer remarks on the new sense of contrast in the *concertato* style, citing examples in the years (especially though not exclusively) 1587-90.

In architecture, the first thoroughly Baroque building is widely held to be S. Susanna in Rome, begun in 1597. Here there is no longer any ambiguity but a complete hierarchy of form, with vertical preponderance and a fully dynamic space. Compared to this, the Gesù facade (c. 1675-84) is both static and dynamic (or neither) and is still somewhat hesitant or ambiguous, as reflecting the mannerism of the 16th century. Nevertheless, in the Gesù the principle of circulation (which is Baroque) is already established, and there is central stress, vertical continuity, and forward motion. The turning point—the point at which we can say that architectural style has become more Baroque than Renaissance (or Mannerist)—must lie somewhere between 1584 and 1597.

In architectural painting, Hendrick van Steenwyck's *Interior of a Cathedral* dated 1587, while not as sweeping as the subsequent interiors of Saenredam or de Witte, is already more Baroque than not. In mural painting, Tintoretto was accomplishing breakthroughs of his own at just the same time. His *Paradise* of 1588 is Baroque in many respects but still Mannerist in its space. Some of the pictures in the lower chamber at San Rocco (done between 1584 and 1588) come very close to achieving Baroque style; consider the *Annunciation* with its free-wheeling action of s-curves, organizing power of chiaroscuro, natural proportions and absence of the fitful Mannerist light which occupies so many Tintorettos. His *Martyrdom of S. Catherine* (Accademia), apparently of 1589, is even more Baroque. It shows dramatic concentration combined with Baroque expansiveness (spinning in and out of a center, with wheels rotating in both two- and three-dimensional activity); the light has ceased to flicker and marshals itself with dramatic cohesiveness; the rhythms are broad and collected rather than nervous and discontinuous. In contrast to the shallowness (or exaggeration) of mannerist space, the depth now is powerful and consistent; the proportions are no longer mannered and the figures are concrete, while the effect is coherent and devoid of obscurities. Tietze said that Tintoretto was "a Mannerist and a Baroque artist"; by 1588-90, at least in some works, the Baroque seems to dominate.

Annibale Carracci's fishing and hunting picture (Louvre) of c. 1590 establishes recession from a foreground stage, a Baroque feature not present in pictures such as his *S. Eustace* of c. 1585. But his older brother and teacher, Ludovico, may have preceded him in the realization of Baroque style. Ludovico's *Bargellini Madonna* of 1588 is cleared of Mannerist ambiguity and obscurity. It is Baroque in that everyone moves and there is no barrier between the natural and the supernatural (people and saints are admitted on familiar terms); there is pronounced chiaroscuro as an organizing principle, even though the handling is still somewhat linear. Ludovico's *Conversion of S. Paul* of 1589 has been called a signpost of the Baroque, and indeed seems to contain nothing not belonging to 17th century style.

Taking music, architecture, and painting together, the time zone of the shift in weight from Renaissance to Baroque style encompasses the 1580s and nineties; within this zone, emphasis lies in the years 1587-90, with special emphasis on the years 1588-89. It is right about 1589, then, that we may situate the shift from the 16th to the 17th century in the stylistic sense.

The 18th Century

For 18th century style we shall have recourse to the term Rococo, using it in the sense Burckhardt made current—that is, as the last phase of Baroque art, comparable variously to the Rayonnant, Decorated, or Flamboyant in Gothic style. In general, this late phase is lighter, quicker, airier, more continuous, more playful, and more decorative than the Gothic of the 13th century or the Baroque of the 17th. In music, the lighter style appears before 1690; following Lully's death in 1687, "his lofty and serious style...gave way to a lighter approach. Entertainment rather than the stirring of strong emotions was now stressed.... Fondness for embellishment, as in the visual arts, became one of the main style characteristics of the musical Rococo" (R.G. Pauly).

The change in the visual arts had begun as early as 1684, for it was in that year that a plan was decided on for a lacquered and gilded apartment, responding to Louis XIV's desire for an interior apartment at the Cour de Marbre which would have more privacy and intimacy (also a Rococo desideratum). By the 1690s, the work of Berain already displayed the Chinoiserie so typical of the 18th century. In Berain's style of decoration (which began to take form in the 1680s), "Le Brun's motifs lived on but underwent a fundamental change. The composition became light and transparent, and the individual forms more slender and lively. Figures and vegetation yielded to geometrically linear ribbonwork" (here is the Cancer century's love of nature being replaced by the Gemini century's love of abstraction). "Above all, the fleshy acanthus tendrils turned into the main theme of the new style, the C-scroll" (W. Kalnein and M. Levey).

In the eighties and nineties Charles de La Fosse was doing work which made him "the pioneer of a new style which led towards the Rococo" (E. Lucie-Smith). Specifically, by 1688 La Fosse was executing a royal commission in a style "altogether lighter than anything that had hitherto been usual at the Court.... La Fosse gives to his nymphs a slender elegance and a rosy flesh-color which foreshadow Boucher. In fact, this series of paintings, which included also works by Bon and Louis de Boullongne the Younger, is the first in which something of the lightness of the Rococo can be traced" (Anthony Blunt). Also to the decorative arts belongs a bronze ewer by Soldani Benzi of about 1695, a work of which it has been observed that the "process of transition from late Baroque to early Rococo is in fact already perceptible" (J.R. Martin).

In easel painting we have the example of Luca Giordano, known in his time as "Luca fa presto" apparently because his father would urge him to paint more and more quickly (a tendency common in the 18th century). In pictures like *Christ and the Money Changers* of 1684, or the *Marriage at Cana* of about 1689, Luca is already closer in style to Tiepolo than to the Baroque. In the north, Meindert Hobbema's *Avenue of Middelharnis*, dated 1689, shows "the exalted spaciousness which often characterizes the Late Baroque, and also a kind of elegance in the elongated, slender trees that goes with the taste of this advanced phase" (Rosenberg and Slive).

Whether we call this Late Baroque or Rococo, its qualities (spacious, exalted, elegant, elongated, slender) are those of 18th century style. The beginnings of this style may therefore be dated broadly to the 1680s and 90s, more closely to the years 1687-90, and centered on the scheduled year of 1688.

The 19th Century

The first great modern artists were Goya and David. That Goya's *Executions of the Third of May* (1814) is thoroughly modern will hardly be disputed, but paintings of 1793 or 1794 such as the *Flagellants* and the *Burial of the Sardine* are hardly less so. Even these, however, do not mark the breakthrough—the point at which the new begins to overtake the old, and from which there is a continuous ensuing development. The *Snowstorm* of 1786 is no longer a Baroque allegory of the seasons; it deals in harsh realities, and there is something ominous, even monstrous about it. F. Licht finds that the blanket thrown over the figures gives them the effect, not of several figures swathed in drapery "but rather that of a multilegged crustacean" and that it suppresses their individual motion which we would expect to be expressive of harmonious body rhythms.

The *Blind Man's Buff* of 1787, like the *Snowstorm*, retains a Rococo decorative sense and a lightness both of tone and mood. Nevertheless it too is a transitional work, for the figures, as Licht observes, assume the posture of marionettes: "Their gestures are stiff and angular, their faces smirk with an unnatural grimace, and any loveliness and grace residing in the picture belong entirely to the costumes." (Beauty or grace is a desideratum of the Renaissance epicycle, truth or reality of the Modern). There is still the echo of the Baroque stage, but the effect is becoming forced. It is as if a "summarily painted, uninteresting, flat backdrop has been lowered behind the figures almost in the manner of a flimsy stage flat" (Licht).

The *Greased Pole* of 1787, ostensibly a swing-like Rococo theme, has adopted an imminent tone in the sky as well as an ominous tension in the pole; the background building, dim and dun-colored, sets off a tipped cart which looks suspiciously like a gun-carriage, and indeed the imagery anticipates Géricault's *Limekiln* (Louvre), also a virtual battlescene despite a workaday content. Goya's *View of San Isidro* of 1788 anticipates Impressionism in the full flood of the sunlight, while his portrait of Don Manuel Ossorio inaugurates modern style in another sense. This picture (Metropolitan, New York) remains formally posed in the center of the picture, all in the Renaissance-Baroque tradition. But the elements of the picture that gain our attention are the birds and the cats, which occupy the more marginal areas of the scene. Thus the composition operates upon a centrifugal principle, sharply opposed to the centripetal one that conditioned all Renaissance and Baroque art, for even the most expansive designs of Rubens or Fragonard always return to a center. The boy portrayed must be three of four years old, and as the inscription on the canvas declares the child to have been born in 1784, a date no later than 1788 for the painting seems inescapable.

In some ways the most astonishing of all Goya's work of this time is the painting of *S. Francis Borja* exorcising demons from a dying man. While a Baroque curtain is still present, its effect (like that of the window) is to abstract the background into a strangely alienated and prison-like scene: a world familiar enough to the early 19th century. Making their first appearance are the monsters and demons of Goya's inner thought world, the modern world of the unconscious, and one commonly associated with Goya only after his terrible illness of the early 1790s. Other modern qualities are somber coloration, dissonances of theme and execution, and expressionist handling of paint. The picture is usually attributed to 1788.

David's *Marat* of 1793 is a modern work in every sense of form and expression, but it is not the first David in which modern qualities come to a head. His *Oath of the Horatii* of 1784, on the other hand, while revolutionary is not yet a modern work. As history, its subject is ancient and mythical rather than contemporary and immediate; the action remains centripetal, the expression rhetorical, the setting theatrical. But the *Tennis Court Oath* of 1790 is centrifugal, contemporary, and immediate. The breakthrough can be traced to the *Death of Socrates* of 1787. While the subject is still ancient history, and centered on stage, the action on the left moves out from the scene, threatening the older principles of centrality and formality. Touches of a realist immediacy appear in the cast shadows of the floor and wall. Here the scratches, lines, edges, and broken marks form a pattern unlike the predisposed patterning of the Renaissance-Baroque tradition, for it reveals the random character so frequent in modern organization—in Impressionism or in Cubism, for example.

In 1788 David began his picture *The Lictors Returning to Brutus the Bodies of his Sons* (exhibited 1789). The subject is still ancient and theatrical, but now the central character (Brutus) has boldly been put into shadow and thrust to a far corner, while his grieving wife and daughters are centered in their area but not in the picture. The central area is occupied by a column, an empty chair, and one of David's familiar outstretched hands—all relatively disconnected and abstract—while the very center is occupied by a prophetically modern still life, detached and insufficiently justified for such a place in such a scene. Here the decentralization has become brutal, while the emptied center utters its modern note of alienation.

Blake's "illuminated printing" (a new method and a modern concept, anticipating William Morris) began in 1787, and his first finished product, *The Songs of Innocence*, appeared in 1789. Alexander Cozens's ink-blot drawings apparently date from 1785 or 1786, as does his revolutionary treatise, *A New Method of Assisting the Invention in Drawing Original Compositions of Landscape* (he died in 1786). Along with Blake, Burns was the first fully romantic (as opposed to pre-romantic) poet; full romanticism belongs to the 19th century. Burns's first major publication (containing some of his greatest poems) came out in 1786.

The 20th Century

The year 1886 enjoyed the last exhibition of the Impressionists as a group; hence they went their different routes, giving way stylistically to late or Neo- or Post-Impressionism, some of which continued until well after 1900. One of the most basic clues to the transition of the middle and later 1880s is the shift in art from nature-realization to picture-making—that is, from an art based on nature to a studio art. Impressionism is nature realization, Pointillism is picture-making. In 1885 Signac adopted Pointillism and Pissarro met Seurat and began to be influenced by their concepts. Seurat added pointillist handling to the *Baignade* probably in 1886, and repainted the *Grande-Jatte* pointillistically during the winter of 1885-6.

Renoir's shift to picture-making is epitomized in the *Grandes Baigneuses* (Philadelphia) of 1885-7. In his later years he recommended finishing a painting in the studio, on the basis of studies made outdoors. This was the same procedure followed by Seurat after 1884; and even Monet, the most nature-oriented and visually sensitive painter of the period, began to shift toward developing the picture in the studio by 1890, if not before. With Monet the dramatic shift to picture-making can be identified in the fall of 1886, when he painted the Belle-Ile pictures. It was at this point that he stopped painting exclusively from nature, but it is also the point at which his approach to the rendering of nature experience undergoes his most radical change.

Compared with the painting Monet had done in the more habitable environs of Etretat in the early 1880s and even down through the summer of 1886, the Belle-Ile pictures suddenly become more expressionist and more abstract. The horizon runs into other elements, or is relegated to a narrow band, or vanishes altogether. Selected elements of rock, sea, and sky are reiterated throughout the painting field. The light no longer reflects the varied and specific conditions of a time of day, temperature, and humidity, but becomes more the product of an inner experience. The color is reduced to two or three major chords, and at times is so abstracted as to be almost monochromatic. The handling changes from a definitively impressionistic to a relatively expressionistic emphasis. In Monet's art at just this time Robert Goldwater detected "the simplification of design, the purification of rhythm, the elimination of contrasting detail, the lessening of perspective, the spread of a dominant color"—all of which are in fact traits belonging to 20th century style with its emphasis on picture-making. This means a primary emphasis on working in the studio or under controlled conditions, and it seems no surprise that during the nineties Monet began to paint "more and more from windows and balconies than outdoors, and the period of retouching in the studio was greatly expanded" (William Seitz). Even Van Gogh, so furiously committed to working outdoors, was from 1887 or 1888 no longer so much a nature-conditioned artist; it has been argued that he was "not properly a painter of 'the effect of light' or a *plein-airiste*, and he was not at all a painter of fugitive moments. Although everything in his painting was executed *en plein air*, even *en plein soleil*, all this was quickly transformed into a smooth and abstract clarity, ideal and decorative in character" (Pierre Godet).

As with Monet (otherwise so different an artist), with Van Gogh the shift in the later 1880s is from a picture which is still primarily a window on nature to a picture which is, as much as anything else, an aesthetic object. Goldwater added to his observations on Monet's change that the picture "has turned into something complete in itself." Gauguin's new style amounted to a comparable aestheticism: he was speaking of "Synthetism" as early as 1887. Toulouse-Lautrec and others "after 1885 paid more attention to the expression of movement within the two-dimensional linear pattern" (G.H. Hamilton), a frequent desideratum of 20th century style.

In the later 1880s all of the major, and some of the minor movements of 20th century art put in their first appearance. Neo-Impressionism emerged with Seurat, late Impressionism with Renoir and Monet (with whom it was to continue into the 1920s, and if we count Bonnard, still longer). Symbolism too appeared at this time. The year 1886 saw the Symbolist Manifesto, but symbolism applies in its way to the later art of Monet, Van Gogh, Redon, and others. Thus Lionello Venturi found a Monet *Haystack* to be "at once a neo-Impressionist painting and also a Symbolist one."

20th century Surrealism must be taken back to Munch and Ensor. Hamilton refers to the "transition from a Naturalist to a Symbolist aesthetic" and observes that by 1885 "Ensor had passed beyond Naturalism to a realm of his own invention." Redon too was an inaugurator—rather than a precursor—of Surrealism: he sought his imagery above all in dreams.

Expressionism must be dated from the later 1880s. J.P. Hodin calls Van Gogh's self-portraits of 1889 and 1890 early examples of Expressionist portrait-painting; they are followed by portraits by Josephson and Munch in the early nineties. But already there is a good deal of Expressionism in Ensor by 1888 if not before, and in Van Gogh by 1886 or 1887. His *Potato Eaters* of 1885 still belongs to realism and romanticism, that is, to 19th century styles. But the pictures of shoes in 1886 initiate the shift to Expressionism, which has been well established by 1887 in the portrait of Père Tanguy: that is to say, the topical and narrative qualities of the earlier works have been replaced by more abstract, decorative, and programmatic "expressions." Kenneth Clark has called Van Gogh the man for whom the term Expressionism was invented.

The programmatic strain in 20th century art and aesthetics can be seen as well in Monet's *Haystacks* and *Poplars*, which might also be considered the first "serial" art, much as Seurat can be claimed for the first "optical" artist. It is even possible to see at this time the beginning of the Conceptual art of the later 20th century: Robert Herbert has noted that in Seurat's work sensations are "felt to be the point of departure for a highly conceptual art" though the term, uncapitalized, actually applies to many styles and movements throughout the century. But the most pervasive of all 20th century tendencies is what is generally called abstraction. The beginnings of abstract art are plain enough in Seurat and Gauguin (and even Van Gogh tried his hand briefly at abstraction), but they are prominent in Cézanne.

Two paintings of Gardanne (one in the Metropolitan Museum, N.Y., and the other in the Brooklyn Museum) were apparently painted in 1885-6. Already in these pictures we find the use of bare canvas as an aesthetic function; an ambivalence of planes as was to become a cardinal feature of cubism; and the emergence of marks which dominate the forms they represent, establishing grids, patterns, clusters, and other congeries of line and plane which belong to picture-making more than to an evocation of nature experience. Cubism therefore can be traced back to certain passages in just such pictures, but not, it would appear, to anything before this time. Picasso called Cézanne his "father." Venturi called Cubism the "renaissance of that architectural consciousness which the 19th century had lost." And where does this sort of architectural consciousness begin if not in Cézanne?

Degas too was to live well into the 20th century and to be in his later years a major 20th century artist; but like Monet, Cézanne, and Renoir, the major change in his art came in the years around and just after 1886. Compare *La Toilette* of 1885 with *Le Tub* of 1886. In the earlier picture the space is still readable and the figures coherent; in the later picture spatial angles are unaccountably though brilliantly mixed, and the figure is occluded, distorted, and dehumanized. The earlier work, though artful, is still naturalistic in effect; the later work, though sharply observant, emphasizes picture-making. Comparable changes can be identified at the same time in ballet and equestrian pictures.

The transition with Degas is datable right around the scheduled year of 1886, as are the key changes in Monet, Seurat, Toulouse-Lautrec, and Cézanne. It was the same in music, where Romanticism was replaced by what is often called Late Romanticism: Curt Sachs called the period 1886-1922 "the age of Debussy and Strauss." According to the timetable, 20th century style in its turn should be replaced by an upcoming 21st century style in and about 1985.

The Structure of a Major Culture 27

The Metropolitan Museum of Art. Bequest of Mrs. H.O. Havemeyer, 1929. The H.O. Havemeyer Collection. (29.100.35)

Plate I
"A Woman Having Her Hair Combed (La Toilette)," by Edgar Degas (1834-1917).

Galerie du Jeu de Paume d'Orsay, Paris.

Plate II
"Le Tub," by Edgar Degas (1834-1917).

C. The Centuries by Astrological Sign

Since there are twelve stylistic centuries in the Evolutionary epoch, it is not surprising that they are representative of twelve cosmic principles, the same principles that are reflected in the signs of the zodiac. What is surprising is that the centuries do not follow the usual sequence of the zodiac—beginning with Aries and ending with Pisces. Instead they begin with Capricorn and end with Aquarius, reading backwards. The significance of this sequence will become clear when we consider the sequences of a cycle of the major cultures (cf. Chapter II) and of the astrological Months (cf. Chapter IV).

The principle governing an Evolutionary century is to be found essentially in the astrological sign, but it may be reflected also in the planet or the house associated with that sign. Therefore primary reference will be made to the signs, but planets or houses may be invoked where particularly pertinent.

The 11th Century

The first Western century is the "eleventh", running from 995-1094. It is governed by the principles of Capricorn, Saturn, and the 10th House. One of the most expressive forms of 11th century architecture is the keep, or donjon: the Tower of London is a good example, with its prison-like massiveness. Rudhyar finds Capricorn signifying man as a maker of forms, forms which have the capacity to become prisons. Pevsner finds that the Norman keep has "the same compactness, the same disdain of embellishment as the Norman church" (these qualities too are Capricornian). The earliest datable keep, notes Pevsner, is that of Langeais on the Loire; it was built in 992—that is, three years before the due date of the century, which puts it on the cusp.

In early Romanesque (11th century) church architecture Pevsner finds a "mighty presence" and further allows that "this plainness is typical of the 11th century, a plainness of statement expressed in the plainness of forms"—all Capricornian traits. Pevsner also finds, "There is no wavering here—as there was none in the ruthless policy of William the Conqueror in subduing and normanizing England."

William as a figure seems to stand for the entire 11th century, and as a figure he is magnificently, as well as severely, Capricornian.

It is not William's personality that counts here, but his policy. The terrible efficiency with which he reorganized the social structure of England is Capricornian in its thoroughness, its ruthlessness, and its long endurance. Pagan gives some leading Capricorn tendencies: ambition and adaptability, industry and momentum, authority and scorn; and conformity no matter how uncomfortable. She finds in Capricorn the thinner or pruner, willing to sacrifice the minority; the capacity to be unscrupulous though not ordinarily cruel; weightiness and impressiveness and regulation. Pevsner describes Norman architecture as "blunt, massive, and overwhelmingly strong." Conant describes the great buildings of Norman England as "all extraordinarily bold, simple, and uniform in style." Capricorn spurns embellishment, and 11th century architecture is remarkably unadorned.

Capricorn is much concerned with power, especially in the sense of organization. William "retained in his own hands forty percent of all England, and was himself by far the greatest baron in the land.... In one word, William established in England a feudal absolutism. Master of his barons, William was no less a master of the clergy. This is remarkable as the reign of William fell in the age of Hildebrand.... Lanfranc was an organizer, not a scholar or saint" (W. Ault). The great Lanfranc (who became William's Archbishop of Canterbury) had already in 1045 at the abbey of Bec "set up a school which soon achieved international importance. The chief Norman monasteries became important organs of the flourishing new feudal state" (Conant). "Feudal absolutism", "master of the clergy", "organizer not saint"—these are pre-eminently Capricornian. The absolutism here is not regal and showy, as in the Leonine 16th century, but severe and strictly ordered, with precise tables of organization, precise rights and duties, and with an emphasis on mutual loyalty and support, especially in the Capricornian vertical direction.

If William and Lanfranc be taken as specifically Norman, consider the salient 11th century role played by Gregory VII. Here (writes Ault) is "the real founder of the medieval papacy. He proclaimed its right to the suzerainty of Christendom.... The pope has the right to sit in judgment on kings; kingdoms are merely papal fiefs" (referring to his program, if not his achievement). "On the whole, this estimate of the great pope seems a just one: He was 'too absolute, too rigid, too obstinate, too extreme to play his part with entire advantage to himself and his cause.' " All these are Capricornian if not Saturnian traits.

By historical principle, Capricorn seems the appropriate sign to initiate a structure of Evolutionary centuries. Capricorn is cardinal, which means initiatory action. And it is earth, which makes it suitable for a grounding, a foundation on which to rear a structure—for the Evolutionary epoch is in fact an elaborate structure, with its three epicycles and other internal formations. By the same principle, it seems appropiate that the cycle of Evolutionary centuries should end with Aquarius, the fixed air sign, fixed meaning stabilizing and air meaning unifying or summarizing.

The 12th Century

The 12th century (1094-1193) was ruled by Sagittarius, and the 9th House, with Jupiterian flavor. By the end of the 11th century there began to appear a "new differentiation. More complex, more varied, more lively forms...less force but more individual expression" (Pevsner). The new century is that of Bernard, of Abelard, of Henry II, of Beckett. They "stand before us as human beings, William the Conqueror as a natural phenomenon, irresistible and relentless." Here is, in broad terms, the move from a cardinal to a mutable sign, from Capricorn to Sagittarius.

If the 11th century is exemplified in William, so Abelard's career articulates the 12th. Abelard's life "throws light on a whole period and a whole society with which it was in so many respects bound up. It shows us the life of the student, travelling...sometimes immense distances to sit at the feet of a famous teacher.... We can feel the excitement running through this small yet rapidly expanding intellectual world, the intoxication with which they handled these still unfamiliar mental tools, and the heroic, almost ascetic light in which they viewed the philosopher and his function.... To his pupils he was a teacher without parallel, with his loathing of stale formulae, his boldness and originality of thought...his sheer intellectual agility and the vigor and clarity of his explanations. Abelard threw his whole personality into his teaching...constantly on the lookout for an argument, endlessly, and not always justly, at odds with the old masters, and ever ready to involve himself in public disputes.... Nevertheless Abelard always displayed a distinct yearning for orthodoxy. When his views were condemned he protested that he had been misunderstood and not that he was right and his adversaries wrong...to some extent he was the victim of his own nature. This made him a symbol of intellectual revolt..." (Philippe Wolff).

Almost all of this is Sagittarian—the eager traveller of long distances, the rapidly expanding intellectual world, the mental intoxication, the heroic view of the philosopher and his function, the loathing of stale formulae, the boldness and originality of thought, the intellectual agility and vigor, a throwing of the whole personality into teaching, the constant lookout for an argument, the readiness to be involved in public dispute, an originality yet combined with a yearning for orthodoxy. Sagittarius is often identified as the teacher, sometimes as the sage, and the 9th House may refer to the teacher, that is, as distinguished from the school. At least until late in the 12th century, the teacher counted for more than the school, and the students were international.

Sagittarius indicates travel, especially that which is distant and enthusiastic. Of all the far and eager travels of Western civilization, none outrank the Crusades; and these belong almost entirely to the 12th century (1094-1193). The First Crusade began with Urban's call at Clermont in 1095, and was in effect from 1096-99. The Second Crusade (1147-9) was followed by the capture of Jerusalem in 1187, which precipitated the Third Crusade, led by Barbarosa, Richard, and Philip of France; this ended in a three-year truce, called in 1192. "The Third Crusade ended the golden age of the crusades.... The Fourth Crusade shocked Europe, discredited the Papacy and the whole crusading movement, and facilitated the advance of the Turks" (Langer).

The 12th century saw the first universities of the West; nor was this Sagittarian interest found only in France, for "Italy in the late 11th and 12th centuries was in an intellectual ferment" (Wolff). The law and lawyers are occupations that "come under Sagittarius" (M. Hone). "Of all the centuries the 12th is the most legal," said Maitland, pointing out that "in no other age, since the classical days of Roman law, has so large a part of the sum total of intellectual endeavor been devoted to jurisprudence."

The "Twelfth Century Renaissance" was distinguished for its poetry, its letter writing and sermons, its philosophy and theology, as well as law—all Sagittarian activities. It was the "age of the sudden but fleeting vogue of this or that school made brilliant by a teacher more eloquent or more subtle than the rest" (Robert S. Lopez). This could sound like Gemini—but the 12th century favored disputations, for example the Cistertian (S. Bernard) versus S. Denis (Suger), or Abelard's *Sic et Non*. The sense of disputation here goes deeper than Gemini, for it has to be, must be reconciled. Furthermore, Jupiter signifies orthodox religion, and Abelard could never renounce orthodoxy.

The 13th Century

The 13th century (1193-1292) was ruled by Scorpio. The typifying crusade in this century was not in the East, but against the Albigensians. It was proclaimed in 1208, and completed in 1226 "after a long chapter of horrors" (Langer). Later in the century Bishop Bernard de Castanet, a Dominican Inquisitor, "persecuted the remnants of the Albigensians with diabolical cruelty" (Frankl). Brutality or bloodshed may be associated with other signs, but deliberate cruelty is Scorpionic. And the appearance of the Inquisitor reminds us that the 13th is the century which invented the Inquisition. The "medieval Inquisition began c. 1233 when the pope commissioned certain Dominicans to investigate the Albigenses of S. France. As it evolved...the Inquisition soon resorted to judicial torture..." (Columbia-Viking *Encyclopedia*). This Western-wide Inquisition is to be distinguished from the one established in 1478 by Ferdinand and Isabella, which, though "far better organized, harsher, and freer with the death sentence than the medieval Inquisition" (*ibid.*), never took hold outside of Spain, and is thus attributable to a (Scorpionic) side of the Spanish character only.

The original purpose of the Dominicans (founded 1216) was the extirpation of heresy, and the Inquisition was formed and administered under their direction. Convinced of the evil of their times, they constituted a disciplined society dedicated to poverty and celibacy. Other mendicant friars also appeared in the 13th century: the Carmelites, the Franciscans, the Austin Friars, all of whom volunteered for poverty and dependence on alms, and were known for industry and learning rather than originality (compare the premium on originality in the 12th century). All this, including the strong sense of extremes—e.g., cruelty and self-denial—is Scorpionic.

A 13th century extremism may further be seen in what Swoboda termed the "co-existence of unfettered idealism and unprejudiced observation of nature," or what Dvorak called Idealism and Naturalism in Gothic art.

Dvorak describes certain 13th century artistic situations in terms that bespeak the Scorpionic. Of the Visitation and the Crucifixion, he writes, "in Romanesque art the scene was conceived in the sense of the typically classical, materially motivated grouping of individual figures; this conception was transformed in Gothic art into an almost motionless, spiritual union...expression was not only intensified...but even those psychic processes...for the first time in the history of art were conceived as something passive—from the quiet, inwardly directed absorption into self to the most powerful emotions of joy or sorrow...." Of the rows of statues on a typical Gothic (i.e., 13th century) facade, Dvorak writes "the majority of the figures are in no way related to one another, but rather they range beyond any form of action over and above symbolic allusion. Nevertheless they are figures filled with an inner tension based not on an act of the will but stemming rather from a receptive psychic process." The emotional intensity of Scorpio contains (according to Pagan) nothing sentimental. Writing of the 13th century cathedral, Pevsner warned that we are "liable to a reaction in these vast halls which is far too romantic, nebulous, sentimental, whereas to the cleric of the 13th century everything was probably lucid. Lucid, but transcendental."

Scorpio, the most powerful of the signs (Cope, among others), governs what is sometimes called the greatest of centuries—in any case it is the century that produced the most powerful architectural system and the most powerful intellectual system of the West. Scorpio signifies the combination of disparate forces in a powerful whole, under the control of an excellent executive—which is in turn an excellent description of what the architect of the 13th century composed out of the experimental forms bequeathed from the 12th century.

Scorpio—and the 8th House—are preoccupied with death. In 1194 the office of coroner was established in England (Scorpio is associated with both death and with the medical profession). In the 13th century all wounds had to be recorded, a practice not much found after that century. The office of coroner was at its zenith in the second half of the 13th century, being second in importance only to the sheriff among county offices; the coroner's office "was filled by slightly less eminent men after 1300 than before" (R.F. Hunnisett), while both county and borough coroners declined in importance during the 14th and 15th centuries. Eventually the coroner was replaced in large part by the justice of the peace. In the 13th century the coroner performed such other Scorpionic functions as holding inquests, hearing appeals and the confessions of felons, and attaching witnesses and suspects. In the 13th century the county coroner was almost invariably a knight; after 1300 this was the exception rather than the rule.

The 13th century at large was a time of hospital building, wherein surgery received special emphasis. The famed Italian physicians were as distinguished in surgery as in medicine, and elsewhere we hear of great surgeons such as Lanfranc, or William of Salicet who like Mondaville wrote treatises on surgery. Dissection was practiced, and surgery separated from medicine. Unlike the 12th century's inclination to intellectual disputation, all this was thoroughly practical. It was in medicine "much more than in law or theology, that the eminently practical character of university teaching during the 13th century can be seen, at least in the form in which it will appeal to a scientific generation"; furthermore, the "standards of the 13th century in medical education were much higher than our own" (J.J. Walsh).

Scorpio is the most mysterious of the signs, and it was in the 13th century that the mystery play was developed and became popular. To Scorpios, Cope says "your eyes tell whole stories"; this sign is generally recognized as the one exemplifying the eye as the window of the soul. The invention of eyeglasses in the West appears to date from the 13th century, possibly attendant on the suggestion by Roger Bacon that convex lenses be used. And the eyes in sculpture and painting are intense.

The colored glass interiors of 13th century churches were dark by comparison with 14th century glass and produced a dim religious light, as if through a glass darkly. Dim but sure. Compared with the experimental gropings of 12th century art, the solutions of the 13th century have a Scorpionic certainty. Focillon notes that the tympana were emptied of their tumult in a single stroke, and finds throughout 13th century art a "rhythm of concealed relationships...whose symbolic significance it translates but does not reveal."

Ruskin observed that from the close of the 12th and throughout the 13th century, color was solemn and deep. And he cited the most frequently used colors of the period as blue, purple, scarlet, and gold, with certain others, but especially green. As against these Scorpionic predilections, the colors of the 14th century tended to be lighter, paler, and gayer: the colors of air.

The 14th Century

The 14th century (1292-1391) was characterized by Libra and Venus. Though still medieval, it was a broad-minded and enlightened time compared to the deeply and jealously religious 13th century. Libra is the sign of fickle pleasure, of elegance and preciousness, of grace and the aircastle and the Rosenkavalier. The rich, dim color of 13th century stained glass was replaced in the 14th century by an effect which Focillon calls "limpidity and optical delicacy." 14th century architecture in every country is light, decorative, open, and airy. 14th century painting is characterized especially by the Sienese school with its courtly grace. 14th century music is represented by the Ars Nova, with its "spirit...aimed at strictness and balance" (Curt Sachs), by the madrigal and the chace, by the rejection of cantus firmus and counterpoint in favor of "an almost chordal, harmonious accompaniment of the melody." To Burckhardt lyric poetry was the chief literary form of the 14th century.

Venus and Libra are dedicated to Love, as is so much literature of the 14th century. Of the top writers of the century, Dante and Petrarch and Boccaccio are all love poets, and Chaucer's *Troilus and Criseyde* is a tale of courtly love. Dante is inseparable from Beatrice; Boccaccio's *Filostrato* was the source for Chaucer's *Troilus,* while Petrarch wrote "the first great love-poems in the Latin language" (Egon Friedell), wherein "all the lover's transports are analyzed with a fullness unmatched before in any work of vernacular literature" (F. Artz). In the 14th century theology itself became romantic (Focillon). The Dance of Death became a romance; it is even possible (for writers have done so) to speak of the romance of the romance. All this, however, was romantic without being sentimental, as opposed to Taurus and the 19th century, which are both.

Libra means elegance—the opposite of grossness—and proportions in 14th century figures as well as in architecture are elegant and slender by comparison with either the 13th or the 15th centuries. As to costume, Mary Houston has noted the "noble simplicity of construction and natural silhouette of the 13th century, compared with the slender elegance of the 14th, and the riot of variety and exaggeration in the 15th."

The 14th was the century of chivalry in the romantic sense; it saw founding of orders of chivalry such as the Star and the Golden Fleece (chivalry distinguishes Venus, while Libra is the gallant lover). It was an age of the court, the courtly and courtship, with a premium on refinement, enchantment, and gentility and exquisiteness of manners. The new music was distasteful to John XXII, who found that it disturbed devotion, intoxicated the ear, and perverted the listener.

Libra is pre-eminently the aesthetic sign; the 14th was a century of art for art's sake, of straining for perfection—as typified in Duccio, Simone Martini, or Petrarch, in whom "everything is aesthetic feeling" (F. Artz) and formal perfection is of supreme value in itself. As against Scorpio, who often finds value in suffering, Libra prefers delight; to Boccaccio man was meant not merely to suffer but to enjoy. In Siena was created what has been called the landscape of happiness, while French mural painting too was given to secular feeling espousing the happiness of life. If the Sienese and the French are the most particularly expressive of (and productive in) the 14th century, we must note the ready acceptance and diffusion of Sienese art in every part of Western Europe, and at the same time note the qualities of delicacy, grace, sensitivity, nuance, and charm in such different artists as Jean Pucelle and Andrea Pisano.

In considering the 14th century naves of Bayonne and Vendome, Frankl wrote, "It can be said, paradoxically, that these architects wanted, as far as possible, to use pure light as their only building material"—Libra being not only an air sign, but one given particularly to "light" in the sense of clarity and illumination. To this the Libran value of "de-light" is related. More Libran qualities appear in another Frankl observation: "The tendency to purity, correctness, and elegant preciosity reaches its full maturity in the church of S. Ouen at Rouen. Here building continued to the plan of 1318...shafts... floating dreamily in space, elegant yet ascetic." In sculpture of the later 14th century Focillon found "equilibrium itself," a "profound repose," and the "harmonious life of the forms."

The Classical Civilization (Greek, Etruscan, and ancient Roman) was Libran, and it is appropriate that an affective rediscovery of this civilization was made in the 14th century. Petrarch was one of the first scholars since Antiquity to propose self-development as a valid ideal (the idea of the ideal, as well as the idea of self-development, is Libran). As to whether the "rebirth" of Classical values of the Renaissance came with the 14th or with the 15th century is a matter of definition. But it may be said that the appeal of the Classical spirit was of greater relative importance in the 14th than in the 15th century.

The 15th Century

The 15th century (1391-1490) was ruled by Virgo. This was a century of Virgoan workmanship, of manual craft, of conscientiousness in medium and exactitude in detail. Compare Schongauer's engraving *Flight into Egypt* with Dürer's (16th century) woodcut of the same theme. In the Schongauer we can hardly see the wood for the trees (another Virgoan tendency) though the trees are fascinating. There is a widespread occurrence in 15th century art of such Virgo qualities as delicacy, sensitivity, refinement, all involved in complex organizations. Not only is the form complicated, but usually the iconography as well.

Virgo—the Virgin—can be prudish. It may be surprising to discover how few nudes were rendered during the 15th century. And of these, fewer still were large, free-standing, or at ease. Donatello's bronze *David* is an exception, though even this figure is not completely nude or natural, while Verrocchio's subsequent *David* is still smaller and less nude. The Western tradition of the nude as we think of it does not really begin until Signorelli and Giorgione, in the 16th century.

The 15th century was well endowed with what Cope has called Virgo's "highly sensitized sensory faculties." The tactile sensations are emphasized in Tuscany and Flanders, the visual in Venice and Holland. Variety is a Virgo trait and no other century shows such differentiation of local styles. This is a Mercurial quality (Mercury is held to rule Virgo as well as Gemini) and is related to Virgo's whimsicality; Frankl observed a whimsical tendency during the 15th century.

Such Virgo qualities as personal reserve and pristine purity, precise observation with humility, nervous articulation and brisk efficiency, are all exemplified in the three most characteristic painters of the century, Jan van Eyck, Piero della Francesca, and Giovanni Bellini. Compare Bellini's humility before nature with the poetry of his follower, Giorgione—also contemplative, but no longer humble.

Virgo is sharply inclined toward critical analysis. The researches of Brunelleschi and Alberti and Mantegna, of Uccello and Piero and Leonardo, all show Virgo curiosity and method. Leonardo Bruni, called Aretino, was the "founder and one of the most profound exponents of the new school of humanist historiography. In his *Historiarum Florentini Fopuli libri xii*, begun about 1415 and still not quite completed at his death in 1444, he set a standard for the critical use of sources" (W.K. Ferguson). The *Historiarum* of Flavio Biondo (1439-53) "is the only history written during the 15th century that can compare with it in originality or influence. It is a careful, critical work...with its plenitude of definite dates, its factual treatment of events...." One last example is the humanist Lorenzo Valla, of whom Ferguson says that for all the diversity of his critical interests, he "remained essentially a grammarian and philologist." What Virgo does not like is theory for its own sake, generalization, or ideal philosophy. Ferguson notes it has been charged that the humanists "contributed little, in this early period at least, to formal philosophy. This...may be admitted. As philosophers they were amateurs. Their philosophy was largely a matter of ethics and good sense, founded upon eclectic gleanings from the antique literary sources. Its aim was simply to aid men to live well." Almost all of this represents Virgo: the eclecticism, the good sense, the philology and grammar—the analytical love of words.

The love of small size and of proliferation of detail is particularly indicative of Virgo. The art of Jan van Eyck has been called "microscopic" but, says Max Friedländer, in fact this artist "never magnified the small—on the contrary he diminished the big without impoverishing it," a beautifully Virgoan process. Richard Turner has found in Giovanni Bellini the "belief that in its smallest detail [nature] reflects without distortion the love and bountifulness of...God." Precisely the same can be said of the Flemish painters of the 15th century—but not of the 16th. This love of multiplicity of detail went along with a tendency to multiplicity in composition; Huizinga found multiplicity to be a "characteristic of 15th century art. It rarely succeeds in finding harmony and unity." Unity and harmony and subordination are the desiderata with which the High Renaissance replaces—in the Leonine 16th century—the fresh, multifoliate purity of the Virgoan 15th century.

Virgo is often associated with Vulcan, who is said to obey patrons without asking why, though with originality and according to his own design, and emphasizing execution. This describes the 15th century artist as against the 14th or the 16th century type. To Virgo is attributed needlecraft. The 15th century is the heyday of Flemish textures and textiles, and while Italy imported her tapestries, the Quattrocento is distinguished for silks, velvets, and embroidery.

Virgo is wiry. Such is the art of Castagno, Rogier, Pollaiuolo, Pacher, or Verrocchio: Compare the fullness of the art of Raphael and Giorgione, Veronese and Bruegel. Similarly, the 15th century's concept of the artist as craftsman was replaced by the 16th century concept—held not only by Leonardo, Dürer, and Michelangelo but also by their patrons—of the artist as heroic creator. At the same time, the brisk efficiency of the Virgoan 15th century was replaced by the relaxed splendor of the Leonine 16th.

There is a dry quality to the 15th century, partly attributable to the dryness of any earth sign, partly because of Virgo's own dissecting and analytical intellect. This dryness may be seen alike in the tempera handling of the Italian painters and in the oil handling of the Netherlanders. By comparison the oil handling in the 16th century (which in the 1490's began to be applied to canvas) is bold and free and energetic. Where Van Eyck and Piero had suppressed the brushstroke, we are now confronted with the *sfumato* of Leonardo and Giorgione, the virtuosity of Correggio and Tintoretto, the bold expressiveness of Titian and El Greco.

Virgo is associated with Mercury, indeed it is in some respects a "mercurial" sign. The music of the 15th century "had been full of ingenuity and intellectual contrivance; what the 16th contributed was the directly sensuous, poetic expression of an idea" (Alfred Einstein). The intellectual ingenuity is Mercurian, the poetic idea Leonine. The same contrast is found in painting if we compare Uccello or Mantegna with Giorgione or Titian.

The 16th Century

The 16th century (1490-1589) was ruled by Leo, which encourages royalty, grandeur, splendor, creativity. We have seen how the 16th century began about 1490 in certain works of Leonardo da Vinci. With Leonardo, said Burckhardt, came a "majesty", and it is one that continues in Raphael and Holbein, Titian and Veronese. In Leonardo's *Last Supper* appears a "calmness and greatness which may be called aristocratic insofar as aristocratic has the meaning of noble; a word which cannot be applied to any painter of the Quattrocento... this air of greatness was to become the common property of the Italians of the 16th century" (H. Wölfflin).

Against the active man of the 15th century Kenneth Clark opposes the heroes and giants of the 16th. The new century expresses not only nobility, as in Leonardo and Raphael, but also heroic will, mastery, even megalomania—all Leonine traits. From the *Last Supper* of Leonardo to that of Tintoretto (S. Giorgio Maggiore) runs an unbroken sequence of sumptuous banquets dedicated to grandeur and generalization, to elevation and majesty. The qualities that Vasari prized in art—*bellezza, invenzione, ordine, richezza*—are prized or practiced from Bramante to Palladio, and help us understand what is shared by Dürer and Raphael. Someone has spoken of Raphael's "proud halls."

Against the multiple variety of the Virgoan 15th century comes the centralized command of the Leonine 16th; grace becomes grandeur, and the devout response to nature's phenomena is replaced by a confident, Olympian ideal. In Raphael, as against his teacher Perugino, Jakob Rosenberg found "a new, powerfully unifying swing throughout the composition, which is simplified and freed of the staccato rhythm of the Quattrocento painting." Leo likes the stately, the spacious, the monumental. In its gigantic scale, massive bulk and unification of stories, the Strozzi Palace is the "direct origin of the four-square block palaces which were to rise in Cinquecento Rome" (F. Hartt); the Strozzi Palace was begun in 1489.

Leo is the actor. The theatrical, writes M. Levey, is "exactly what separates the lucid, human 15th century world from the new stage-like grand manner in which emotions are acted out by people who, like antique classical actors, seem masked, strangely robed...." The actor is masked, yet he has his Leonine personality as well. In the 16th century "the personal style of the great artist is what was valued" (Panofsky). Leo is the most widely creative sign of the twelve; in the 16th century arose the "belief that art possesses divinely creative energy" (Levey). All signs have creative power, but Leo's seems related to the abundance associated with solar energy (the Sun is Leo's ruler) and with the sense of "mastery" associated with Leo's sense of rulership. Such mastery must be purchased at a price; in terms of centuries, the price was the pristine and ingenuous freshness of the 15th century. Kenneth Clark saw that Leonardo's *Virgin of the Rocks* (c. 1483, Louvre) "is Leonardo's last Quattrocento picture and still shows the graces of that enchanted interval. Mastery of execution has not overlaid the freshness of the types." A decade later his *Last Supper* was to do just that.

By this time the heroic had triumphed over the trivial, dramatic unity over the fresh variety of nature. Subordination of detail to grouping and organizing principles is a familiar distinction of the High from the Early Renaissance. Leo organizes and delegates. Art historians speak of the formalizing, summarizing, and harmonizing character of the High Renaissance: Pagan says of Leo, "This power sums up and harmonizes the characteristics of all the others," and of Apollo (ideal ruler of Leo) that he "perfected the lyre invented by Mercury [ruler of Virgo], adding to it many strings and drawing from them harmonies unheard before." In the 16th century, Panofsky noted, "artists would fashion Christ in the image of Apollo."

Leo is characterized by exaltation and dignity, symmetry and clarity, glory and majesty; and produces works of large scale and grandeur, of monumentality and ambition. In such qualities we may find the underlying unity between such otherwise contrasting artists as Dürer and Raphael, Leonardo and Holbein, Titian and Michelangelo. In the 16th century the Virgo love of detail—so green in the 15th century—is now surrendered; Leo (says Carter) likes to "deal with the large issue," and leave the detail to others.

The voyages of discovery of the 15th century seem spurred by Virgo-like curiosity; those of Columbus were moved by what Santayana called "the soul's invincible surmise." The 16th is the century of the Reformation and irreconcilable religious struggle; Leo has been called the sign of "invincible belief."

Leo is royal, majestic, and monarchical. The ultimate royal form in the history of the European state was absolute monarchy. Great claims of absolute monarchy were made by James I of England, and great success was made of it by Louis XIV of France. But both of these were latter-day derivations; absolute monarchy itself was a creation of the 16th century.

Along with the Tudors (from 1485) rose strong monarchies in other countries of Europe. The Medici, from being first citizens, became Grand Dukes. Isabella and Ferdinand united Spain. With Charles VIII and Louis XII of France appeared what Burckhardt called "the newly formed royalism." In 1500 it was "not yet the nation but the monarch—the prince—that was worshipped.... The prince was becoming a sort of god" (C.J.H. Hayes). The two most famous books of the century were to be Castiglione's *Courtier* and Machiavelli's *Prince*.

The doctrine of the divine right of kings came from France: not in the 17th, but in the 16th century. While absolutism was not consummated in France until the 17th, or in Germany until the 18th century, it was consummated in the 16th century by those leaders in political form, the Spanish and the English. Charles V, greatest of Hapsburg emperors, inherited an empire on which the sun never set; in 1527 he made a prisoner of the pope himself. His son, Philip II, sought absolute power along with the extirpation of heresy. From Loyola sprang Jesuit absolutism.

In England, the real founders of despotic government were the Tudors. The Parliaments of Henry VIII and Elizabeth were highly tractable, while those of James I more than once did "resist him and defeat him" (Maitland). With James, the doctrine of divine right is a posture borrowed from France. The English citizenry, which had accepted all manner of arbitrary government under the Tudors, by the 17th century were moved to depose and execute a monarch, in stark opposition to the oldest monarchical tradition in Europe.

In the 16th century the sovereignty of the king, or of king in Parliament, existed both in fact and in theory; it applied to religion, and it had no need of a standing army. This was quite different from medieval sovereignty, and the Protestant revolution contributed by encouraging the king to extend his authority over religious as well as civil affairs.

The doctrine of sovereignty was "implicit in Machiavelli, and possibly also in Marsiglio of Padua, but it became explicit in the *Commonwealth* of Jean Bodin" (H.J. Randall). The theory of sovereignty held that the state was founded on the family (a Leonine orientation)—not, as in the Middle Ages, on the group. Only the sovereign was able to make or to repeal law. All over the world, as H.G. Wells put it, "the close of the 16th century saw monarchy prevailing and tending towards absolutism."

Nor was the Leonine sense of power confined to kingship. In general, 16th century man "gave himself up to a pursuit of power.... This was the primitive age of power" (G. Bazin). The Reformation and Counter Reformation were deeply involved in power struggles, and in the dramatic struggles of hero and martyr. Rudhyar says that under Leo the hero "thrives on tragedy.... Some group...must be dark and evil." There must be pagans "condemned to the eternal shadow of hell, if the 'man of God' is to show forth his inspired mind, and his God-energizing faith, either by converting the unillumined, or by dying the martyr's death at their hands." And he calls Leo the sign of rebels and dramatists, of movers and shakers. "They bring tragedy in the form of ruthless awakenings." Luther, Servetus, Calvin, Loyola are invoked by M.P. Hall's description of Leo as a "combination of idealism and fatalism."

Of fashions, Friedell observed an "imposing majesty of Italian dress" of the time, or in the north "a dignity proper to pedagogs, parsons, and princelets," along with "a conscious mannerism... period costume...theatrical disguise...stage fever"—all Leonine, and accompanied by the introduction of the Italian (Ariosto), the Spanish ("Celestina"), the French (Jodelle), and the Elizabethan theaters. It has been reported that the color red was so popular with the nobility that peasants were forbidden to wear it: Red is Leonine and royal. Referring broadly to the 16th century, F.B. Artz sums it up as "an age of royal and princely culture."

The 17th Century

The 17th century (1589-1688) was ruled by Cancer. Compared with the theatrical roles of 16th century leaders—Julius II, Charles V, Henry VIII, Philip II, Elizabeth—the leader in the 17th century was likely to play a concealed role. Richelieu, Colbert, Mazarin, and Olivares often surpassed their monarchs in power. Cromwell was never more than Lord Protector, where Henry VIII had been King as well as Protector and Only Supreme Head of the Church and Clergy of England.

Cancer is the lunar sign, the most nocturnal of the twelve. Caravaggio substituted nocturnal light for daylight. Elsheimer established a landscape art of feeling and tone (Cancer) in which the moon and nightlight play major roles. The moon reflects. The 17th century is the age of the mirror and of myriad reflections, from Caravaggio's *Bacchus* or *Narcissus* down to the *Galerie des Glaces* at Versailles (begun 1678), which sums up a century of walls of glass that reflect one another and the spectator. Pools of limpid water bejewelled the art of formal gardens. 17th century Baroque created an "orgy of colors and light, glaringly reflected from the polished marble armor of spacious colonnaded halls" (O. Hagen).

Such glittering effects, epitomized in Velasquez, Claude, or Cuyp, signify both the Moon's reflection and Cancer's quality of shine. The painting and sculpture of the 17th century attained the most shimmering illusion of reality in Western history. Cancer is a water sign, which undoubtedly contributes to the moist atmospheres and deep mists that abound in Baroque painting. A "baroque villa without water is almost unthinkable; it was the period's favorite element" (Wölfflin). And the century was rich in maritime activity; it was the golden age of the Dutch fleet, it saw the inauguration of a French navy by Louis XIV to meet the Dutch, and the creation of the English navy by the soldier Blake.

Cancer is a romantic sign, the most personal of the twelve. The 17th century is the only period before Romanticism proper about which historians are tempted to use such a term. Romantic is applicable to Claude, Rembrandt, Seghers, Ruisdael, Salvator Rosa, whereas in the 16th century Altdorfer and Grünewald were expressionists, and Hubert Robert in the 18th is better called picturesque. Cancer is the sign of moods; Elsheimer created the landscape of mood, which was followed by so many others in the century; but this applies even to the "modes" of Poussin, which were but a classicizing form of moods.

Cancer is the sign of loneliness in the crowd, of centering in the self. Think of Seghers and Rembrandt, but also of Velasquez, whose masterpiece, *Las Meninas*, is a demonstration of the artist as introvert. Cancer reveals a fascination in the eternal feminine. Rich female characterization leads the portraiture of Hals and Rembrandt and Van Dyck; it is striking in Rubens and Philippe de Champaigne and Bernini; and the female is by far the leading subject in Velazquez and Vermeer.

In overall subjects, in all schools of the 17th century, it may be noted that previously popular themes such as the Annunciation are replaced by martyrdoms and depictions of saints in ecstasy—that is, themes which are at once watery, emotive, romantic. In such an area we find links between artists otherwise so different as the Italian Bernini, the Spanish Ribera, the French Poussin, the Flemish Rubens, and even—at moments—the Dutch Rembrandt.

Cancer can refer to people in touch with the public, while the Moon can signify the "people" itself. In the 17th century the Dutch "people" threw out a powerful invader and established what was, for its time, a popular form of government. Cromwell said, "If my calling be from God and my testimony from the people, God and the people shall take it from me, else I will not part from it." In the 17th century, not the American nation or government, but the American people was founded.

The Moon governs magnetism. In 1600 appeared William Gilbert's *De Magnete*, the pioneer study of the subject. The moon also governs biological clockwork, which man translates into mechanical clocks. The 17th century was the great period of clockmaking (previously there had been few clocks other than in church towers or public squares). Leibnitz saw the universe as clockwork. Also prominent in the 17th century in general and in Holland in particular was the Cancerian interest in optics—from optical effects in painting to optical instruments, from reflection and refraction to the mirror and the lens.

There is no sign more suspicious than the Cancerian; Friedell observed that "the Baroque never did trust itself." Cancer's crab goes two ways at once, and even the glyph for the sign is suggested in W. Hausenstein's remark, "Baroque means the unthinkable: the river with two mouths." In formal style, the Baroque is invoked in Jocelyn's description of Cancer as "this spiralling, evolutionary force." M.P. Hall terms Cancer in the occult sense the sign of "Nascent

Mind. Mind in its original state. The beginning of mind. The mind in its first and unmingled condition." Descartes spoke for his century when he found that man is real because he uses his mind.

Overall, the 17th century can be described as ruthless and adoring, relentless and contrite, glaring and concealing, ecstatic and mysterious, real and illusory, opaque and crystalline, rushing and languishing, sympathetic while enjoying the sweetness of pain. All are Cancerian traits.

The 18th Century

The 18th century (1688-1787) was ruled by Gemini, which anatomically rules the nervous system. The 18th was the century of "nerve"—think of Marlborough and Casanova, Voltaire and Dr. Johnson. Gemini is the most articulate of signs, the 18th the most articulate of centuries. Gemini expresses particularly through the wrists, hands, and fingers: In no other art are these so pronounced as in that of Watteau. One page of drawings shows nine single hands in action. The de Goncourts spoke of the nervous life of Watteau's hands, which "seem to possess the faculty of thought." A nervous quickness also distinguishes the art of Tiepolo and Guardi, Fragonard and Gainsborough, Vivaldi and Haydn.

Marcel Brion cites the "mobility of feature and character of 18th century man, his lively emotions and his responsiveness," referring also to the "restless glance" typical of the period. This is very Geminian. Jakob Rosenberg found in Watteau's drawing the visual equivalent of the charm, wit and accent of a lively Parisian tongue. In Fragonard, passion is translated into play, and the expression is far more an articulation of nerves and senses than of any profound feeling. Play and pleasure should not be interpreted here as superficiality in a merely frivolous sense, for Gemini truly enjoys the superficial, and the 18th century really believed in pleasure. What the 18th century did not believe in was enthusiasm, that is, in the self-deluding or over-zealous sense.

The de Goncourts found in Watteau the witty epigrammatist—wit being, even more than with Libra, a Geminian trait. And the 18th is the century (above all in Paris, but also in London, Venice and Vienna) of the witty jest, the play on words, the unexpected way of seeing things. Wit on the one hand is related to fun, which is familiar enough in 18th century intercourse, games, and festivals, but which applies no less to the sheer fun in the painting of Hogarth or Fragonard (who was to die of a stroke while eating ice cream). The Rococo was always "free to amuse" (H. Read). Wit's quickness or repartee is at its best never obvious or vulgar—a distinction between Watteau and some of his followers, and a Geminian connection between artists so different as Fragonard and Chardin.

Rudhyar speaks of Gemini's "search for new relationships over the whole world of experience." He might have been speaking of the 18th century. This is accompanied by "a peculiar abandon and lack of concern for ultimate results" which "seeks temporary intellectual control through verbal formulation." Compare Friedell's characterization of the 18th century. "Men thought no longer in laboriously built-up...systems...but in close piquant polemics, faceted epigrams, time-killing satires, peppered pamphlets, and razor-edged aphorisms; or, again, in *poésies fugitives*, lyric-epigrammatic *niaiseries* that had only a shimmering streak of any train of thought in them."

The 18th century talked a great deal about "sentiment", a quality we would naturally identify with signs like Cancer and Taurus—not with an air sign. But the sentimentality of the 18th century was not the deep feeling of Rembrandt or of Wordsworth; it was the calculated sentimentality of Sterne's *Sentimental Journey*. At a lower level it was the fraudulent sentimentality of Greuze (Gemini can enjoy fraud). Otherwise it meant sensibility, a Mercurian quality. Crébillon said, "We take each other without loving; we leave each other without hating." For the 18th century it was not the grand passion of Milton or of Crashaw, but the sweet, frothy cream of love that was sought. In love affairs, the stress was on the affair. E. Lucie-Smith refers to the century's libertinism (a Geminian predilection). At times family life actually came to be considered bad form and conjugal fidelity improper. Lady Montague wrote from Vienna that it was a serious insult there to invite a lady to dinner without both the husband and the official lover. Gemini is called a sign marked by no great fidelity; this applies to 18th century morality; but also, as Friedell said, the "Rococo mind lacked integrity."

Gemini is a mutable sign. The colors characteristic of 18th century painting are no longer solid and clear like those of the 17th century, but are composed of mutations. Gemini is an air sign. There is a wonderful symbol of this in the garden swing—popular in 18th century art and epitomized in Fragonard. Another symbol may be found in the prevalence of powder, which was used in place of bathing, which was flung to the ceiling to float down on the head (with face protected), and which (Friedell claimed) was "no freak of fashion, but the most eloquent symbol of the age."

Mutable air likewise signifies the *word*—whether spoken or writ—but in a brief and changing form. Voltaire said, "I find all books too long." Favored over the ponderous tome were the article, the journal, the letter, the newspaper. The first daily paper (the "Daily Courant") was started in London about 1700. Addison founded the "Tattler" and the "Spectator"; Dr. Johnson edited the "Idler" and the "Rambler"; in Italy appeared the "Observatore" and in France the "Spectateur francais", "Le Pour et le Contre", and the "Mercure de France"—even the titles are Geminian.

It was the age of the editor, the journalist, the correspondent, the essayist, the novelist (the novels often appearing serially in periodicals). The Mercurian and especially the Geminian love of language had its serious side: "The 18th century saw the origin of two currents of thought.... Linguistics, or the empirical science of language...[and] that which has appropriated the name of Comparative Philology" (A.L. Kroeber). Love of talk and language meet in the art of conversation, at which the 18th century exceeds all others. It was the age of generally well-read, competent conversationalists and interlocutors whose performance was not unlike that of the virtuoso on violin or piano; and of the Conversation Piece as a favored subject in painting.

Along with the art of conversation came a new art, that of letter-writing. While it could be casual, this proved a leading form of intercourse, and included not only private letters but circular ones. "Letters were called 'soul-visits'; one fell in love by letter and corresponded passionately with people with whom one never became personally acquainted" (Friedell).

A Mercurian interest appears in the 18th century development of the dictionary. Modern lexicography is said to have begun with Nathan Bailey's *Universal Etymological English Dictionary* of 1721; it was followed by his *Dictionarium Britannicum* of 1730, which Samuel Johnson used in preparing his *Dictionary of the English*

Language (1755), Johnson's definitions proving basic to subsequent lexicography. William Kenrick was the first (1773) to indicate pronunciation with diacritical marks and to divide by syllables. Noah Webster, whose major works appeared in the 19th century, got his start in the 18th: His *Spelling Book* came out in 1783. Even actors (Thomas Sheridan and John Walker) published dictionaries.

Is it appropriate to see the duality of Gemini (the Twins) in the invention of bifocal reading glasses? They were invented by Benjamin Franklin. Certainly there is an evidence of twinning in the abundance of couples represented in pictures of the period. There are romantic couples (as in Watteau) and unromantic ones (as in Hogarth); there are people presented in pairs: two nudes, two goddesses, two children, two actors—even two couples. The pictures of Tiepolo, Boucher, Gainsborough, Longhi, Chardin are marked by twinned phenomena to a degree noticeably greater than in any other century.

Gemini is a merry sign, with a highly developed sense of fun. The 18th century was a merry period: rollicking with Fielding and Hogarth, Richardon and Rowlandson. The French were less boisterous but second to none in the fun of their wit, which could be visual and aural as well as verbal. Joy sounds oft in John Gay and Handel, Sheridan and Haydn, reaching a culmination in Schiller's *Ode to Joy* of 1785. Where Cancer tends to pessimism or reserve, Gemini tends to an unabashed optimism. Frankl distinguished between 17th century pessimism and 18th century optimism, noting the shift from a "tragic resistance against an immense, overwhelming power to a cheerful response to every puff of wind" (Gemini is an air sign).

The turbulence so frequent in 17th century style is replaced by the surface play favored in the 18th century. "Irony, wit, and a willingess not to take oneself too seriously are intellectual commodities more readily found in the 18th century than in the 17th" (Julius Held). These again signify the replacement of water by air.

Gemini has been called the most enlightened of the signs. This quality is identified in the 18th century movement called the Enlightenment, with its open, liberal, and rational trends of thought and its freedom from prejudice or superstition. But it is also evident in the century's unprecedented flooding of light in architecture and the shedding and movement of light in painting. The "enlightened" character of Gemini is also expressed in the premium on being well-informed, a premium found not only in the European capitals but in the outlying colonies of North America.

The 19th Century

The 19th century (1787-1886) was ruled by Taurus, the sign which anatomically relates to the jaw, neck, and throat. 19th century figure painting recurrently emphasized the neck and throat, sometimes the lower jaw. This is particularly striking in many of Courbet's figures, with the head doubling the chin or a thrust of the lower jaw, but such traits represent postures of the period. Consider the importance of jaw, neck, or throat in Goya, in David's *Marat* or *Lepelletier*, Géricault's figures, Delacroix's *Chios*, *Sardanapolis* or *Michelangelo*, Ingres' *Valpinçon* and other *Bathers*, Daumier's *Uprising* and *Saltimbanques*, Manet's *Olympia* or *Folies-Bergère*, even Hunt's *Awakening Conscience*. In Cézanne's *Conversation* of 1872-3 the figures are all neck; his *Gustave Geffroy* of 1895 is all head (in 1886 began the 20th century, governed by Aries which rules the head).

The two main trends of 19th century style are Romanticism and Realism; most any sub-style belongs to one or both. It is in this context that contemporaries so differing as David and Goya, Turner and Constable, Courbet and Manet are related to each other as well as to their century. Seemingly antithetical appellations such as Romantic Realism, or Romanticist reality, indicate this underlying connection, which is a combination of Taurean traits.

The Romantic side of the 19th century—from Novalis and Burns to Brahms and Van Gogh—is an expression of Taurean sensuous warmth. Taurus is the most ardent of the signs. The primitivism that recurs in the 19th century style has other connections, but is probably also encouraged by romantic urgings, and the fact that Taurus is (according to Lloyd Cope) the most intense and primitive of the earth signs. The lyrical bent of 19th century Romanticism—so strong in painting and music as well as in poetry—is also Taurean (especially through the Venusian connection). The unexampled identification with nature in the 19th century has to do with the modern age in general but with Taurus in particular, for it is a romantic nature, even in a realist like Courbet.

The romantic side of Taurus may degenerate into sentimentality, a popular weakness of the century—as late as 1883 Pissarro found that the "most corrupt art is the sentimental." The higher spirits (Goethe, Goya, Beethoven, Daumier, and some others) rose, like Rembrandt and Milton in the Cancerian 17th century, beyond sentimentality,- though other great spirits (Wordsworth, Turner, Dickens, Courbet, Mark Twain) were not immune to this Taurean proclivity.

The Realist side of 19th century style was a function of Taurean materialism, earthiness, and love of the tangible. Sometimes this took the form of an overemphasis on detail or handling: Delacroix (himself a superb technician) protested that a "silly manual skill is the supreme goal." In a happier sense Taurean materialism appears in the love of *matière*, of the relation between the matter of paint and the nature-substance evoked, of paint as tangible poetry. The great 19th century painters are either punctilious technicians in the sense of Friedrich, Ingres, Degas, or poetic handlers in the sense of Constable, Courbet, Manet and the Impressionists. With the later Cézanne and Seurat, however, the rich sense of *matière* dries out and becomes abstract and refined, while with the late Monet and Renoir the balance between the matter of nature and that of paint is replaced by an abstracted expressiveness.

Taurean Realism also meant an earthy matter-of-factness. It is this which permitted and encouraged the representation of things simply as they are. Thus Courbet (the ultimate Realist) is anticipated by Géricault, and Géricault by David; and thus Impressionism comes out of Courbet. The subjects of 19th century painting that had the most coin were portrait, landscape, still-life, and the figure—all realist subjects.

Taurean materialism was expressed in the 19th century's love of the art object, and in turn of almost any kind of object. The 19th century loved its collections of bric-a-brac—it was the period of the junkman's paradise. Materialism also led to the glorification of Work: with Ford Madox Brown, with Zola, with Carlyle, who at the same time was dismayed by the materialistic paralysis of 19th century England. But 19th century materialism was cultural as well. Meyer Schapiro has spoken of the materialization of art; there was dialectical materialism, a materialism in scientific thought, as well as strong tendencies to sensationalism or sensationism (Mach).

Money as material property is Taurean (whereas money as nurture is Cancerian). It has been said of Taurus that money is the dominating force (the Taurean need not be rich but he takes money much to heart). To Comte and Balzac, not to mention the Gold Rush, money was the motivating force. The 19th was the century of the businessman, the banker, the broker, and the financier, as well as that of the cattleman, the industrialist, and the art collector—all of them Taurean types. Burckhardt felt the reason why his contemporaries could no longer respond to the Antique was "the total egoism of today's private person who wants to exist as an individual and asks of the community only the greatest possible security for himself and his property, for which he pays his taxes and sighs...."

Materialism was not the mark only of a money-mad middle class; it also distinguished the Mills, Huxley and Darwin and Wallace, Spencer and Buckle—and not the English only, but Comte and Marx and Ranke as well. 19th century science tended to be slow and plodding in its procedures, emphasizing the mechanical and the technical (20th century science has been more theoretical and sudden); 19th century science revered the quantitive, as if to say, "To measure is all."

Taurean amplitude is revealed in 19th century body types, not to mention the gargantuan menus; it was a period of the trencherman, the portly waistcoat, the full beard—all Taurean features. L. Kronenberger described the Victorian age as "something massive, pious, philistine, stuffy." Taurean style too is ponderous, and the 19th was a century of full, elaborate signatures, of many-volumed books, of interminable paragraphs and sentences. Much of the difference between Dickens, Carlyle, or Twain, and Pound, Stein, or Hemingway lies in the difference between a Taurean and an Arian temper.

The Taurean is especially a nature-lover, and his taste for the out-of-doors is unexceeded in any other sign. Such appetites are expressed in 19th century landscape art, and also in daily life. In the 18th century a solitary walker "was viewed with almost as much suspicion as he is in Los Angeles today. But the Wordsworths walked continually.... Even the unathletic Coleridge walked. They thought nothing of walking sixteen miles after dinner to post a letter. And so, for over a hundred years, going for a country walk was the spiritual as well as the physical exercise of all intellectuals, poets, and philosophers...in universities the afternoon walk is no longer part of intellectual life" (Kenneth Clark). Taurus is fixed earth, and exceeds all other signs in its immersion in nature. Outdoor painting began towards the end of the 18th century; it ended, in effect, by 1890.

The 20th Century

The 20th century (1886-1985) is characterized by Aries and Mars. Both are inclined to be sudden and immediate. The tendency to impulsiveness and abruptness in 20th century living is self-evident. Compared to the broad, slow, massive, and comfortable quality of 19th century life, ours is headstrong and headlong. Speech and communication—from advertising to academics—seem always in a hurry, and it is significant that the pace of musical conducting has speeded up. The 19th century took its time. In the 20th century, brevity has been carried to the point of abbreviation: William Henry Harrison, Henry Wadsworth Longfellow, James Fenimore Cooper have been replaced by F.D.R., J.F.K., L.B.J.,—not to mention the host of agencies that go by initials.

Bodily emphasis has shifted from neck and throat to head and brow. Focus on the head in art begins with the Symbolists and Post Impressionists, and continues with the Expressionists and Surrealists (it seems no accident that Van Dongen's painting of the soprano singing conceals the throat with a broad necklace and stresses the head instead). From Modigliani and Picasso and Rouault to de Kooning and Lester Johnson and Dubuffet the head has received a disproportionate emphasis. This is reminiscent of the head emphasis in old West African art; and indeed it is possible that the enormous popularity in our century of African art is intensified by an Aries affinity. Both the 20th century in the West and the entire African culture enjoy an Aries rulership.

Accordingly cubism is found in both, and qualities of expression, even expressionism, are advanced. Aries is the primal fire sign, and fire purifies; cubism is a purifying or reducing process. Aries is also given to expression, or pressing out. Much as the African masks and large-headed figures tend to pronounced expressions, so expressionism has been one of the two main traits (the other being cubism or abstract art) from Van Gogh and Gauguin and Munch down to the abstract expressionists and the neo-expressionists.

The Structure of a Major Culture

According to Rudhyar, Aries is liable to dreaming expressionist or surrealist dreams. Expressionism, dreams, and surrealism are all critical to 20th century art and literature. Solipsism too is Arian, and has been in the van since Van Gogh (the self-portraits in which man is the world itself) and the later Nietzsche (*Beyond Good and Evil*, 1886; *Will to Power*, 1888; *Thus Spoke Zarathrustra*, 1883/91). Solipsism lies at the core of 20th century Existentialism, which is likewise enlivened by a love of confrontation—another Arian trait.

Aries and its planet Mars can hardly be ignored in contemplating the warlike character of 20th century society, whose militant intensity appears unexampled. It is a militancy that takes form not in wars only, but in armament races, militant political action, strikes and demonstrations, violent crime and police response. We have wars limited and unlimited, pre-emptive and retaliatory, interventionist and non-interventionist: Talleyrand said prophetically that non-intervention is a philosophical and metaphysical term and means about the same as intervention.

Arian too are the fiery weapons (flame-thrower, napalm, fire-bombing) which contrast with chemical warfare—dropped by mutual agreement after the First War—while the biological tends to be used in outlying areas and with strong disapproval. Arian heatedness applies also in more peaceful intercourse: political or intellectual debate, economic or social interchange.

20th century life tends to be busy and public, hardly favoring the contemplative. It is progress-oriented (Progressivism keeps recurring in various forms). Groups, like individuals, tend to see only their own point of view; articulate advocates outnumber judicious judges. Leaders are not distinguished for looking before they leap, or if they do they tend to look the wrong way. There is a strong ingredient of self-righteousness, especially in the strongest leaders, and an acceptance of fanaticism in frequent contrast to the 19th century, when it was unusual and suspect. Everywhere in the West (for these are Western centuries only), competition is the order of the day. All this is Arian.

Our century prefers to live in the present, to throw the past behind. Constantly we crave to be original and avant-garde; if tradition is to be regarded, it is better for it to be the tradition of the new. All this is part of an Arian focus on the present, for Aries has no more commitment to the future than to the past. Immediate consumption is the 20th century bent. Aries is "not concerned with planning ahead, which detracts from spontaneity, nor with the results that might occur" (Meyer and Wickenburg).

Enthusiasm is one of our most highly prized qualities, though as Rudhyar notes, in Aries enthusiasm can turn into neurosis. We view sex as release, and espouse action for its own sake. An immediate Cause will have more appeal than some abstract or distant verity. Discipline is interpreted as a term of opprobrium: Aries is not so much interested in self-control as in rebellion. And Mars is "as of madness" (Edgar Cayce) in a century whose psychological states range from alienation and the abyss to the indulgence of criminal insanity.

At its highest, however, Mars stands not for war and madness but for energy and effort; it is embodied in the initiator, the pioneer. Whether in art styles or scientific approaches, the 20th century has been unusually inventive and daring. While the century lasts we may still expect to see outpourings typical of the Aries soul, which Pagan sees as expressed above all in "hope and courage and enterprise."

The 21st century is due in 1985, and will be governed by the Pisces principle. The 22nd century will be due in 2084, to be governed by the Aquarius principle. This will complete the Western cycle of the Evolutionary centuries. It will not mean the end of Western power or vitality, but it will conclude the sequence of twelve centuries associated with astrological signs. In other words, only the core part—the Evolutionary epoch—of a major culture shows astrological correlations, but each major culture, taken in its entire chronological and geographical span, is itself correlated with a sign.

II

The Major Cultures by Sign

A cycle of twelve major cultures runs in order, but it does not begin with Aries and end with Pisces; rather it begins with Aquarius and ends with Capricorn. The Aquarius to Capricorn cycle of major cultures is the same as the cycle of the twelve centuries of the Evolutionary epoch except that the latter works in reverse. This is not surprising when we consider the reversed order of the astrological Months (see Chapter IV) whose sub-ages run forward. In each case the inner cycle, by a principle of reflection, runs in reverse to, but with the same start and end as, the larger cycle.

The present Western culture, governed by Capricorn, is the last of its cycle; the present Russian culture, governed by Aquarius, is the first of a new cycle. The old cycle can be identified as follows:

African	Aries
Indus Valley	Taurus
Babylonian	Gemini
Egyptian	Cancer
Chinese	Leo

Indian	Virgo
Classical	Libra
Levantine	Scorpio
Ancient American	Sagittarius
Western	Capricorn

A glance will show that these cultures overlap in time as well as in area; nevertheless the time and area of each culture have discrete identities.

Dating

The African culture originated in Central West Africa, during the fifth to fourth millennium BC. There are rock paintings in the area going back possibly to 5000 BC; surviving terracottas and bronzes from as early as 500 BC represent very late echoes of original styles. The area in general was sub-Saharan, and the Evolutionary sequence of centuries was probably over by the time the Egyptian sequence began.

The Indus Valley Culture is represented in present archeology by the Harappa and Mohenjo-daro remains, which are clearly those of the late phase of a major culture. Piggott dates these remains within the millennium 2500-1500 BC, during which time "there was little appreciable change in the fabric and pattern of this enigmatic civilization"; this suggests a late, petrified stage, so that a dating of the Evolutionary centuries from the mid-fourth to the mid-third millennium is appropriate.

The Babylonian culture's Evolutionary sequence ran from about 2800 to about 1600 BC. During the final two centuries Babylon assumed the central power of the civilization—a power previously exercised by Akkad and Ur—thus giving her name to the culture originating in the area of the Two Rivers, much as the Ch'in Dynasty was to take over and give its name to the culture originating on the Yellow River. "Mesopotamian" would be a more accurate name for this culture, but "Babylonian" has better coin.

The Egyptian culture provides the very model for the three epicycles which comprise the Evolutionary epoch. The Old, Middle, and New Kingdoms represent the three epicylces, with the First Intermediary period belonging to the Middle Kingdom, and the Second Intermediary to the New Kingdom, or Empire. According to Langer, the first signs of trouble in the empire and of decadence at home appeared in the late reign of Amenophis III and mounted in the reign of Ikhnaton, which began in the 1370's. It is reasonable to date the end of Evolutionary, therefore, as around 1390 BC. The end of the first epicycle can probably be determined by the end of the 6th Dynasty, which was overthrown in 2185 BC (H.W. Janson). These two dates confirm a timing of the beginning of the Egyptian Evolutionary at about 2580 BC. The end of the Evolutionary was due 1188 years later (twelve centuries at 99 years each), or shortly after 1390 BC. According to H.A. Groenewegen-Frankfort, with the XIX Dynasty the vitality of Egyptian art had spent itself: This is an apt description of the end of an "evolutionary" epoch. The XIX Dynasty is now considered to have begun in the 14th century, perhaps around 1350 BC.

The dating of the Chinese Evolutionary epoch can be based fairly precisely on the conclusion of the period of the Warring States, in 221 BC. This date corresponds in the Classical with the establishment of the Roman peace (31 BC) or of the *imperium* (23 BC). It gives us a date of about 90 BC, or immediately thereafter, for the end of the Chinese Evolutionary, and thus a dating of the entire epoch at about 1280 to 90 BC.

The Indian Culture, being ruled by Virgo, did not produce the clear-cut empires of Rome or China: India's imperial tendencies were marked by confusion and multiplicity (the disintegration of Asoka's empire after his death, however, does not mean the failure of an "imperial" system but rather that it was too early). We can identify the end of the Indian Evolutionary within a few decades, nevertheless, since powerful barbarians "poured down into India toward the end of the first century BC and established their rule over a large slice of northwest India, modern Afghanistan and part of the Oxus River basin" (de Riencourt). This exemplifies a breakdown of inner resistance typical of the end of an Evolutionary epoch. Thus it is logical to locate the Indian Evolutionary centuries as running from around 1200 to roughly 10 BC.

The Evolutionary of the Classical culture began around 1100 BC and ended around 100 AD. Precise dating will be discussed later.

The Evolutionary epoch of the Levantine culture began almost at the same time as the end of the Indian: about 15 BC. The evidence for so close a dating depends upon a system of configurations which must be reserved for analysis in a subsequent volume. Certain clues to the Levantine dating are discussed under their different headings in Chapter III. For the moment, however, we may observe the conclusion of the Levantine Evolutionary, in the 1170s AD. In the late 12th century, the entire Byzantine Empire began to disintegrate. It is true that Islam picked up many of the pieces, but even in Islam radical changes were in evidence: During the 12th century the whole of the Seljuk empire (excepting Rum) fell into the hands of the so-called Atabegs or regents, that is, captains of the Seljuk armies (W. Langer); the situation is reminiscent of "contemporary" developments in ancient Rome.

The evolution of Byzantine cultural forms came to an end at the same time. While art and architecture were to revive in subsequent periods, even with splendor, it was not the same. S. der Nersessian has observed that the art of the 13th and 14th centuries, "in spite of its beauty and its undeniable technical mastery, did not show the development that one might have expected after the experience and successes of works" of earlier centuries. This cessation of further "development" is exactly what is meant by the end of an "Evolutionary" epoch.

The outstanding cultural creations of the Islamic sector of the Levantine civilization lay in philosophy, science, and literature. Kroeber locates the end of Islamic (including Jewish) philosophy of importance in the last part of the 12th century (Abubacer, c. 1110-c. 1185; Averroes, 1126-1198; Maimonides, 1135-1204). Islamic science seems to have ended in the first quarter of the 12th century (though with a brief aftermath, following a long gap, in the 13th century). Arabic poetry and belles-lettres lasted into the later 12th century; after this there continued to be writing in history, travel, and journals, but not in the realms of what is ordinarily considered artistic or creative literature.

The dating of the Levantine culture is therefore quite far removed from that of the Babylonian. The two cultures are often confused because of their geographical overlapping. The distinction is further clarified when we credit each with its proper sub-cultures. The Babylonian sub-cultures include the Sumerian, the Akkadian, the Babylonian, the Hittite, the Chaldean, the Assyrian, the Phoenician. The Levantine sub-cultures include the Persian, the Judaic, the early Christian (including Coptic), the Byzantine, the Islamic. Furthermore, the two major cultures differ in the nature of the entities they produce. The Babylonian entities are principalities, the Levantine are religions, or religious states.

The Ancient American culture embraces the pre-Columbian civilizations of Mexico, Central America, and Peru. Its Evolutionary epoch runs from the third quarter of the first century AD to the third quarter of the 13th century. It follows almost as closely on the Levantine as did the Indian on the Chinese, but in locale it is far removed; indeed it is the only major culture which spans two continents from its very beginnings.

The Western culture may be found today in Europe, the Americas, and Australia. In its formative period it occupied Western Europe, whence it is almost universally recognized as the Western culture. It should not be confused with "western" civilization when this term is used to include Greek, Roman, and other societies, as opposed to "eastern" civilizations. For the Western culture is limited mainly to America and Western Europe, and did not begin until after the birth of Christ. The Western Evolutionary epoch opened in 995 AD and is due to close in 2183. The Evolutionary period of the Russian culture began in 1866 (see Chapter III). Despite this overlap with the Western Evolutionary, and with the Redundant stage of the Levantine culture, the Russian actually belongs to a new cycle of major cultures, a fact which might still further emphasize the differences between Russia and the rest of the world.

The major culture is not merely the most significant but is the only definitive form of civilization in history. Toynbee was referring to this general order of being when he wrote of "institutions of the highest order—institutions that is, which comprehend without being comprehended by others." All of the enduring religions and sciences known to history have been conceived within some major culture. "None of the great art styles and systems of thought which have had so much influence throughout the world can be ascribed to a secondary civilization" (Philip Bagby). Having thus an absolute identity, a creative soul, the major culture is related to its fellows not in any discernible rhythm, but by an order in accordance with that of the astrological signs.

A. The African Culture

The Arian culture of the fourth millennium BC that originated in western Africa is only the earliest that can soundly be identified. It seems quite plausible that the preceding Piscean culture was located in what is called Old Europe (The Balkans, Greece, Crete, and southern Italy), with an overall span of, very roughly, 7000 to 3000 BC. But positive identification is not presently possible.

The African culture survives in latter-day arts and customs which must be separated by the historian from superimposed Egyptian, Muslim, or Western forms, but which are still characteristic whether amongst Africans or Afro-Americans. We should not be misled by the "primitive", stereotyped, even caricatured African sculptures which have so influenced the Western artist and excited the public. In seeking traces of this major culture it is more revealing to look to the old Yoruba sculpture, for example, which is much better than the modern, which was made of stone (e.g. quartz), terracotta, and bronze (rather than wood) and which evinced convincing proportions and a keen fidelity to nature rather than conventional features. There are old portrait heads better even than those of Benin.

According to their own oral tradition, the Bini learned bronze casting from the Ife, and who knows what lay beyond? We should adduce the Nok terracottas, and the stone-built complexes of southern Africa. According to Daniel McCall, African art could conceivably be as old as the European paleolithic, though it must be emphasized that here we are not looking for rock painting, which is probably pre-civilization and which in Africa is found in the Sahara, the east and the south.

That there is no native historiographical tradition may mean that such have been lost, or that this Arian culture was never interested in the past. Of the signs, Aries and Libra are those most focused on the present; thus the Libran lack of interest in history among the ancient Greeks is particularly striking against the background of record-keeping by the Cancerian Egyptians.

Aries is the sign of the ram. There are very old rams' heads, both stone and bronze, in Nigeria. The part of the body ruled by Aries is the head, and the agglomeration of sculptured heads—not only rams' heads but also human—found in ancient sites is startling. In later sculpture, the head is very frequently pre-eminent in size as well as in expression. Even today, African huts often have pointed domes and look like helmets.

Isabel Pagan describes Aries individuals as reckless and fanatic, with "a sense of fun and a real gift for enjoying a situation." She also finds them unaffected and sincere, while energy and enthusiasm are their greatest gifts. She emphasizes their religious enthusiasm, their practical jokes, their superabundant vitality which finds inaction intolerable. She notes "their splendid bodies," their deification of athletes, and their tendency to be attracted into the army. Given to sudden bursts of fury and ferocity, they favor pugilism and the warrior. Physically, the bones tend to be large, the body muscular, the hair crisp, wiry, curly or thick and of strong color, the forehead fine, with short nose, powerful jaw, and an orator's mouth (they tend to prefer oratory to literature). Movements are quick and impulsive, and the whole personality is intensely alive.

Does this not describe the characteristic African as we know him still today? And in characterizing the black race may we not often be adducing traits that can now be seen not as racial but as derivative from this Aries civilization? Consider the observations of Lothrop Stoddard: The black man's "outstanding quality is superabundant animal vitality. In this he easily surpasses all other races...extreme fecundity...ability to survive harsh conditions of slavery under which other races have soon succumbed."

M.P. Hall cites "the building of the body of the native of Aries," and C.E.O. Carter invokes all extreme activity, especially physical, seeing here a sign given to action rather than to theory. An expression of physical activity for its own sake is the dance; Africa had produced what has been called "a history of danced art." The dance on the one side involves rhythmic music, which is one of the strongest features of Afro-American culture but is also an ancient creative tendency: there is evidence of African musical influence as far as Indonesia. "African Art in Motion" was the apt title of a show at the National Gallery in Washington.

Another side of the Arian African dance is its military postures and gestures correlative with violent ritual songs. Compare the militant character of African political movements with the pacific tendencies of India, a culture ruled by Virgo. Correctly proverbial are the athletic instincts and accomplishments of African and Afro-American alike. Gauquelin invokes the Mars temperament in relation to sports champions, and we may ask again whether this athletic distinction should be attributed to race or to a derivation from the African culture ruled by Aries.

B. The Indus Valley Culture

Existing evidence of the Taurus culture lies at Harappa in the Punjab, and at Mohenjo-daro in the Sind. This evidence is of the late state of a civilization that had its own identity; it must not be confused either with the Indian civilization which followed much later in an overlapping area, or with the Babylonian civilization which followed closely in time and in an adjacent area. The Indus Valley was, according to J.B. Noss, in touch with but "differed markedly from the Sumerians and Akkadians." In Babylonian art, animals are shown mainly in themes of combat or pursuit; in the animal depictions of Mohenjo-daro "the feeling here is of affection, and when animals wear human masks, even of identity" (Jane Gaston Mahler). In contrast with later India, the Harappan ethnic structure was predominantly Mediterranean with natives and foreigners (Piggott). As against India's "sacred cow" the Harappans emphasized the holy bull—a Taurean image.

The Harappan script has no discernable affinities with any known ancient script. B. Rowland noted that in the Indus Valley remains there are no buildings identifiable as temples. Religious works belong to the early stages of a major culture, social works to the last. In the Indus Valley remains Piggott found a "combination of elaborate social and economic organization over a huge empire" with unusual isolation, effectively ruling out any connection with another culture; he added that an origin outside India is inherently improbable. At Harappa he found "the first really organized industry in Western Asia, as distinct from that of a craftsman guild," again clearly antedating both the Babylonian and the Indian. Cylinder seals (a Sumerian invention) are as rare in Harappa as in Egypt.

According to Piggott "the mature Harappan civilization—and it must be repeated that this is the only phase of the culture we know at present—flourished within the millennium 2500-1500 BC...during that time there was little appreciable change in the fabric and pattern of this enigmatic civilization." From this we can postulate an Evolutionary epoch for the Indus Valley lasting from the mid-fourth to the mid-third millennium. This sense of "little appreciable change" indicates the very late, Redundant phase of a major culture, and also emphasizes its Taurean character—Taurus being of all signs the least fond of change. There is a "terrible efficiency about the Harappan civilization which recalls all the worst of Rome, but with this elaborately contrived system goes an isolation and a stagnation hard to parallel in any known civilization of the Old World.... The remarkable uniformity of the Harappan Culture is in fact expressed not only spatially, but also in the dimension of time...the innate conservatism of thought that is repeated through the centuries...a total duration of the two cities...for over a thousand years, is theoretically not impossible" (Piggott).

The following descriptions of Harappan culture suggest further Taurean qualities in high degree: "uniform products...monotonous regularity of a highly organized community...absolute uniformity in the products...must have been a strongly established commercial code and a standardized technique of production which could control the size of bricks, the capacity and type of pots (turned out on the wheel in a variety of depressingly utilitarian forms), and the system of weights and measures...heredity of land tenure and trade...great granaries strangely foreshadowing those of the Roman army...continuity of government was somehow assured throughout this long time ...tradition was transmitted unimpaired and of constant validity" (Piggott).

Taurus is the sign of the Earth Mother. At Mohenjo-daro are countless mother-goddesses (Mahler). At Harappa there must have been "some form of worshipping a Mother-Goddess" (Piggott), and there is the suggestion of "the idea of an earth-goddess concerned with vegetation" (the idea still survives in India, but its priests are not Brahmins, and represent pre-Aryan traditions). In the Indus Valley, "agriculture must have been one of the chief industries" (Mackay). Taureans are agricultural, loving both nature and animals. Mahler emphasizes the "love of animals" manifested at Mohenjo-daro (where a number of streets have rounded corners to ease pack animals). Animals appear interminably in clay toys and on seals. The favorite toy was a small pottery farm cart; no war chariots have been found (Mackay); Taurus is associated with peace-loving Venus. On Kulli ware are many cattle, and when fish or felines are occasionally depicted the heads may have ears in the manner of cattle (Piggott). The Indus Valley inhabitants were undoubtedly flesh eaters (Mackay), a Taurean penchant contrasting with Virgo's preference for a more purified diet, which has been so strong in the Indian culture.

Returning to the Taurean bull, we note that among many animals on seals we find "notably the magnificent series of humped and dewlapped bulls, monumental for all their miniature size" (Piggott). Indeed the bull was far the most popular subject of Indus Valley art (Rowland). To the bull (or ox, or buffalo), the goat is always "secondary on the seals" (Mackay).

Of the human body, Taurus rules the neck and throat. Striking among clay figurines that have survived from the Indus Valley are those of women who seem to be all neck. Other human representations stress the throat and the concommitant activity of singing, and there was an evident popularity of songbirds. Unlike subsequent India, no carved snakes have been found at Mohenjo-daro, and only one at Harappa.

C. The Babylonian Culture

While the Babylonian and Egyptian cultures overlap a great deal in time, and are often treated as contemporary, actually the Babylonian Evolutionary period began and ended at least two centuries earlier than the Egyptian. L. Woolley was right in discerning that the Sumerian civilization was ahead of the Egyptian and influenced it. The Babylonian Evolutionary began around 2800 BC. By about 1800 the culture had been definitively unified under the Babylonian empire; by 1600 the Evolutionary was over. Unlike Egypt, the area of the culture showed no underlying unity but instead endured local rivalries, foreign incursions, sudden upsurges and collapses. This fragmentary and diverse character suggests Mercury, the ruler of Gemini.

Gemini itself is a dual sign, often called the Twins. The Babylonian culture is the most dual that we know. Its seedbed is the land of Two Rivers. Its ruler was designated "King of Sumer and Akkad." Its art depicts a man standing between two men, or two bulls, or two lions, or a hero embracing two human-headed bulls; it shows the two-headed snake, or two stars (as above Naramsin), or lions in pairs. There is a predominance of figures flanked in pairs on gates, or reversed on seals or reliefs. It devises a motif not known to other traditions: a sculptured block (e.g. the N.Y. Metropolitan's *Guardian of the Gate*) carved as in the round when seen from the front, and as in relief from the side, so that the creature has two right front legs.

Some students lump the Babylonian and the Levantine cultures under one rubric called Near Eastern, or the like. However, a look at the difference between an air sign like Gemini and a water sign like Scorpio shows the contrast between these two cultures. While Early Christian and Byzantine buildings all turned inward, glowing in the dark, the Babylonian turned outwards and emphasized height, lightness, and air. Babylon built roof or "hanging" gardens, and staged towers (ziggurats) stepping up into the sky, with stairways on the outside which led to a sanctuary on the top. Ziggurat meant "temple tower", or "to be high". Henri Frankfort noted that "although not all sanctuaries included a temple tower or Ziggurat, all were given a token elevation above the soil." By comparison Byzantine churches seem cave-like, almost as if dug into the ground. The Ziggurat was typically high in relation to other dimensions (the Tower of Babylon was indeed a tower), while both the Egyptian and the Levantine temples were low in profile.

"Air" in a sign also connotes superficiality, whether in good or bad sense. Superficial can refer to the outward surface: The art of Babylon and Assyria is one of articulate facades, endless reliefs, brilliant glazes. Columns were covered with cone mosaics, walls with glazed bricks. Compare the polished but unadorned surface of the Egyptian pyramid, or the unarticulated exterior of the Byzantine church.

In Western astrology the symbol for Gemini is the Twins; in Chinese it is the Tiger. Mesopotamia—unlike China and India—had no tigers. But it did have the Asiatic lion, migrant from Greece and central India—and this played a favored role in Mesopotamian art.

Gemini is the mutable air sign. No assignment could be more fortuitous for astrology, which deals with the appearance of movement in the sky. Most civilizations produce astronomies and many produce astrologies, but there are none known to compete with the Babylonian. Egyptian astronomy was particularly concerned with timekeeping, as reflects Cancer's fascination with time and records. Babylonian astronomy was concerned with celestial activity. As for astrology, all astrology "in whatever part or period of the world, seems in fact to be reared directly on Mesopotamian foundations" (A.L. Kroeber).

Intellectually Gemini, while capable of superficiality, is quick and incisive. It has the darting Mercurian intelligence and is often called the brightest of the signs. The Babylonians have been called the brightest race known to us.

Physically Gemini rules the shoulders, arms, wrists, and hands, the nervous system and nervous energy. The Gemini projects love of life and action; he is quick, alert, merry, and vivacious. Mesopotamian art—as no other—stresses shoulders, arms, elbows, wrists, especially in wiry delineations. There is a distinctive motif of wringing hands, and others of figures who talk with the hands, or with sensitive lips (Gemini being the most talkative of the signs). By comparison the lower body is hardly stressed at all: Often it is difficult to tell if the body stands or sits.

Frequent in Mesopotamian art are eyes and faces that look up and out—in contrast with the inward stare of the Levantine eye, or the half-shut eye of the Egyptian. How many smiling faces are to be found in Byzantine or Egyptian art? They are frequent in Babylonian and Assyrian: smiling, alert, vivacious, sparkling, with bright eyes and quick, nervous rhythms, and gestures of greeting. Only the figures in the art of Ancient America smile so much, and they rather grin (as is more characteristic of the Sagittarian).

Geminians love business activity. Mesopotamians, on down to the Phoenicians, were outstanding businessmen as well as tradesmen, and also showed a high degree of interest in Geminian activities like measuring, numbering, and accounting. Gemini is the most literary of the signs. Babylonian and Assyrian art are rife with narration; the Phoenicians developed the alphabet, while the Sumerians, before 3000, had invented writing. Later Babylonians were to become prolific letter writers. And all manifestations of Babylonian culture, even their religion, evince a pervasive Geminian sense of humor and delight.

D. The Egyptian Culture

The Evolutionary period of the Egyptian culture began about 2600 BC and ended about 1400. One clue to the end of an Evolutionary is the beginning of depopulation in the core regions. In Rome this began in the second century AD; in Egypt it was apparent in the XIX Dynasty—that is, shortly after 1400. The three successive Egyptian Kingdoms—Old, Middle, and New Kingdom or Empire—stand as archetypes of the three epicycles that make up an Evolutionary epoch.

In the 19th century, dating of Egypt's three Kingdoms tended to suppose very long periods; more recently these periods are seen as much shorter. Since the early 20th century, as Roger W. Wescott has pointed out, a rough consensus has emerged which sets the interval between the founding of the Middle Kingdom and that of the New Kingdom at about 400 years (the length of an epicycle).

The Egyptian civilization was ruled by Cancer, which is the cardinal water sign. Cardinal means direct action. Where mutable water (Pisces) invokes the oceanic roll, and fixed water (Scorpio) the deep still pond, cardinal water is expressed in the living river and the straight fall or cataract. Egypt looks as if it is designed for Cancerian activity: The Nile is the straightest of the world's great streams, its cataracts are legendary. On the Nile the annual alluvial shift is tide-like; as M.P. Hall put it, "the cardinal strength of Cancer is like the inevitable slow rise of the tide."

Cancer is a creature of the shore—whether ocean, lake or river—and Egyptian art is replete with a sense of the littoral: the fauna and flora of the river's edge, and man himself poling and wading. With Egypt the Cancerian qualities of prudence, foresight, and self-protectiveness are emphasized, qualities that persist through millennia of Egyptian history—which, whether in its political, religious, or artistic traditions, shows a natural conservatism. Cancer is described as very shy, and if we change this possibly pejorative term to "reserved," we have at once the whole expression of Egyptian imagery. Even the theology of Egypt always remained in what has been called a "fluid state"—hidden and secretive, like the tombs, statues, and mummies.

While the astrological signs do not have the same meanings as the planets which "rule" them, still there are intimate correlations between signs and planets. The planets themselves can be assigned numbers. The correspondence of planets and numbers is treated differently by different numerologists; this problem, however, is ready of solution if we relate numbers to astrological aspects. The aspect is identified, in this context, by the number of times it divides into 360 degrees.

Thus the aspect for the number one is the conjunction; for two, the opposition; for three, the trine; for four, the square; for five, the quintile; for six, the sextile; for seven, the septile, for eight, the semi-square; and for nine, the novile. To see which planet corresponds to which number, we simply relate the character of the aspect to that of the planet. This has been done in an article by Charlalee B. Sedgwick in the *Jupiterian*, 1980; and the results come out the same as the correlation of numbers and planets found (without mention of aspects) by Lloyd Cope. Thus the unitary and inclusive character of the conjunction indicates the Sun, the harmony and balance of the trine indicate Venus, the blockage and constriction of the square indicate Saturn, and so on. The result of this method gives the following:

One	Sun
Two	Moon
Three	Venus
Four	Saturn
Five	Mars
Six	Jupiter
Seven	Mercury
Eight	Uranus
Nine	Pluto

Returning to Cancer and its association with the Egyptian culture, we then associate Cancer with the Moon and therefore with the number Two. The kind of Two involved here, however, is not like the double or twinned images related to Gemini as a "dual" sign. The Two of the Moon is the Two of the opposition aspect and means reflection and polarity.

The polarity in Egyptian life was that of the South and the North, of the Upper and Lower Kingdoms. These sought ever to be united under one crown, and from Zoser until late Pharaonic times they usually were.

The Egyptian polarity of politics and religion was expressed in the tension between monarchy and priesthood, resulting in a theocratic structure. Herein, monarchy and priesthood reflected one another (reflection is a principle of the opposition aspect): There was a theology of the kingship as well as a politics of the priesthood. Egyptian theocracy thus appears different from the more fused theocracies of Byzantium and Islam, which represented Scorpionic single-mindedness.

The lunar connection of Cancer is further revealed in their veneration of the cat, what we call the housecat (Cancer is the most domestic of the signs). Cat forms appear widely in Egyptian religious and artistic imagery, and the cat itself was long considered sacred (at least in certain times, to kill a cat was punishable by death). Why the cat? Apparently because the cat is that lunar creature of the night, wrapped in the darkness and secrecy we associate with the moon, Egypt's planetary symbol.

Physically, Cancer rules the breast, an area which may include the chest and stomach. It is precisely these areas that are emhasized in Egyptian sculpture. Compare the hand and arm emphasis in Mesopotamian art, or the torso emphasis in Classical. Indeed the upper part of the Egyptian figure was often more completely carved than the legs or feet.

The Western symbol of Cancer is the Crab. Some astrologers give as a variation of, or addition to, the Crab that strange creature the Scarab, a dung-beetle which when its wings are folded is rather crab-like. The Scarab (with wings folded) was one of the most favored of Egyptian images in stone, gem, and seal, as well as in imagery and ritual.

Cancer tends to display a "moon" face, to show tender family feeling, to "make a good wife," to have sympathy for animals: All these qualities may be found emphasized in Egyptian art from hunting scenes to joint portraits of king and queen. Cancer is silent. The figures in Egyptian art show a taciturnity equalled only by figures in Levantine art; furthermore Egyptian religious practice was frequented with vows of silence. Cancer is secretive. In addition to the pyramids and temples with their concealed entrances and secret chambers is that wondrous Cancerian invention, the Egyptian labyrinth (the Great Labyrinth had some three thousand chambers, half of them subterranean). Cancer likes a special room of his own. The Egyptian pyramid focused on a particular, secreted chamber, and the temple interior led to a sanctuary along an increasingly arcane and hieratic pathway.

Egyptian art is, at its highest, sculpture in stone, or an architecture especially sculptural—that is, solid, massive, heavy, dense, and hard. The Cancerian is hard-shelled, like the crab. Egyptian architecture had a harder shell than any comparable kind of building, and Egyptian sculpture, while it covered a range including wood, metal, and softer stones, showed a preference for the hardest stones known to any great sculptural tradition.

The number Two, the lunar number, is usually taken to symbolize involution into matter—in particular, as John Addey put it, into "the *objective* expression of a thing" (his emphasis). Here is the character of Egyptian imagery from sculpture to hieroglyph. The Egyptians believed that "anything correctly reproduced might by appropriate ritual be called into being" (*Oxford Companion*), thus preserving existence and producing "a rational objective truth independent of time and space." Material technique was particularly stressed; according to Diodorus, Egyptian artists were classified by the material in which they worked, while Greek artists were classified by their artistic ideas (which is a Libran predilection). The Egyptians did not distinguish the arts and crafts, as did the Greeks, who emphasized the literary and intellectual role of "art".

Egyptian art favored squared-off qualities, cubical forms, with heavy and secure foundations. This applied not only to pyramid and temple, but to statuary with its unmistakably "cubic" character. "In Cancer the human person is like a square or a cube—a foundation," says Rudhyar, who adds that the Cancerian can be "the most helpless or the most determined in a strange, silent way"; that the Cancerian principle will reproduce "as clean-cut and as permanent an image or impression as possible"; and that Cancer will "bring these forces of formation and growth *to the clearest possible focus*" (his emphasis). Such qualities are persistent in Egyptian art from small sculpture to vast pyramid, for which were often used the hardest stones, even if they were not locally available.

Why this hardness? Cancer is crusty. It is the shell of the crab again, and it has the character of endurance as well as perseverance. Cancer, says Carter, will proceed "cautiously, almost imperceptibly" (like the Nile, or Egyptian history itself), and has "the greatest sticking power of the signs" (the pyramids and mummies are still there).

Cancer loves the past, and old things. "Egyptian art resembles the treasure chamber of an old and distinguished family, which preserves the jewelry of its ancestors in active use together with what the present generation with its indefatigable energy adds to the collection" (H. Schäfer).

Cancer never forgets. While Hindus or Greeks seem hardly to have noted the past at all, Egypt kept the most extraordinary records of any ancient civilization. Cancer is conservative and lives in the past. The "natural conservatism" of Egyptian art and society are proverbial. Cancer has a strong domestic bent. Think of the contents of Egyptian tombs, as well as temples and shrines that were living quarters for the gods. Cancer invokes the womb. Think of the layered protection of the inner chambers of temple and pyramid.

Cancer is said to symbolize the bursting of the bud: Observe this motif on Egyptian capitals. Cancer likes to write things down: Consider the scribe as a frequent artistic image. Cancer signifies heredity (the Egyptian dynastic principle) and the teacher: Even the Greeks, who liked self-instruction, sat to the Egyptians. Cancer has a strong sense of personality: Egyptian portraiture is unsurpassed in this aspect. Cancer is associated "with the inner soul-life" (V. Reid), the very meaning of ancient Egypt.

E. THE CHINESE CULTURE

The Evolutionary epoch began shortly after 1300 BC. Revised chronology gives Shang at Anyang from 1300 to 1028, Chou from 1027 to 256. Of Shang and Chou bronzes C.O. Hucker writes that they take more than thirty shapes, and that "variations in decor have been sorted out so minutely that specialists can now date a vessel almost to the decade on stylistic grounds." This is an excellent description of what "evolutionary" means; the same stylistic dating can be applied, say, to Western sculpture from 1000 AD to the present.

A striking change in the style of bronzes occurred in the period around 900 BC, which would correspond to the beginning of our Renaissance. It was called the "second phase," and was marked by robust and heavy treatment, with greater relief. The period from about 480 to about 220 is called that of the Warring States, and corresponds in the West to the period that began in 1789 and continues through the present; or in the Classical to the period from 290 to 30 BC, that is, from the Third Samnite War to the peace of Octavian. The appearance of Ch'in on the stage (221-207) corresponds to the full-dress appearance of the Roman Empire, as well as giving a final name to the Chinese culture. The Han dynasty (206 BC to AD 8) has specifically been compared in character to the Roman Empire. In 111-110 BC conquests in southern and eastern Yueh rounded out the frontiers of China proper and gave "the Chinese all the best lands in their known world" (Langer). 108 and 102 saw further conquests of petty states. Overall, the years 127 to 101 represented the second expansion of the Chinese empire (Garraty and Gay). The first regent was appointed in 87 BC. A date in the rough vicinity of 100 BC, and probably between 90 and 80 BC, is logical for the end of the Chinese Evolutionary period.

China's ruler is Leo, whose planet is the Sun, signified by the number One and the principle of unity. Amaury de Riencourt speaks of the permanent tendency of the Chinese toward unity, and observes that the number One, for the Chinese, was "not the beginning of a new series...but the center of the mathematical world. As such it was privileged to represent the Totality and to have, therefore, the highest rating of all numbers." Furthermore the number One, "the Totality, occupied the political position of the Emperor in the mathematical world" (de Riencourt).

Leo represents the family in the sense of a stable organization obedient to authority. De Reincourt notes, as perennial traits of Chinese culture, the authority of family elders, and "the extreme stability of the family, its complete, unquestioned devotion and obedience to the chief of the clan." Leo means kingship and royal power. Already in Shang times there is evidence of monstrous royal funerals, and the focus of Chinese society has ever been on king, prince, emperor, or supreme ruler. Even the Chinese communists tend to deify their ruler in a way the Russians are wary of. From early times, according to D.B. Richardson, "it was the Chinese emperor, not Yaweh, who was the leader and Father of the people."

The aim of Chinese politics has usually been the self-sufficient, well-administered empire. Leo represents "the greatest amount of power...in the widest sense" (C.E.O. Carter). Leos are born leaders and autocrats; their scene is one of patronage, often accompanied by flattery and favorites—a good description of the proverbial Chinese court. Leo is a fixed sign. Confucius stated that "the sovereign who reigns by virtue is similar to the polar star. He stays immobile in the center and everything regularly revolves around him." Leo tends to be placid.

Leo's animal is the lion. The early Chinese sculptural tradition, according to Hucker, was "carried over into the early Empire primarily in the form of carved lions and other animals, real or imaginary...." In Chinese astrology itself, however, Leo's animal is the dragon. It is a familiar enough creation as it runs through Chinese and Japanese art, but it was more than a favored artistic image. L. Sickman calls it "the very incarnation of the Tao," and the Japanese writer O. Kakuzo said of the dragon, "We associate him with the supreme power or that sovereign cause which pervades everything, taking new forms according to its surroundings.... The dragon is the great mystery itself."

Leo's color is gold—"the flame is golden and luminous and burns steadily" (M.P. Hall)—here is an image of Chinese art and manner all in one. Even the glyph of Leo (like a lion's tail, or serpentine like a dragon) may suggest the meandering character of the Chinese "way", whether of garden path, of implied direction in painted space, or of philosophical progress.

Physically, Leo rules the chest and upper back. In Chinese art, praying is often shown with hands to the chest, which in turn is accentuated by drapery or even by being exposed. Animals and athletes favor a swelling chest; vases and mountains are chesty. Associated with the Sun, Leo appears in the sunny smiles of Chinese rooflines, and in the radiant qualities of Chinese society, whether we think of hospitality, generosity or the radiating of empire. It is the civilization of the Sun king.

Leo is one of the most enduring of signs; Chinese society today is the oldest more or less intact society on the world scene. The radiant and the enduring combine to give an expansive tendency; 20th century China has done pretty well at expansion, considering that it started almost without an industrial base. Leo is self-confident. Of all cultures known to us, the Chinese have evinced the supreme sense of cultural superiority, tending to look at others either with scorn or patronization. Leo is the most creative of the signs, if not in depth at least in breadth, and tends to excel in many areas. Chinese literature and philosophy, music and drama, architecture and painting, sculpture and crafts, are all highly distinguished—though it is hard to find one that is distinguishably a world leader in the sense of Egyptian architecture, Greek poetry, or Western music. But the Chinese standard in all the arts together is probably as high as any. And in at least one art China was a world leader: she produced the finest pottery of any Stone Age civilization.

Leo is the sign of the actor. Both the Chinese and the Japanese traditions are rich in the theater, which continued to produce as long as any other art form. The Chinese believe in acting *as if* a certain condition were so, and by acting out the part thus to make it so. But it is the entire Chinese way of life—with its posture and gesture, its staging and ritual—which, more than with any other culture, becomes drama in itself.

F. THE INDIAN CULTURE

Geographically, the Indus Valley overlaps only marginally with the subcontinent of India, locus of the Indian culture. Temporally the difference is still greater: Between the last significant Indus Valley activity and the first indications of Indian culture lies a millennium of no remains save some entirely utilitarian pottery and some latter-day Indus Valley figurines. The seed people of the Indian culture, the Aryans (corresponding to the Dorians in Greece, the Northmen in Western Europe), did not arrive in India until the second millennium BC; the occupation of Mohenjo-daro ended around 2750. The Indus and Vedic cultures, says John Marshall, "were unrelated"; the Vedic was later and "had an independent development."

The Vedic or Indian culture was one of the least historically minded of known cultures (Virgo is said to perceive only the present). Therefore dating is tenuous, but a few basic clues provide sufficient framework to support the hypothesis of an Evolutionary structure beginning in the 12th century BC and ending in the first century AD.

De Riencourt gives the age of *Upanishads* as 800 to 500, calling it at once a "reaction against the medieval ossification of the *Brahmanas* and a bold leap forward in man's understanding of the world and of himself. It is the end of what could be called the 'medieval' phase of Brahmanism, and the beginning of a true Indian 'Reformation'." The period c. 800-500 would then correspond to the Western period c. 1400-1700, giving us, by interpolation, a date for the beginning of the Evolutionary epoch around 1200 BC. This dating is further supported by the arrival of Buddhism, the last of the great Indian religions. The Buddha lived from c. 563 to 483. The last of the great European religions appeared in the 16th century, so that again, rather roughly, around 500 BC in India compares to around 1700 in the West.

Taurus likes warm fields and fertile plains and bright flowers; Capricorn likes rugged, aged mountains, with somber, soaring peaks. But the other earth sign, Virgo, favors deep valleys where nameless secrets lie hidden and a gloomy sadness prevails (M.P. Hall). Here is the appropriateness of the Indus Valley landscape for Taurus, of the mountains of Western Europe for Capricorn, and of the valleys and jungles of India for Virgo.

The western symbol for Virgo is the Virgin, reflected in Indian monasticism on the one hand and female emphasis on the other (it is said that in India the man gains dominance over the woman by becoming even more feminine). In Chinese astrology the symbol for Virgo is the Serpent. In Indian art the serpent plays a role comparable to that of the dragon in Chinese art, and Indian art is permeated with serpentine motifs. In India the serpent means wisdom and, together with the cow, the serpent is sacred to Hinduism. Anatomically, Virgo rules the hip or the loins, areas which received pronounced emphasis in Indian art from Yakshis to Buddhas.

Virgo is the sign of purity, and the Indian culture has shown a passion for purity. Beside a limpid stream, the Indian sustains himself on the simplest dish of nuts and fruits. "The practice of such austerities hardly smiles upon us in our northern clime; but in far-away forest and desert and cave many a Virgoan follows the calling still...." (Pagan thus describes a Virgoan type, but it also sounds like a typical example of the Indian culture.) Virgoan purity means keeping oneself unspotted by the world, untouched by it: India is the society that invented a whole caste of Untouchables. In general the Virgoan, like the Indian, obsession with diet and with cleanliness is proverbial.

As Leo glorifies the ruler, Virgo's psychology is that of the servant—not in the servile sense but in the higher sense: to serve. As China looks to the Prince, so India aspires to discipleship. More than any other sign, Virgo must have a master; or, as Pagan puts it for Virgoans, "to enter the service of the Master is the chief event of their religious life." To become a chela is often the chief event of the Indian aspirant.

Concommitant with dedication to service is Virgoan self-discipline, which may (extreme Hindu and Jain) or may not (Buddhist) take the form of asceticism. And along with these—both in Virgo and in India—goes an absorption in "technique" (yoga), purification (bathing and breathing as well as physical culture and diet), and self-revitalization (prana). Obedience—to the law, or to the master—is indispensable.

In Indian psychology may be observed such Virgo traits as nervousness (meaning either highly strung, or simply of the nervous system); highly sensitized faculties of awareness; a tendency to classify everything; a habit of introspection and self-scrutiny, and a pervasive humility (passive resistance). As compared with Gemini (the other sign associated with Mercury), Virgo is more interested in discrimination and immaculateness—a satisfactory distinction between Indian and Babylonian cultures. India is particularly given to the institution of the mendicant monk, a nicely Virgoan combination.

Indian art displays such Virgo characteristics as unusual skill and craftsmanship; variety, multiplicity, complexity and the many-faceted; elaborate rituals and hierarchies; a sensuousness, frequently voluptuous, which is at the same time intellectually analytical; an additive composition; an endless ornamentation and elaboration, even incrustation, yet combined with a native drawing-back or indigenous restraint; a suavity, delicacy, intricacy, and grace; a linear perfection and instinct to calligraphy, with exquisite detail; a sinuousness of line and of the dance, especially the dancing girl; a taste for the very small (in miniature images and pictures, in spires and pavillions); a flowing humor and unusual whimsicality; a taste for richness and preciousness paradoxically combined with a dislike of clutter.

According to Rowland, the stupa at Sanchi shows no unified iconographical scheme, but has disparate subjects without order or sequence, haphazard combinations, and an extraordinary variety of buildings. This Virgo situation is found equally in Indian society, which, as de Riencourt noted, is distinguished by "political plurality" where Chinese is distinguished by "political unity."

Rowland spoke of the isolation and the self-absorption of the Indian tradition—both Virgo distinctions. The Indian today continues to make an excellent secretary (or otherwise to shine in a serving role); to make plans and appointments and discard them just as easily; and to display overall the natural resilience of the character of mutable earth, with a Virgoan lack of regard for outward show.

G. The Classical Culture

Although the Greeks were not given to keeping records, we know enough about later Classical developments to date the Evolutionary epoch with some precision. The earlier developments can be given only approximately. The Greek "Middle Ages" have ofttimes been identified with the period from around 1100 to around 700 BC. This is correct. The period marks the first epicycle of the Classical Evolutionary and corresponds to Old Kingdom Egypt, or to the Romanesque-Gothic period in the West.

The Western Crusades, which began one century after the beginning of the Western Evolutionary, appear to be echoed in the first Greek settlements in Asia Minor, which are dated about 1000 BC. The Trojan War must be dated sometime in the 13th century, and corresponds to the first trans-oceanic drives of the Northmen, in the 9th century AD.

The Classical "Gothic"—that is, the second half of the first epicycle—would then be the "full" Geometric of the 9th and 8th centuries. The Doric temple as we know it is a creation of the Classical "Renaissance": In Homer there is no indication of the "classical" Classical temple, and columns are mentioned rarely by comparison with "high roofs."

The second Classical epicycle is occupied by what we call Archaic and Classical style, dating from around 700 to around 300 BC. The third epicycle (300 BC to 100 AD) comprises Hellenistic and Roman developments. A number of students have found similarities between aspects of Hellenistic style and mannerism, or even Rococo. This is not correct. The "mannerism" of the Hellenistic—for example the Pergamum Altar—is not properly mannerism but rather a kind of Wagnerian rhetoric. And as J.J. Pollitt has observed, while Hellenistic works have sometimes been described as "rococo", in fact "they represent the most intense drive toward realism which ever appeared in Greek art"; and are otherwise correlative with trends of the 19th century in the West.

The end of the third epicycle is the end of the Evolutionary. The scene now is Rome, whose population began to decline in the 2nd century AD. The continuity of Greek into Roman values endures in the Roman reverence for Greek architectural forms and orders. This lasts until the end of the first century AD, whence Roman style changes radically, putting arches directly on columns, breaking up orders, producing curves and other irregularities.

The wars of Trajan, especially the second Dacian campaign, were "the last wars in which the empire was victorious without difficulty and without disappointment" (J. Carcopino). Under Trajan the empire reached its maximum extent (Donald Strong). In the Dacian wars of 101-107, Trajan "first seriously exceeded the limits set to the empire by Augustus" (Langer). "The last conquests of the Caesars" were the conquest of Dacia (106), of Arabia (109), and the Parthian campaign of 115. In 117 Hadrian was recognized as emperor. "Almost immediately he abandoned the new provinces across the Euphrates" (Langer) and began consolidations, including the wall across Britain. Unlike Trajan, "he was opposed to territorial expansion;" he renounced Trajan's conquests in the East and "carefully delimited" Rome's "well-defended frontiers" (*Encyclopedia Britannica*). Under Trajan was "attained the highest plane of ancient civilization.... Latin literature was soon to run so nearly dry" (Carcopino).

The end of the third or "Roman" epicycle may thus be placed somewhere between 101 and 118 AD. We can come still closer to a precise year if we examine two key turning points in Classical history, the turn from the first to the second half of the second epicycle, and the turn from the second to the third epicycle.

The turn at the middle of the second epicycle is familiar in the West as the shift from Renaissance to Baroque. As shown in the discussion of the Western centuries (Chapter I) this may be dated at 1589 AD. The corresponding point in the Classical evolution is the shift from Archaic ("renaissance") to Classical ("baroque") style.

Observing the Strangford Apollo, J.J. Pollitt sees "the outward humanization which characterizes much of late Archaic sculpture" (the "late Archaic" would correspond to the art of Bruegel and Veronese). He concludes the work "must date from 490 or 485," noting that it is still fundamentally like the earlier "kouroi." In sharp contrast is the Kritios Boy, who "might turn and ask you a question"—a work which "stands at the very beginning of the Early Classical period." It is one of the first works to embody contrapposto (albeit incomplete)—contrapposto is one of the "classic" Greek inventions—and it introduces the naturalism which in the West appears with Caravaggio. Pollitt dates the Kritios Boy at probably just after 480 BC.

But the Kritios Boy is not quite the first known example of the new ("Classical" or "Baroque") condition. "Our earliest instance of 'living balance' in a Greek statue," Rhys Carpenter observes, appears to be the "nude adolescent male from the Acropolis entered in the Acropolis Museum catalog as item 692." This he concludes must be appreciably later than the "Theseus" which "belongs in the last decade of the sixth century," and which predates the more advanced Kritios Boy.

Pollitt further observes the contrast between a fallen warrior from the west pediment at Aegina and one from the east pediment. While the earlier west pediment still uses strong silhouette (a Renaissance desideratum) and a "dignified court tableau" (a "16th century" trait), the later east pediment is distinguished by a new stylistic fusion and unification, with a novel expression of naturalism and emotion (all Baroque characteristics). Pollitt dates the earlier work at around 490, and the later at around 480. From the two contrasts (the two free-standing and the two pedimental works), and by combining the findings of the two specialists, we arrive at a date for this transition from Archaic to Classical which must be no earlier than 490 and no later than 480 BC.

The second key point is the shift from the second to the third Classical epicycles. It is at this point that the spotlight moves from Greece to Rome, from Europe to America. In the West the third

82 HARMONICS OF HISTORY

epicycle began in 1787; this was not a critical year in Europe, but in America it was marked by the creation of the U.S. Constitution and therefore the beginning of America as a formal polity. What is the corresponding point in Roman history?

"By means of a political 'strike' in 287 BC, the plebeians" gained the concession "that their decisions...should have the force of law" (Rostovtzeff). This was established in the Hortensian Law, which now "fully equated the *plebiscita* with the *leges*.... The plebs had thus achieved complete legal equality with the patricians, but the old problem remained in the oppression of the poor" (Langer). Comparably, with the United States Constitution, legal freedom was established, but the institution of slavery was excepted. Furthermore, neither constitution was pursued much further at the time. The United States Government remained republican, hardly yet contemplating democracy; and in Rome "when the plebeians were victorious, their leaders were not at all anxious to continue the fight; and the rank and file...did not procede to radical changes in the constitution" (Rostovtzeff).

The constitutional crisis was accompanied by political consolidation. With the U.S. Constitution, one unified government replaced a congeries of nearly autonomous colonies. By the time of Hortensian Law, "Rome had now established her supremacy throughout central Italy" (Langer); central Italy represented the core of the rising Roman polity, and corresponded to the newly consolidated eastern seaboard of America. As of these points, Rome and America had begun their corporate careers.

From this we must conclude that there is no alternative to equating the crisis of 287 BC with that of 1787 AD. Computing 99 years to the century, we arrive at the year 485 for the shift from Archaic to Classical, and the year 110 AD for the end of the Roman growth. Comparable dates for the Classical and Western cultures may now be aligned:

584 BC	1490 AD
485	1589
386	1688
287	1787
188	1886

89	1985
11 AD	2084
110	2183

True to its Libran character, the Classical culture occupied a modest space. Greece itself is small, and is composed chiefly of hill and sea. The mountain pockets and abrupt islands might suggest an earth sign; the sunny clime (relatively rainless) a fire sign; or the fact that in classical times there was hardly a major center more than forty miles from the sea might suggest a water sign; but in fact the Classical is ruled by an air sign.

We are sometimes misled by the stolid remains of Greek temples into overlooking their original appearance. Painted in bright colors and surmounted by articulated roofs, these temples sprang easily into the air. Not too far, nor with too much emphasis—for Libra is the sign of balance and moderation—but with a distinctly light touch. To see these temples with a Greek's eye we must consult not modern archeological reconstructions (which tend to be Capricornian because our culture is) but those rare renditions surviving on classical vases. Here (e.g. the Würzburg Krater) we become aware of an airiness around the columns, a bright articulation of entablatures and pediments, and above all an emphasis on sculpture and decoration above the roof line, which have been either lost or misread in today's trunklike remains. Instinctively we look for Capricornian thrust and counterweight. Yet the original effect of the Doric order was just as Rhys Carpenter found it: "the sensation of stone poised aloft as though it weighed nothing...using it for a free fantasy of imaginative construction."

The refinements of a classical temple had several purposes and effects, but none was more important than a pulsating or "breathing" quality—the same quality that can be found in even a fragment of a carved classical face. Both buildings and statues—with a few special exceptions—stood in the open air. "Antique art, in its best period," as Focillon surmised, "saw man surrounded only by light." Yet this effect of light is not confined to the "classical" period (cf. our Baroque) of the Classical culture, but may be found in any post-Mycenaean art of Greece. Mt. Olympus was the apex of the Greek cosmos, and Homer described it in terms possibly surprising to the

Western Capricornian reader: "Not by winds is it shaken, nor ever wet with rain nor doth the snow come nigh thereto, but most clear air is spread about it cloudless and the white light floats over it."

Amongst human faculties, air represents the mental and the supermental (M.P. Hall). The Greeks were intellectuals. Their science was rarely utilitarian. "Archimedes, the greatest inventor of antiquity, refused to leave behind him any practical treatise, and his biographer—Plutarch—commended his decision" (H.J. Randall). Their philosophy is still unexceeded, for all the incisiveness of Arab or the profundity of German thought. An Arab proverb relates that "God gave the Greeks skill with the head, the Chinese with the hands, but us Arabs with the tongue." And as Delacroix (no mean critic) observed, the beauty of Homer and Virgil is more rarefied than that of the Bible. (It was a Scorpionic culture that produced the Bible, and Scorpio is a water sign.)

As the product of a culture ruled by a cardinal sign, Greek architecture shows far less change, invention, variation, ambition, or daring then either the Egyptian or the Western; and much the same must be said of Greek sculpture. But these are "earthy" media, and if we consult the "airy" ones—poetry and drama, philosophy, geometry, elocution—we find daring and invention enough. Literature was "by long odds the first product of Greek culture," said Kroeber. Rhetoric was the last. The cardinal mind is "quick, fertile, insatiable," said M.P. Hall in what might serve as a description of the Greek mind.

The cardinal signs divide into pairs with regard to their sense of time. Aries and Libra experience time in the present—a pure present, eternal and timeless: the eternal moment of the classical Greek. Cancer and Capricorn look to the past for the meaning of time. Cancer loves memory, Capricorn history. Egyptian and Western historiography seem endless. Of their own past, the Greeks wrote down almost nothing, and the Greek of the 5th century knew incomparably less of Greek history than we do today, through Western historical investigation. When the Greeks did discover "history"—from the time of Herodotus—it was chiefly in the sense of storytelling, biography, or travel: there is hardly ever a sense of the passage of time. Libra has been called a sign of short memory. To us this seems a lack, but we lack the Libran Greek capacity to live in the present moment.

Manilius (in the time of Augustus) gave certain astrological associations which are generally found in our own time, such as the arms and shoulders for Gemini, the sides and back for Leo, or the legs for Aquarius. For Libra he gives the buttocks. To think of the emphasis on the size, musculature, and geometry of the buttocks represented in Greek figures—no less the male and especially in the Archaic—is to suspect that such a designation may be not without significance.

Librans are wont, presumably from their love of symmetry, to part their hair in the middle (this is so pronounced that persons whose ascendant has progressed into Libra are known to give their hair a middle part when they have never done so before). Greek sculpture shows hair centrally parted with considerable frequency, much more so than in any other tradition. Otherwise Greek hair is shown not parted at all but arranged in some symmetrical shape, as well as being generally short, modest, and regular in formation.

Libra signifies the kidneys on the inside of the body: on the outside the area is that between navel and pubes. This is precisely the area distinguished in Greek painted and sculptured figures, and it is an area not emphasized in other known traditions. In Archaic sculpture, the form in this area is a sharp V-line; later this is modified to that combination of curve and angle which is the Libran glyph upside down.

Plate III

Above is the Libran glyph.
Astrologers have observed that this corresponds to classical pediments or domed porticos; these are of Greek and Roman origin. The architectural motif at the end of the 'Canopus' at Hadrian's Villa, Tivoli, perfectly shows the Libran glyph across its top.

Plate IV

Libra prefers a variable and temperate climate: this applies to Greece today but was still more true in Hellenic times when the climate was both cooler and moister. Libra is associated with the vine: remember Homer's "wine dark and deep," and consider how "another factor in Greek humor was their use of wine. Hellenic

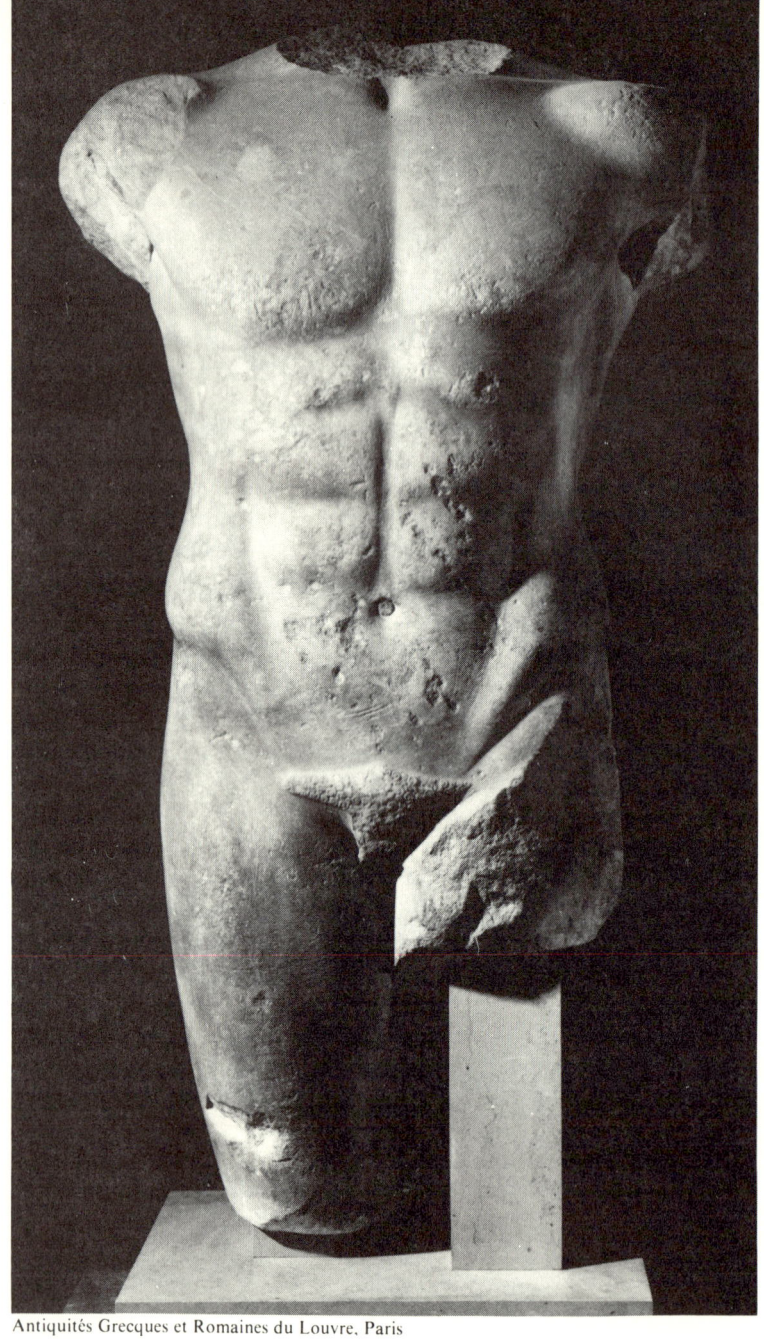

Antiquités Grecques et Romaines du Louvre, Paris

Plate III
Torso de Milet

Tivoli, Italy.

Plate IV
The "Canopus," Hadrian's Villa.

territory grew wine and olives, and in some places little else. Wine was always to play an important part in their way of life, their own being a rather inferior stuff by current standards—Samos perhaps excepted—but constantly mentioned in all their literature" (C.N. Parkinson).

According to Chinese astrology, the animal associable with the sign Libra is the horse. The Greeks (typically of Libra) were not interested in animals as such, but they had an unusual number of words related to "horse." And while they did not usually allow animal parts, at least in the Classical age, to be represented in major sculpture in the round, the centaur was sometimes excepted. Another favorite Greek subject, the satyr, while generally considered to be part goat, was often depicted by the Greeks with a horse's tail.

Venus (whose primary association is with Libra) is related to the fig, the cypress, the pomegranate, the almond, the apricot, as well as the vine. All are distinctive of the Greco-Roman landscape to this day. In ancient days the fig was a staple, at times the only item, in the diet of slaves. By contrast the moon (Cancer and Egypt) signifies the palm tree; and Saturn (Capricorn and the West) the pine, elm, willow, cypress, and yew. The Classical and Western cultures overlap in the cypresses of Italy and southern France.

The planet Venus, "ruler" of Libra, is represented by the number Three. Three was a number compelling to the Greeks. The Classical Three was not a Trinity, however, but a triad—that is, a combination of three discrete and equal parts. Greek classicism is sometimes given three aspects: humanism (the anthropomorphic and anthropocentric), idealism (the abstract and archetypal), and rationalism (number, ratio, and proportion). To Pythagoras, Three embodied the idea of contemplation and a symmetrical whole, and in the Pythagorean concept of numbers, Three is the first real number as it has a beginning, a middle, and an end.

This was the Classical concept of how a story should be divided. Plays were combined into trilogies. Drama was given three unities (time, place, and action). Three actors were employed, even for six parts. There were three Graces, three Fates, three goddesses from whom Paris chose. Three multiplied three times is 27; "neither Plato nor Aristotle, who knew the forces effective in nature, went beyond the number 27 in their analysis of the world" (R. Wittkower). Plato "had to content himself with the harmony of airy thought-structures that lacked weight, and with a paper surface that lacked depth. The step from three to four brought him sharply up against something unexpected and alien to his thought" (C.G. Jung). Compare this situation with that of the early Western civilization, which is ruled by Capricorn, Saturn, and the number Four. Even though the medieval West was Christian and thereby required to elevate the number Three of the Trinity, still certain of the medieval philosophers (e.g. German mystics) "tried to include matter in the Trinity as God's fourth aspect" (Marie-Louise von Franz).

The Greek love of Three appears throughout the Doric order, which represented the culmination of their architectural thinking. The Doric order is composed of three main parts: a horizontal base, vertical columns, and a horizontal entablature. The base has three steps. The column has three parts in the sense of discrete shapes: shaft, echinus, abacus. But the capital also has three parts, because the necking (which in shape belongs to the shaft) is actually part of a single block including abacus and echinus. The entablature has three parts (architrave, frieze, and cornice), and the triglyphs on the frieze are three-formed.

In stressing the fact that Libra is an air sign, emphasis has been put on the airy and ideational aspects of Greek works of the imagination. This is correct and should come first. There remains, nonetheless, a sculptural or body-like impression in Greek cultural forms: the corporeal polis, Euclidean "figures", a highly sculptural architecture, a painting that deals almost solely with the figure, and a figural sculpture that appears to have dominated the visual art forms. Physical development was so important that it was held worthy as an offering to the gods, as in the games.

How account for such body emphasis in an air sign? For one thing, the body is pre-eminently human, and "human" is Libran. The other sign signifying "man" is Aquarius, but where Aquarius might be designated by the term "humanitarian" the designation for Libra would be "humanist." Humanism, properly used, means the study of Classical forms, and Classical means Greek and Latin. In the visual arts the most completely "human" expression must be the externally realized body or figure—whether realized in a life-sized, proportional statue, a frieze-like painting, or a body-like building.

But there is a further explanation of the Classical body, and this is to be found in esoteric astrology. For the esoteric designation of Libra, M.P. Hall gives the "dense physical body. The form compounded from the gross elements which serves as a vehicle of the higher nature while it manifests in the material world." Discussing the Libran "scales" which weigh and evaluate, Jocelyn noted that "mass is fundamental because it evaluates an object...in terms of...gravitation."

Venusian Libra connotes love, and amatory diseases are called "venereal". The Westerner likes to think he invented romantic love, but this is only in the sense of yearning, a Capricornian trait. Where the Western lover is focused on the object of his yearning, the Greek was in love with loving. This loving could be of man with woman, of man with man, or (apparently less often) of woman with woman. Libra, says M.R. Meyer, is "often, though by no means necessarily, a significator of male homosexuality."

More strictly speaking, the Greek male was given not so much to homosexuality as to bisexuality. Actually, homosexuality was "the object of contempt and malicious jokes. The normal pattern was a bisexuality" (M.I. Finley). And the courtesan too had a significant role in this amatory confusion, the explanation for all of which may be attributable not only to the Venusian idealization of love, but also to the Libran traits of ambiguity and indecision.

Venusian also is what Evangeline Adams called "aesthetic beauty." It is a happy combination. Aesthetics by itself can become dry intellectualizing, while beauty can be pursued sensuously, without thought. The Greeks put aesthetics and beauty together; and the Romans pursued this, albeit with a heavy hand. "The civilizations of Greece and Rome," wrote Wilhelm Dilthey, "produced an aesthetically sensuous culture." Guglielmo Ferrero (speaking of Rome as well as Greece) observed that "art occupied in the ancient world the position which science occupies in modern civilization." And he stressed that this "was not a refined luxury for the few, but an elementary and universal necessity." H.J. Randall observed that "the Greeks were shocked, as we are not shocked, by lack of beauty in common things."

The Classical aesthetic was Libran in its being based on a keen sense of the appropriate. Things must fit—as the parts of the Doric order fit one another (a factor more important than their structural function); as the shape and size of a mirror or vase fits its concept and use; or as it was fitting that a sculpture of a human be life size. Vitruvius even indicates that a temple to Mars should be masculine in form, a temple to Venus feminine.

The sense of the appropriate relates the Libran interest in justice (let the punishment "fit" the crime) to the Classical penchant for jurisprudence. We think of the Law as the Roman's greatest accomplishment, but to the Spartan the "law" had been the final appeal, while the theme of Plato's most important book was justice, and the just man. "Justice is their love," said Jocelyn of Librans. Where the prime concern of Roman law was "equity", that of the Common Law is precedent. Here the Classical mind betrays its preference for balance, equation, and justice in the sense of reasonableness—all Libran traits—while the Western shows its insistence on historical continuity and the weight of tradition—Capricornian predilections. Comparing the two in their time sense, Spengler found that "all Western law bears the stamp of the future, all Classical the stamp of the moment."

Related to the Libran love of equity is its desire for equilibrium in the form of bilateral symmetry. As a human biological need, symmetry is found in some form in most arts. With the Greeks it is a subject by itself. In the best Classic art the symmetry is never rigid, yet never off-balance. The classical athletic figure was not daring. The Greeks never equalled their predecessors the Phoenicians in seamanship or exploration, but insisted that all activities should be to scale. While scale has to do with proportion, it also has to do with the "scales" of justice, the symbol of balance.

When a system of modest action and moderating counterbalance has been established (as in Greek contrapposto), symmetry and harmony become much the same thing. Harmony means a balance of rest and activity, one of the secrets of Greek art. The Greeks found it more expressive of their sense of the moment to show the figure in some motion than at complete rest, yet (in the classical period) the action is never violent nor even restless. It is as if they had heeded Evangeline Adams' advice to Librans, that they should "avoid too violent exercise."

Balanced too, in the literal sense, is the Greek view of virtue. Courage, for example, was not conceived as the opposite of cowardice, but as an equilibrium between the two extremes of fearfulness and rashness. Such balancing often produced in Greek psychology a concommitant Libran trend: indecisiveness. "They did not see a choice between reason and passion, Apollo and Dionysus, the eternally perfect and corrupt transitory, but the necessity of living with both, with all the resulting ambiguity and uncertainty. And 'they' means nearly all Greeks..." (M.I. Finley). This is sheer Libra, as is the observation by J.J. Pollitt on the effect of contrapposto in Greek sculpture (contrapposto in the sense of displacement of weight) which was "to create a figure which seems to hesitate and to be uncertain about what it is doing and where it will go. It seems conscious of its surroundings and faced with alternatives which ask for judgment and decision."

Libra may be equated with the Golden Mean (Else Parker). The Greeks invented the Golden Mean. The Mean means moderation, balance, harmony, poise. It means the avoidance of extremes: the Greeks allowed Dionysian ecstasy, but they never allowed fanatics. Libra (says M.P. Hall) should "as far as possible bring his emotions under the guidance of his reason". This, and not some Panathenaic procession past or present, is the true theme of the Parthenon frieze. "The Antique", said Delacroix, putting it as well as anyone has, "is full of that unaffected grace which we see in nature; nothing jars; nothing is to be regretted; nothing is lacking; nothing is in excess."

If nothing is lacking and nothing in excess, then there must be measure. The Latin word Libra identified the sign of the zodiac, along with which it meant balance or level, but it also meant the Roman pound (twelve ounces), whence we have Italian "libbra", Spanish "libra", French "livre" and English "pound" (also, sterling). Weights and measures. Mensuration and the weighing of things, invoked Plato.

While contrapposto deals in weights, it is inseparable from the concept of proportion, with which the concept of measure also is involved. Proportion means that a sculptured figure implies the sense of scale of a human figure, but proportion also means the measured set of ratios of which the sculpture is composed. The Greeks created measured proportions for the sculptured head and figure very much as they established ratios in their architectural orders. These ratios were highly standard within a given generation, varying in accordance with artistic evolution rather than by individual invention.

This sense of a common coin—of a universal norm—is also Libran. The proportions in Renaissance architectural orders or figural depictions, with their idiosyncratic variations and play of individual invention, should serve to highlight the Libran clarity and order of the Greeks, especially when we consider the extent to which the Renaissance is supposed to have imitated the Classical antique.

As a value in itself, the Greek love of proportioning appears attributable to that love of harmony, appropriateness and relationships which lies in the essence of the Libran soul. Perfect proportion resides only in the realm of the Ideal. The intimation of it on earth is, then, both an aesthetic, a philosophic, and a religious proposition. Kenneth Clark describes a profoundly Libran situation when he says that "in every branch of Hellenic thought we encounter a belief in measurable proportion that, in the last analysis, amounts to a mystical religion."

Measure and proportion require the art of constant adjustment. The "refinements" of the Parthenon amount to an elaborate set of displacements or modifications of what seems at first glance a simple proposition. They serve to adjust the differences between what logic requires and what the eye experiences. Adjustment is also a key to the refinements of Greek diplomacy and Roman law, two distinguished products of the Classical culture. At the same time Libran wit can involve itself with turning the argument—thus the Sophists and our word sophistry.

The root meaning of Libra is free. The Greeks invented the free-standing statue as well as the free-standing building (the structures on the Athenian Acropolis differ in size, shape, orientation, and elevation). The statue should further be free of encumbrance, and so the Greeks introduced the nude figure (the Nude is defined by Clark as "an art form invented by the Greeks"). The Greek polis could never submit itself to an enduring alliance, much less a superior power. But if Greek freedom came close to anarchy, it is also true that slavery was relatively open, especially for the ancient world. The Greeks were free of snobbery, and pretty much so of the alienation of classes; "Athenian society was singularly free from barriers that depended on status" (Kitto). On the other hand, Greek freedom did not encourage rebellious or eccentric genius of the type of Michelangelo or Beethoven, Caravaggio or Van Gogh. To do so would have threatened the harmony of the social family. Libra is ever on "the lookout for the ideal group" (Rudhyar). The Greeks reduced the gods in number, and made them into a family and a family council. Greek art, like Greek democracy, was essentially communal and social. It is in this sense that Greek culture has been called "popular"—a trait which, in either the democratic or the derogatory sense, is likewise Libran. A Libran, says Cope, can even be "popular for all the wrong reasons"—think of Alcibiades. The Libran is capable of neglecting the children for the mate (in Greek art there is expressed small interest in children, and none in children as children). The Libran is not given to fixed opinions, yet neither does he favor the maverick. He may be an opportunist, and not morally staunch, nor long on initiative; he tends to like elegance; he does not like to live alone. "There is no place in Aristotle's scheme for the man who cannot live in association with his fellows. Rousseau, on the contrary, thinks of individuals as relinquishing rights to the community" (W.S. Carpenter).

The Libran art of persuasion is related to the art of drama; the Libran is given to theatrics because he likes to influence (M.P. Hall). Greek drama was accompanied by Greek oratory and followed by Roman oratory as among the leading creations of the Classical culture. In Greek literature and philosophy, the supreme virtue is *arete*, for which our word *excellence* is the best though by no means an adequate translation: *arete* is an excellence having to do with a perfected function and a proportional ideal. Man can approach this ideal, not by willful invention, but by perfecting the material counterpart of the archetype—which truly exists only in the Ideal.

Thus the Greek artist is not the inventor in the sense so admired in Western civilization. To the Greek, variation is valuable to please the eye or tease the ear. To the Westerner, variation signifies a strong and bold innovation. It is the difference between cardinal air, with its clarity of ideal, and cardinal earth with its romantic dynamism. Herman Melville could have been addressing Libra, though it was the Greek classical temple he described in the words:

> Not magnitude, not lavishness,
>   But form, the site.
> Not innovating willfulness
>   But reverence for the archetype.

H. The Levantine Culture

The difference in territory between the Levantine and the Babylonian cultures has been indicated in the introductory summary. The Levantine was born outside the original Babylonian area; it did not include Sumer, but was centered in Persia, Palestine, and Arabia.

The term Levantine was introduced by Roger Wescott to refer to the urban cultures of Anatolia, Syria, Lebanon, Palestine, and bordering regions. It points to the major culture that Spengler calls the Magian or Arabian, a culture of which he is the original discoverer (though he notes that some later Arab writers seem to have been aware of it). This is about the same as the civilization which Philip Bagby calls the Near-Eastern. The term Magian is apt but lacks coin; the term Arabian is evocative but too limited, while Near-Eastern is not limited enough.

The term Levantine seems the most appropriate. The word Levant connotes the East, helping to distinguish it from the Classical which it overlaps geographically. It refers generally to the area now made up of Palestine, Lebanon, Turkey, Syria, Egypt and Greece; this amounts very closely to the core area of the Levantine culture in, say, the fourth century AD. Bagby himself observed of this civilization: "There has long been a common-sense recognition of this cultural entity. The inhabitants of countries bordering on the Eastern Mediterranean, whether Muslims, Greeks, Jews or Copts, have been popularly classed together as Levantines."

The Copts (native Christians in Egypt) and "Greeks" have nothing to do with the ancient Egyptian or Greek cultures; in the Middle Ages Greek meant Byzantine—as in "El Greco". A people—the Jews, for example, or the Italians—may belong now to one major culture, later to another. But as sub-cultures, the Jews like the Muslims belong to the Levantine culture, further distinguishing it from the Babylonian, as well as from the Egyptian or the Classical.

The Levantine culture is governed by Scorpio, the fixed water sign. The Egyptian culture was ruled by Cancer, the cardinal water sign. Her state was built upon a straight, long-running river, and her art expressed a continuous progression in a single direction, whether along an architectural way, or in the gaze and stance of her sculptured figures. It is not that the Egyptian culture expressed the Nile, but rather that both signified cardinal flow. Major cultures choose their geographic sites with impressive aptness.

As fixed water, the Scorpionic Levant expressed still bodies. The Levantine landscape is marked by contained seas and lakes: the Caspian Sea, the Sea of Galilee, the Sea of Marmora, the Black Sea, the Red Sea and the Dead Sea—the names of the last three being particularly appropriate to Scorpio. A sense of still water is immured in the faces and figures of Byzantine mosaics, with their deep moods, their "fixed" stares, their immobile and radiant garments, rippling quietly as in a pond.

That Scorpio is a water sign surely is related to the abundance of motifs from the plant kingdom in Byzantine and Persian art, a choice which once again distinguishes the Levantine from the Babylonian cultures, since Babylonian and Assyrian art emphasized the human kingdom, (along with a few selected animals, notably the lion of Gemini, in hunting scenes).

The emphasis on baptism by water also indicates a water sign. While the widespread use of baptism by water during the past two millennia is rightly associated with the Piscean Age, still baptism is a practice found in many cultures, and it remains significant that the practice of baptism by immersion was inaugurated in the germinating days of the Levantine culture, at the hands of both Zoroastrians and Jews. It is also the Levantine culture which invented the Baptistry as an architectural form, and used it far more extensively than other cultures have. Baptism was usually performed in a fixed pool of still water.

The depth and mystery and inwardness of Scorpio are not only expressed in Levantine art, but also they seem to contribute to the fact that this culture was as productive of enduring religions as any culture known. Against the Indian culture's Hindu, Jain, and Buddhist religions, which continue to dominate East and Southeast Asia, the Levant offers the Zoroastrian, the Mithraic, the Judaic, the Christian, and the Islamic, to mention only the most prolific. The Zoroastrian, while strongest in the centuries before Christ, is still alive today with the Ghebers of Iran and the Parsis of India.

The Mithraic, which derived from the Zoroastrian, was in the 2nd century AD (a time of Early Church Fathers and Neo-Platonists) more widespread than Christianity. The Judaic, the Christian, and the Islamic continue to dominate religious adherence in the West, the near East, and Africa. Religions are seldom confined to the scene of a single major culture, but they are always spawned in one, and retain significant aspects of its zodiacal character.

Scorpionic religiousness favors ceremony and ritual: Catholic ritual and Byzantine ceremony were creations of the Levantine culture. Scorpio is less inclined to verbal articulation and prolixity than is Virgo. From the Indian culture, ruled by Virgo, come the Vedas, Brahmanas, the Upanishads—unsurpassed in richness; and the Ramayana, the Mahabharat, the Gita—unsurpassed in beauty. Compared with these, the Avesta, the Bible, the Koran are relatively brief and succinct (the Vedas originally contained 100,000 verses).

The Indian religions are intricate and contemplative. Virgoan too is Indian yoga, with its complex and refined manipulation of bodily apparatus and sensuous experience. The Levantine religions are ethical and prophetic. What more ethical than the Zoroastrian or Judaic, what more prophetic than Judaic, early Christian, or Muslim? (Scorpio is a prophetic sign.) Scorpio's code of morals, says Pagan, is "high and somewhat stern," and she adds that Scorpio likes to invoke: "Cursed is he that breaks the law." Generally recognized of Scorpio is the unwavering devotion to principles, and the grave, unbending quality that likewise marks the ethical force of the Levantine religions.

Of world religions, only Judaism, Christianity, and Islam may be said to be truly exclusive and intolerant. Cope says of the Scorpio that he can be intolerant without remorse. Bernard Pares notes that the Tartars showed a "remarkable tolerance to all religions, and spared their ministers" but that this tolerance "disappeared after the Tartars became Mahometans."

Scorpio, says C.E.O. Carter, has few flabby characters, and is given to heroes and villains. We may think of Ohrmazd and Ahriman, Light and Darkness, Good and Evil, God and Satan, life and death—the heroes and villains of the Levantine religions. Such oppositions are hardly to be found in the Indian religions, where Evil does not exist and Good is relative. The Levant is the homeland of the chosen people; Scorpios, says Pagan, are "confident of their own salvation." Scorpio is the silent sign according to astrologers, and Edgar Cayce said that to learn silence is the great lesson of Scorpio. Spengler described his Magian (our Levantine) culture as a "consensus of silence."

That the Levantine is an eastern civilization is appropriate in consideration of Scorpio's "oriental impassivity" (Pagan) and its "immense reserve"—traits expressed in Early Christian, Coptic, and Byzantine art. The Levantine arts, however, for all that they reveal, are subsidiary to the Levantine religions, which amount to the culture's strongest expressions. Pagan goes so far as to say that with Scorpio we find "seldom or never an irreligious man."

Scorpio is the sign of degeneration and regeneration—and thus of conversion and transformation. Scorpio, says Jocelyn, raises from the dead; it is the vice of Saul and the virtue of Paul. The physical location of the degenerating and regenerating process is the sexual area. This is Scorpio's specialty—whereas sex as recreation and procreation belong to Taurus. While the Capricornian priesthoods of the West were willing to give up sex (in order to cure simony) but not alcohol, puritanical Islam prohibited alcohol but allowed sex even unto polygamy. All the Levantine societies have a strong sexual consciousness. Byzantine law showed a "preoccupation with sexual behavior" (H.J. Muller). It has been claimed that in the early days of the Church, certain Christian sects engaged in sexual activities as part of their religious worship. Scorpio sees the church as the Bride, says Jocelyn, and is exemplified by mystical sex seeking union with the greater whole.

Both with Scorpio and the Levantine religions, mystical sex is tied to death and transfiguration. The 8th House (ruled by Scorpio) is the house of "death", and Scorpio is the sign of regeneration and transfiguration. Hence its emblems range from the death-dealing Scorpion to the regenerating Phoenix. And so do the Levantine religions range from the "destroying force" in Zoroastrianism to the physical resurrection in Christianity: "O death, where is thy "sting"?

It may be significant that medieval astrologers held the Jews to be ruled by Scorpio, as modern astrologers hold the Arabs. With the Arabs it is the sexual and sacrificial predisposition that obtains, with the Jews it was more a magnetic quality which may in fact be extended to the Levantine culture as a whole. Spengler called this the Magian culture, a word which appropriately invokes magic, wizardry, and the occult; he called it the culture of secrets and seals and the philosopher's stone, in all of which he might have been speaking of Scorpio just as well.

Jocelyn called Scorpio the "mightiest of alchemical signs," and the Levantine is the culture above all to seek the world of alchemy: the very word is Arabic, as is elixir. In Arabic "alchemical thought, *al-iksir* was the substance which when added in projection...to any imperfect thing brought about a change for the better in the balance...of its qualities, i.e. a transmutation...the *iksirs* were naturally thought of as drugs, the 'medicines of man as well as of metals'...the idea of a medicine of eternal youth was exceedingly un-Greek...there is in fact a great deal in the Arabic alchemical literature on elixirs of life and everlasting life." Thus Joseph Needham, in descriptions of an Arabian alchemy which can only be interpreted as Scorpionic, and to which should be added: "There is one very important theme of Arabic alchemy which seems never before to have been set properly in the context of elixir doctrine, though Krau gave it close and learned study. This was the so-called Science of Generation...concerned with the artificial asexual *in vitro* generation of plants, animals, and even men..." On top of this, the Arabians produced an exceptional genealogy.

Levantine religions are monotheistic. Indian religions (speaking here of the cultural level, not the esoteric) are given to a rich and varied polytheism, such as suits the Virgo temper. The Scorpionic unwillingness to do anything by halves—plus the magnetic and messianic aspects—accord well with Levantine monotheism. David B. Richardson refers to the "personal, absolute, and transcendent God" of the early Levantine period.

Rudhyar writes of Scorpio's surrender of the ego's desire to remain separate: The very word Islam means submission. Cope finds in Scorpio "one of the toughest challenges in the zodiac: an identity crisis." The Levantine seems to have suffered an identity crisis more than any other culture. The Egyptians knew they all belonged to one civilization; and as for the Chinese, they thought it the only one. Greeks and Romans, for all their oppositions, knew they shared a culture. But even what Spengler termed the "pseudomorphosis" (wherein a young culture grows up in the neighborhood and under the shadow of an older one) does not account for the identity problem of the Levantine culture. For while it suffered this relationship to the

Classical, so also has the young Russian culture suffered in relation to the Western. Even today the identity of the Levantine culture is only beginning to be recognized, whereas the Russians have known Holy Russia from early times, and have recognized themselves as a cultural entity vis à vis Europe since at least Danilevsky. The difference seems less one of timing or circumstance than of Aquarius versus Scorpio.

While in western astrology Scorpio is signified by the scorpion (or eagle or phoenix), in Chinese astrology it is the sheep. If the importance of the Fish in early Christianity is attributable to the Piscean Age, how account for the importance there of Sheep and Lamb and Shepherd other than as symbols of Scorpio? The eyes in Byzantine mosaics have been called sheep's eyes. The Scorpionic eye—large, deep, bright, dark, and mesmerizing—is one of those ubiquitous features that relate all of the various Levantine traditions. It is found in Early Christian and Coptic art, Byzantine and Hebraic (as at Dura-Europos), Persian and even Arabic art, where the latter filters up into the old Spanish imagery. The Byzantine and the Spanish, in this sense, echo in the great shining eyes of El Greco. This Scorpionic eye is frontal, luminous, impelling, mysterious, and magnetic. It is truly the eye as the window to the soul, and it removes almost all emphasis away from the body. To call Byzantine art "Greek", as is often done, can be very misleading: Byzantine is "eye" art; Classical Greek is "body" art.

Byzantine architecture favors the central, or "Greek cross" plan, and likes the elevation to be surmounted by a low dome, often surrounded by other, lesser domes. The architecture of this culture is what Spengler called "the architecture of the central dome." Baldwin Smith saw the dome as "the outstanding feature of Byzantine and Islamic architecture." This dome is not the soaring cupola of the Baroque but an enclosing, inward-turning form typical of Scorpio.

The preferred plan of a Byzantine church is the central plan (the basilican plan, often used in Italy, was a Roman inheritance). Scorpio rules the most central areas of the body, that is, the reproductive and eliminatory systems. In Early Christian and Byzantine painting there tends to be a strong emphasis on the central area of the human figure; frequently this produces a V-shape or cross-shape or other accentuation about the groin. These figures are never nude unless the story absolutely requires it. Being Scorpionic, the figures are concealed by drapery, yet the drapery (an unconscious artistic expression of great power) cannot help but reveal its culture's predilections. Comparable expression may be found in a repeated gesture of the hand, or (in Persian painting) by folds around the crotch or an emphasis in the low belt buckle.

The dome on wall in Levantine architecture accomplishes not only the special emphasis of Scorpio upon the interior, it also creates a peculiar underground world. Pluto rules the underworld, and one has only to think of the catacombs at Rome, of the Tomb of Galla Placidia at Ravenna, or of subterranean basilicas, to recognize an "underworld" sense. It is not like that of the rock-cut tombs or temples of Egypt and India, but has an inner, glowing glory and a mesmerizing flow, like the rhythm of an Early Christian arcade, like the interior of S. Vitale with its "floating and welling of space from the center into the surrounding outer layer, the extent of which remains in semi-darkness" (Pevsner). And here, quite possibly, is the explanation of the Levantine love of gold, as seen from alchemy to adornment. It is not for gold's sunny radiance, as in Chinese gold, but rather that inner gleam "as in the gold mosaic of a wall," a quality deriving from the fact that gold as it occurs in nature is not only precious but is underground and hidden.

The 8th House (ruled by Scorpio) is the House of legacies and wills, of settlements and testaments. Testament signifies to bequeath or to testify, and both senses are involved in the Old and New Testaments. Where Scorpio signifies regeneration and transfiguration, the 8th house invokes regeneration and life after death (whence legacy and testament). We may be reminded of the remark of Edouard Schuré, that "the nature of a religion is revealed in the civilization to which it gives birth."

While the Evolutionary centuries of the Levantine are far behind us, the culture still produces characteristic forms, whether in the resurgent states of Israel and the Arab nations, or as wandering individuals and groups within the context of other major cultures such as the Western and the Russian. We still make coin of Byzantine "deviousness", sometimes called "Byzantinism". Egon Friedell (himself Jewish) observed of figures in Dostoevsky (himself Scorpionic) that they were "Byzantine" in the way they "fix their torturing, searching glance on the observer."

Modern Jews may reveal either the ancient ethnic tradition which has been well guarded, or the Levantine cultural tradition which is scarcely recognized. Thus the Jewish interest in the law in general appears to derive from the ethnic culture, whereas an interest in the criminal law in particular would suggest a Scorpionic inheritance from the Levantine civilization. As Scorpio is "preeminently the physicians' sign" (Pagan), so the traditions of Jewish and Arabian medicine are attributable to the Levantine cultural tradition.

Taking the Levantine culture as a whole, we may note that a jealous scrutiny and suspicion is widely recognized as a Near Eastern trait. These qualities, along with an emphasis on the deep and sometimes dark recesses of the mind, are evident in the Persian (Iranian) and Judaic, the Byzantine and Arabic cultures alike, and are perennial Scorpionic traits.

I. The Ancient American Culture

The Sagittarian civilization occupied what is now Mexico, Central America, and the northern Andes. Its Evolutionary epoch began in the 7th decade AD and ended in the 5th decade of the 13th century. The Maya correspond to the Europeans; the earliest pyramids are dated to the first or 2nd centuries, corresponding to our Romanesque churches or to the Old Kingdom pyramids of Egypt. The Toltecs correspond to the New Kingdom or Empire, the Romans, and the Americans (indeed the Toltecs in Yucatan were called the "New Empire" by Morley).

The Aztecs began to arrive in Mexico in the 14th century, and correspond approximately to the Turks in the latter days of the Levantine civilization. The Ancient American civilization was thus two centuries past the end of its Evolutionary epoch when the Spanish destroyed the remains. The Evolutionary epoch had begun with a cultural explosion "in the first centuries AD, after gathering strength during a late archaic epoch" (S. Linné). At this time "the high cultures of Mexico suddenly burst into life. This first golden age...is marked by an incredible amount of activity." It is the same suddenness that appears in Old Kingdom Egypt and Romanesque Europe.

Around 500 in South America emerged the classic Tiahuanaco,

corresponding to our classic Renaissance of 1400. The "classical" phase of the Mayan culture endured until around 900, corresponding to the end of our Baroque just before 1800. By this time the early civilizations had begun to falter, giving way to the Toltecs, who "inaugurated a new era" (Linné), much like the Romans in Hellenistic times.

The "Romans of South America" is a term that has been given to the Inca from around 1200 (which is to say, approximately the time of Tiberius). In the Andes, "master craftsmen" had been identified from the first century AD (i.e., the beginning of the Evolutionary), and an "expansionist" development from around 900 (i.e., around 1800 in the West, denoting both European and American expansiveness).

That the "Peruvian" and the "Mexican" civilizations belong to the same major culture can no longer be doubted. Their chronologies correspond; they share an unusual number of social values; their arts have the same inner form; they indicate the same zodiacal traits. Recently there has been a growing recognition by archeologists of contact between the two sub-cultures and, as Lytle Robinson observes, there is evidence that Incas "migrated to southern Mexico and fused with the Mayas. There is also recently discovered evidence that the Mayas drifted southward and mixed with the Incas." Olmec influence appears throughout Meso-America and probably as far as Peru. There are special features, writes H.D. Disselhoff, "common to American art objects that distinguish them from those found in other parts of the world" (for example, a formal accentuation to the point of abstraction). The same writer concludes: "There can be no doubt that the peoples of Mexico and South America were in contact with one another in ancient times."

Both the Maya and the Inca constructed sacrificial roads, often very long ones. Long distances and journeys are characteristic of Sagittarius, short distances or trips are characteristic of Gemini. From Mexico City to Tiahuanaco is a matter of thousands of miles, from Sumer to Nineveh a matter of a few hundred.

Sagittarius is a fire sign. In this culture, sun-worship seems to have been frequent and endemic. Images of the sun god are familiar, along with other fiery images. The planet connected with Sagittarius is Jupiter; to Jupiter corresponds the number Six, which is represented by the sextile, an aspect of ease. Ease was an essential characteristic of this culture; children, for example, were not severely disciplined, and prisons of any kind were rare.

In content and character the arts of South America are reminiscent of those of Meso-America, but there is at least one important difference: In South America there is a rich and incisive portrait tradition (in statuary and painting alike), for which there is hardly any evidence in the north. This sounds like the situation in Western Europe, where the portrait has been rich and strong in the north as against a generalizing or typifying tendency in the south—except that in the Ancient Americas, north and south appear to be reversed.

In Chinese astrology the symbol for Sagittarius is the monkey: consider the frequency of the monkey effigy vessel amongst other ape lore in Pre-Columbian art. In western astrology the Sagittarian symbol is the hunter, often a centaur with bow and arrow. It is a particularly athletic image, and we may be reminded of the abundance of figures of athletes, along with acrobats and warriors, and of the prominence of sports like the ball games, in addition to the hunting rituals. In esoteric astrology, Sagittarius is represented by the "animal or emotional mind" (M.P. Hall), suggestive of much expression of color and theme as well as form in Ancient American art.

As in Egypt so in America the pyramid was a prominent architectural form, important, and often of vast size. Yet the American pyramids are surprisingly unlike the Egyptian. The pyramids of Egypt are lower than they are wide (except for a few very late and small examples). While there are some long, low American ones, there were many that were quite tall and steep, as can be seen in paintings. The Egyptian pyramids were pointed, with the working parts inside; American pyramids were flat-topped. Rather than culminating in sanctuaries deep within, they were flanked by outside steps leading to sanctuaries cresting the summit. Inca temples are said to have been "open to the sky" (Disselhoff). Inca shrines were built at the highest point on hills. The high point and the summit suggest Jupiter, the ruler of Sagittarius, one of the most extroverted of signs, while Cancer is one of the most introverted.

Egyptian pyramids look very much the same, with square plan and triangular face. The plan of American pyramids varied from square to circular to oblong, and the profiles varied widely, manifesting a Sagittarian (mutable) variety. Cancer prefers to stay close to home, to be contained, even concealed, and inwardly oriented. The Egyptian pyramid is like a giant repository when compared with the American type, which acts as a mount to support and elevate the activities— rites and sacrifices, performances and plays—that took place on its steps and its summits. In Mayan architecture there is very little interior space. Meso-American homes do not seem to have been particularly habitable, and they were often of perishable materials. Egyptian housing was more ambitious and durable (Cancer is an intensely domestic sign). And then there was the tomb—the site of so much Egyptian art—which represented the eternal home.

Sagittarius has been called the sign of great social migrations and the love of exploration (Alan Oken). Migration seems to have been a way of life in Ancient America, especially Peru. Also Sagittrarian are the Maya of Yucatan, who still today are exceptionally honest, good natured, and fair-minded; they are socially inclined, with an attitude of live and let live; they are considerate of others and thoughtless of the future; they are sparing as hunters but not particularly kind to animals.

It is held that before the conquest, Mayan civilization was distinguished by a lack of greed, of debt, of strife, murder, or robbery by violence. Peru developed a theocratic socialism, abstractly organized, in which law had high religious sanction. In Mexico, judges were independent even of the king, and held office for life. Ease, tolerance, and trust are Sagittarian; the law is a leading vocation of the 9th (Sagittarian) house; and Sagittarius itself is given to legal, civil, and theological codes of the masses, and to the establishing of the moral foundations of society.

Sagittarius is the most extravagant of the signs (Pre-Columbian art is extravagant in color and motif), and one of the most expressive—a quality involved with the love of spectacle in Ancient America. Sagittarius has an incomparable love of laughter; Ancient American art is studded with grimaces and grins—e.g., the "Totonic smiling head"—against which the Greek archaic and the Western Gothic "smile" seem pale and occasional. The image of the laughing or smiling infant has been traced back at least to the Olmec. The American Indian grinned under torture, and it is proverbial that Eskimos when in desperate situations resort to laughter instead of anger.

Intellectually, Sagittarius is a metaphysical sign, expressive of the higher mental faculties. The Maya were masters of mathematics (they used zero), adept in astronomy and chronology, and extraordinarily sophisticated in calendrics. The Peruvians were distinguished in astronomy, geometry, music, and philosophy.

In terms of the body, Sagittarius rules the area of the loin, hip and thigh. To survey a large number of figures in sculpture and ceramic from the traditions of Ancient America is to be impressed by the frequency with which this area of the body is stressed. Figures (including even babies, and animals) like to sit up—as against the sitting down or reclining favored by Classical figures. They like to squat, even in a standing squat; they like to turn at the hip. They sit with the knees up (stressing the thigh), or with one up and one down. There is a lot of leg thrust, sideways, or forward and back. Figures kneel, sit on haunches, or recline with a hip twist. They often look like frogs. They sit with hands on knees; they recline with knees up; they crouch. They like to spread the leg from the thigh (compare Babylonian figures who spread Geminian arms). It is even possible to speak of "hipped" pyramids.

J. THE WESTERN CULTURE

Quite unlike the Classical culture, with which it is often coupled as members of a "western" or "European" civilization, the Western culture had its root area in the mountains of Switzerland, France, and Germany; the root area of the Classical was in the islands of the Aegean. Even in Italy, where the two cultures overlap, the difference is that the Classical cultural origins lay from Rome and Volsinii south, the Western from Assisi and Florence north.

The Western Evolutionary epoch began in 995 AD, and has since spread to the western hemisphere, notably to the United States (which is its "Rome" in terms of constitutional development). This major culture is ruled by Capricorn.

To those brought up in this culture, its zodiacal character may at first be less readily discerned than the sign of another culture, or less readable than to the native of a non-Western tradition. To the Chinese, all Western music sounds like march music, a reaction incomprehensible to most Westerners. Similarly all Russian music sounds sad to Westerners, while the Russians say this is not so to them at all. In our group soul we are Capricornian, and if we do not see this from the outside, then self-observation must reveal it.

Capricorn is the cardinal earth sign. Where cardinal means force, and earth means nature, the result is a sense of the forces of nature, or of an entity as a "force of nature." No culture has probed the forces of nature in a way to compare with the Western. Our heroes (Goethe's Faust, Milton's Satan) or outstanding figures (William the Conqueror, Oliver Cromwell) convey the image of a "force of nature" unapproached by heroes like Odysseus or figures like Pericles.

The cardinal form of earth's landscape is the mountain, and it may be more than incidental that the very center of the Western civilization—the Alps, the Vosges, the Dolomites, the upper Rhineland—is peaked. Consider the role of mountains in Western landscape art: not only in Cézanne of Mt. St. Victoire and Altdorfer of the Austrian Alps, but also in Turner of London, Van Gogh of Holland, Bruegel of the Flemish plain.

The mountain is the "cardinal" form of nature because of its thrust (as opposed to the fixed fields of Taurus, the shifting sands or mutable jungle of Virgo). The mountain is also specifically Capricornian that it evokes the Saturnian growths and ruins of time; and in that it is to be climbed step by step. It is the habitation of the Goat.

The Capricornian Goat may be either the mountain goat, or the Mer-Goat or sea goat (which can also take the form of an amphibious hind). And so emerges the other prime image of the Western landscape: the sea. The Capricornian Westerner is not especially attracted to plains, ponds and pastures, nor to swamps or jungles. If he likes dense wood, it is on the mountain side—not the flat forest of India or Russia. He is drawn to the extremes (also Capricornian) of nature: the towering hill and the endless sea. And this sea is not the limpid, limited "Sea between Lands" of the Classical Culture; it is the Ocean Sea, of which Columbus was made Admiral: the primal sea of unmeasured breadth and depth and history, the realm of Moby Dick.

The towering hill of Capricorn is manifested in the Western architectural facade from the 9th century on. At Corvey, Centula, Maastricht, at the great Romanesque abbeys and Gothic cathedrals, at the Medici Palace in Florence, the Pied Piper's House in Hamelin, or

Richardson's jail in Pittsburg, what we confront is a mountain rockface. It may invite us to a climb, or it may tower imminently over us, but it is a Capricornian hillside all the way.

Saturnian symbols include the oar (relating to the Capricornian sea) and the hour glass and scythe (expressive of Saturnian time, and expressed again and again in Western imagery). Another Capricornian symbol is the Unicorn, or so Jocelyn discerns, saying that this is as yet seldom known. He sees the Unicorn as a triumphant being, "victor in all strenuous tests." Both the strenuous and the testing are Capricornian, and the single horn suggests the singleness of thrust of this highly focused cardinal sign, along with the hard, bony quality of the Capricornian body. Furthermore the Unicorn, while equine above, may have had the legs of an antelope, and the antelope is closely related to the mountain goat. The Western unicorn has a goat's beard and a long corkscrew horn from the Arctic narwhal.

What has all this to do with the Capricornian Western culture? It is true that the unicorn's meanings are myriad, and its origins long predate the Western culture. Nevertheless its ancestry is uncertain, and the point probably is that the unicorn, as we know it, is an invention of the later Middle Ages. Before then it played a minor role, but in the later Middle Ages and in the Renaissance it became a favorite subject.

Four is the number of Saturn, the Capricornian planet. What the trilogy was to the Classical culture, the quartet is to the Western. The quartet appears at its fullest in the most characteristic Western art, music. The vocal quartet has long been popular, from *Rigoletto* to barber shop, and the typical ballad is a quatrain. But it is in instrumental music, with its severer logic, that four-part forms are most fully realized.

The string quartet abounds with Schubert, Brahms, Bartok, Hindemith. Haydn wrote 84 string quartets, Mozart 24 (with one clarinet quartet and six quintets), Beethoven only 16—but they represent the most important single form in his work. In the development of Western Musical structure, the acme is reached in the sonata form. In the Anglo-American tradition, sonata form is given three parts, but in the German tradition, which may be more significant, it is given four. In any case, the number of movements (each of different tempo) into which a major composition is divided is characteristically four.

The Saturnian Four also appears in the concept "four-square", where one side represents the firm foundation, a second the forthright position, the third side rectitude, and the fourth the rigidity of the rectangle. Western building from Romanesque to Wright has been obsessed with foundations. The most characteristic Western styles are forthright. Rectitude is a requirement from Suger to Alberti to Ruskin; and the rectangular plan is overwhelmingly favored throughout Western architecture. Likewise the rectangle is the ordinary shape of a Western picture. We take this for granted, but we ought not: the Chinese used a scroll, the Egyptians a continuous wall, the Greeks a medallion. While the defining rectangle of the window-picture belongs mainly to the Renaissance and Baroque, Giotto had already divided his continuous wall series into firmly shaped rectangles, and even in our own experimental day the irregular frame or shape is infrequent.

Capricorn governs the bones, the skeleton. Is there an architecture so skeletal as Gothic—unless it is modern? Are the art forms of other cultures so concerned with the "framework" of a poem or philosophy, of a painted or musical composition? This skeleton includes the "function of tendons and cartilages" as well as the "articulation of bones" (M.P. Hall), thus articulating the organic and dynamic quality of the Gothic and Romanesque, Baroque and Renaissance alike, for even Raphael is dynamic compared with Phidias. Compared with the Classical, Western art is both skeletal and muscular: against the Classical set of external harmonies and proportions, it sets up an inner dynamic of thrust and tension, push and pull.

The anatomical focal point for Capricorn is the knee. Phrases like "weak-kneed" or "stiff-kneed" are natural to us. In other cultures, prayer varies from prostration to the *orans* position, or the stance with arms and legs down and apart; in the West the preferred prayer is "on your knees"—and the recognition of higher power brings us to our knees. Obeisance takes varying forms in different cultures; in the West genuflection—i.e., touching the right knee to the ground—has from at least the 15th century replaced the profound bow.

The knee is used not only to bow, but also to spring. Romanesque arches and Gothic vaults "spring" from the solid grounding with a vigor unknown in other architectures, and there is a spring-like tension in countless figures of Western sculpture and painting. The spring is the characteristic movement of the mountain goat of Capricorn. In Classical Greek art, the emphasis within the figure is about the hips, and the result is a Libran poise verging on hesitation. In Renaissance art the emphasis is on the action of one knee against the other, and the result is a Capricornian thrust. Even Raphael will introduce an extraneous step for a figure to raise his foot upon. The knee-action in Western art can be traced at least from the 10th century, and even when the subject calls for a figure in repose, the bending of the knee, or an emphasis on the knee area, is as pronounced as is the emphasis upon the loin area in Byzantine figures. "Knee-action" may be found in Western forms from Romanesque buttress to modern machine.

Plate V
Plate VI

It is no accident that the advanced machine is a special product of Western civilization. Every civilization attains some kind of advanced science in its later stages, and the late Classical, for example, or the Arabian, was far more developed scientifically than the young cultures that followed. But each major culture produces sciences typical of its zodiacal character: the Egyptian scrutiny of internal organs, Classical statics, Levantine healing. The Western is the most dynamic of known sciences; it is also the most technological. Indeed the Western mind does not always distinguish between technology and science, as the Classical mind clearly did. Classical man pursued Science in the literal sense: in order to "know." The Western researcher ordinarily feels he must justify his investigations on a pragmatic basis: How will these results enable us to construct, to control, to predict? The Classical mathematician was overwhelmed by the beauty of his subject; the Westerner more often wants to know the use of it.

Western man, said Jung, "can turn everything into a technique." Architectural structure, painting technique, musical instrumentation become far more complex, and more essential to the aesthetics of the West than of any other culture, as do the techniques of political or legal practice. But it is in science where technique (or technic) is most fully realized. In Western science the object is to get the thing to work—and the thing may be a machine or an idea; as Spengler observed, the "working hypothesis" so basic to the West is meaningless to other cultures.

Also with Capricornian technique and "working" must be included

The Pierpont Morgan Library.

Plate V
Winchester Crucifixion c.1000-1050.

The Metropolitan Museum of Art, The Cloisters Collection, 1930.

Plate VI
Joseph; from an Adoration group; high relief. Stone. About 1188.

the Saturnian aspect of science. The scientist himself is Saturnian in procedure and often enough saturnine in temper. Gauquelin has devoted a volume to the Mars temperament as evinced in sport champions, and another to the Saturn temperament in men of science. According to Max Dvorak, the Greek conception of science was "an anthropological philosophy of nature which sought to explain the world of the senses in terms of metaphysical systems." In a word, Greek science could be described as a handmaid of philosophy. In the West, philosophy has generally been the handmaid of science; the philosopher has more often been the scientist than the other way around.

To consider the technology of a Gothic vault, a Flemish painting, a Miltonic composition, a Bach fugue, is to be mindful of the deliberate difficulties involved. No art forms are so inherently difficult as those thrown up by the West. An Egyptian pyramid is immensely difficult in terms of sheer effort and patience (a Cancerian combination); an Indian temple is difficult in its Virgoan intricacy. But many a Western form is difficult in the sense of being nearly impossible. Western structures, at their most characteristic, entertain ambitions loaded with contradictions (the Gothic support systems, the sculpture of Michelangelo, the etching of Rembrandt). It is not a matter merely of a love of resistance, though that is frequent enough. The Egyptians liked to find the hardest stone to carve; the Westerner might use the hardest or the softest, but he is tempted to force it into some form never tried before. Capricorns are said to learn everything the hard way, and it is the harder rather than the softer that the Westerner prefers, for hardness—of skin or bone or temper—is a Capricornian feature. To the word "hard" meaning difficult we must add "hard" meaning rough or recalcitrant: the engraving tool, the scratched surface, the firm resistance in the art of Donatello or Albrecht Dürer or Jackson Pollock.

"Hard" meaning difficult is related to Capricorn's driving ambition. N. Devore cities Capricorn's "emphasis on the personal ego." C.G.M. Adam calls it "the most ambitious sign of any"; M.P. Hall speaks of Capricorn's "continual effort and a tremendous will power often with unfortunate arrogance." Such ambition may take the lower form of social climbing—or the higher one of Romanesque spires and Gothic vaults, of Rembrandt and Beethoven, where ambition becomes aspiration. The distinguishing outer features of Western architecture are the tall dome, the tower, and the spire. Not the "topless towers of Ilium" but the tower surmounted by a lance to "pierce the sky." The spire is related to "aspire", and aspiration is the higher form of Capricorn. As Western building has reached higher than any other so likewise have the aspirations of Michelangelo and Shakespeare, of the top Western thought systems and speculative sciences.

The driving force of Capricorn not only aspires up, it also digs deep. According to M.P. Hall, Capricorn shows of all signs the highest and deepest ambition, even if this is less evident than in the more expressive signs. The Goat is the mountain-climbing goat (N. Devore) but it has the fish's tail, "signifying extremes of height and depth." Thus the Capricornian Westerner is the climber (the Indian had "known" Everest for millennia, but it was the Westerner who had to climb it), but also the digger. Digging is expressed in the mining so prevalent in Western Europe and America. Indeed Western science is said to have begun with mining operations in the Harz and Erzgebirge. It is also expressed in the archeological "dig", which is specifically Western in that it penetrates the earth physically while penetrating the psyche of other civilizations and societies through "unearthing" their customs and values. Westerners like to "dig" for facts; Capricornians like to be "students of ancient sciences and languages; Egyptology interests them" (M.P. Hall). Once every year, observed Will Cuppy, the Nile overflows its banks, depositing a layer of rich alluvial soil; then it recedes "and soon the whole countryside, as far as the eye can reach, is covered with Egyptologists." Mainly Westerners.

The advantages enjoyed by Western archeology, anthropology, and comparative history in reconstructing past civilizations are not based on a subtler psychology (most Eastern cultures have keener psychologies than western ones). Rather they lie in the Capricornian penchant for digging, that is, for penetration. At the same time the Capricornian has an ability to identify with the collective unconscious (Rudhyar). Here the traditions of Jung and Spengler join.

Accompanying the West's ambition and drive is a restlessness sometimes leading to loneliness and hyperseriousness. Capricornians' whole perspective "is bound up in themselves. Their own purposes assume cosmic proportions, and if they fail to attain their end they regard it as a cosmic disaster" (Hall). Here are Hamlet and Don Quixote, Beethoven and Cézanne. The "average Capricornian does not know how to be happy" (Hall); he is subject to the "despair of loneliness and frustration" (Rudhyar). It seems a loneliness attendant on extreme independence. Capricornians are "deeply introverted," writes Hall; "they have a deadly fear of dependence"—consider Cromwell's Independents, the many Western wars of independence, the social role of the Western artist or philosopher as compared, say, with the Classical type.

Capricornians "crave power, yet power fails to satisfy—and they know it"; Rudhyar adds that this is the sign given to political machines and the control of public opinion. Consider the following description: "the lonely Wanderer on the heights of snow-covered peaks; the solitary individual...." It sounds like Spengler on Western man; it is Rudhyar on Capricorn.

Another distinctive Western type is the historian. A curiosity to recover hidden facts is accompanied by a fascination in history as aging and evolution, as form and direction. This process of history is never-ending, from the foundations of time. Capricorn is the long-lived sign, the sign that achieves in age and dominates in the latter part of human life. And Saturn is the planet of cosmic memory. Little wonder that Western historians have already made the Chinese, the Egyptians, or the Arabians look like dilettantes. To the Greeks, history meant written accounts—to the West, history means the study of growth.

Dilthey expressed not simply the modern period in the West, but the entire Western culture, in his remark that man can know himself only in his history and not through introspection alone. That history is fundamental to all fields of Western knowledge is manifested in Weizsäcker's *History of Nature* and is becoming recognized even in the physical sciences (R. Coulborn). The most the Classical could say of history is that it was philosophy teaching by example.

To the Capricornian, the idea of history is inseparable from that of tradition. Our very breaks with tradition are dependent on it, and even when involved in an avant-garde we like to call it a "tradition of the new." Part of the meaning of tradition in the Capricornian experience of history is a keen "sense of direction" (Evangeline Adams). This is precisely the spatial factor which distinguishes

Romanesque building from its Roman and Byzantine ancestors. In the first emphatically Western structures, of the late 10th century, the architecture is spatial—not the "magic, floating" space of the Early Christian and Byzantine, but "spatial in an organizing, grouping, planning way" (Pevsner). Here we are confronted with another fundamental characteristic of Western art: its Capricornian insistence on organizing. As for Western society, has any other been so absorbed in programs and problems, policies and plans? What did the Greeks care about any of these?

Being planners, Capricorns make exemplary architects; but in social planning they may assume "too much responsibility regarding the destiny of others" (E. Adams). Responsibility itself is implicit in the fatherhood role of Saturn. The result is a tendency to apply Western institutions to other societies, or to adopt some form of paternalism. Likewise we have the phenomenon of the "protector": the Keeper, the Lord Protector (the highest title Cromwell would accept), the "protector of the Faith"; or the Protectorate as a territorial institution.

"Character" belongs to Capricorn more than to any other sign. Not only Western education, even our sports are character-building. The sports of classical Greece aimed at beauty and balance—Libran desiderata. Western sports, from Eton to West Point, are based on competition, but this is not directed exclusively to winning; the primary aim (as football coach Lombardi noted) is to prepare to win. In preparation is character formed.

Character extends to characterization. The faces in Greek statuary epitomize Libran idealizing; and even Hellenistic portraiture evinces not character but personality (it is different with Roman portraiture, but this is precisely because ancient Rome was herself ruled by Capricorn). The faces of Western art, right from the Romanesque, are charged with character; it matters hardly whether they are portraits or not—indeed it is often hard to tell. Even in these rare Western artists who eschew portraiture—Bosch, Michelangelo, Bruegel, Poussin—the imagery overflows with characterization. And if we do not expect our artists to be gods, or even heroes, we do like them to be "characters".

The classic Greeks made subtle, non-emphatic differentiations between the adult and the aged (often just an adult man with a beard); between the mature and the child (often just smaller); between male and female, or Greek and barbarian (the barbarian usually more "characterized"!). Western art likes to characterize sex, to distinguish races and civilizations by their character (consider the portrayal of blacks by Rubens or Rembrandt, not to mention the Moorish Magus in countless Adoration scenes); and above all to characterize age, and aging. "There is a history in all men's lives" (Henry V, Pt. 2).

In the West, character involves not only characterization, and a certain "cragginess", but also character formation as the product of hard experience, and expressive of a Saturnian sense of responsibility. "The English heroic ideal," writes George Barker (and it is Western as well), "got itself perfectly enunciated in *Paradise Lost*. It is an ideal of Justice. The hero is a man prepared to take the consequences."

The Capricornian work ethic is a profound element of most Western societies. The West prefers to ask not "who" a man is, but, "what does he do?" Here lies his identity. The Western mind is less interested in the name of a thing, than in: Does it work, how does it work, why doesn't it work?

Among "workings" that appear most to fascinate Western man are the workings of the cosmic universe, and the "works" of that preeminently Capricornian invention, the time-piece. Chronos (Saturn) was god of Boundless Time and the Cycles. Attempts to calculate time relationships particularly distinguish Western historiography. Westerners feel themselves moving through time; the Greeks on the other hand conceived of themselves as stationary, with time coming up behind, catching them, and moving on, so that the future became the past. The Greek word *opiso* sometimes means "behind" and sometimes "in the future" (Clyde Kluckhohn).

The Westerner experiences time in a measured, sonorous beat: step by step like the Pilgrim's progress, like the progression of the Romanesque facade or the Gothic nave, like the Scholastic argument where "the reader is led, step by step, from one proposition to the other and is always kept informed as to the progress of this process" (Panofsky).

This sense of beat and measure makes Capricorn the most fundamentally musical of all signs, makes music the characteristic Western art, and makes Western music the most accented—and therefore the most like "march-music"—of all. As Westerners we naturally expect all music to show the inevitable quality of accent that marks our own. Spengler observed that "we ourselves have accent in our blood and therefore do not notice it."

Accent can mean emphasis, or it can mean stress; both are Capricornian. Stress shows not only in Western music but in all other arts. In Greek drawing (from the evidence on vases) the line is almost always without stress. In Western drawing—even with "classical" artists like Michelangelo or Matisse—there is constant emphasis: heavy and light, thick and thin, cluster and dispersal, compression and extension.

Stress can mean pressure, a trait both Western and Capricornian. But essentially stress means beat or rhythm. Rhythm is basic to the time sense of Saturn and of Western culture. We "got rhythm." Titian got it, and Milton, not to mention Handel. The very evolution of Western architectural styles can be treated no more revealingly than by rhythmic form. Rhythm is something that the Western politician understands, where the Classical politician understood personality and oratory. Timing is our watchword, and timing means regard for a rhythmic process. To the future Western historian, the rhythmic process, in all its complexity and beauty, may become central to historical understanding.

The last part of the sonata form (a Western invention) is the recapitulation. To recapitulate means to reconstruct the rhythmic process, to repeat and to restore. Western styles recurrently have involved revivals: Greek, Gothic, Roman, Renaissance. And Westerners like to restore the object itself; they are not content to keep and preserve like the Cancerian Egyptians, but must dis-cover and re-constitute. To recapitulate and to reform are of Capricorn.

K. The Russian Culture

Russia is not a country, like France, but a major culture, like China. The Russian Evolutionary epoch began around 1866. For an extended examination of this and related dates, see Chapter III.

That Russia is ruled by Aquarius is accepted by astrologers. Aquarius is an air sign. Russians love their sky, their steppe and open plain with its limitless expanse. Airy too is the Russian love of talk and of theorizing. All the air signs are given to relationships. With Gemini, relationships are especially those of a sibling nature; with Libra, of partnership or marriage. With Aquarius relatedness signifies common motives and mutual responsibilities; and these are Russian proclivities long pre-dating Soviet socialism.

While it is an air sign, Aquarius is also known as the "water-bearer". Jocelyn writes that this sign "symbolizes the Son of Man who pours out living, spiritual water, which gives on-going" motion. Bernard Pares writes that Russia is "before all things a country of waterways, which are among the finest in the world." Jocelyn writes that the evolved Aquarian bespeaks "an *intense inner repose.*" Pares adds that, in Russia, "the river taught peace."

A common symbol for Aquarius is the Man. Helen Muchnic describes Russian as "the tongue of those whose faith is given entirely to man...who see the only hope for the world in his realization of his own complexity, and of both the grandeur and the meanness of which he is capable and for which he alone is responsible." Another symbol for Aquarius is the bear: Russia was long referred to as "the bear who walks like a man." In Chinese astrology the Aquarian symbol is the dog. Of all animals, the dog is the most domesticated, the closest companion to man in home or work. It may be symptomatic that the first orbiting capsules sent up by the Capricornian West contained machines, while those sent up by the Russians contained dogs.

The part of the body ruled by Aquarius is the lower leg, above the foot, notably the calf and ankle. The Russian dance is the ballet. It is not a refined activity; it is a cultural institution, and it places much emphasis on leaping, on walking or running on the toe instead of the foot—in a word, on the operation of calf and ankle. The ballet is a "dance drama in which the poetic idea, in which music, costume, and decoration should unite in inspired naturalness with a technically finished but not self-sufficient dance," wrote Curt Sachs; and this is what "is realized at the beginning of the 20th century in the Russian ballet."

Aquarius is the only sign of the zodiac usually referred to as future-oriented. Aries is a pioneering and adventurous sign, but its time sense is in the present, like Libra's; while Capricorn's and Cancer's are in the past. Aquarius lives in the future, and Uranus is prophetic. "Russian literature is the most prophetic in the world; it is full of forebodings and predictions," said Berdyaev.

The prophetic religions, so called, are found in the Levantine culture and involve a different meaning of prophecy. The prophecy of the Old Testament and Islam is transcendent; it speaks of fulfillment. Fulfillment emerges out of germination and "germination is a Plutonian process" (Rudhyar); the Levantine culture is Scorpionic and thus Plutonian.

The "prophetic" literature of Russia is concerned with what is going to happen in the near future on this plane of experience; it is future-oriented. Much of what was prophesied in the literature of the 19th century was realized in the Russian Revolution, even if not in the anticipated form.

Some sort of revolution, however, was likely enough simply through the Aquarian instinct to rebellion. Aquarius is given to experimentation and new thinking, and "on a lower level of expression, these tendencies are rebellion against form and tradition" so that Aquarius is "perfectly willing to let the old foundation fall to pieces" (Sylvia Carroll). Aquarius looks to the new order. The Russian revolution may be seen in the light of an Aquarian "rebellion against form and tradition." For it was not strictly necessary (better reforms had already been begun), in the sense that the American Revolution appears to have been unavoidable.

The West has not had revolutions like the Russian. The American was not properly a "revolution" at all, but the reassertion of local government which had already been well established and was subsequently threatened. The French was indeed a Revolution, but not a willful one like the Russian. The French must be viewed as one of the many revolutions attendant on the breakup of the Renaissance epicycle and the emergence of the modern—revolutions such as the industrial, the agricultural, and those in social custom and the arts. In a word, the French Revolution was a particularly explosive expression of a change of epicycle. All changes of epicycle are revolutionary in nature, whether or not in expression. The change from the medieval world to that of the Renaissance was a change of epicycle, and "so far as anything can be revolutionary the Renaissance was revolutionary" (H.J. Randall).

The Russian Revolution was in no way related to a change in epicycle (the first Russian epicycle had begun in the 1860s). It was an Aquarian example of willful rebellion—the sort of thing which has actually been quite rare in the West. Despite some lip-service (mostly from the French and Americans) the West does not really believe in revolution. Capricorn is conservative and preservative. The French Revolution and the English Civil War (which really was a revolution) were followed by restorations. There has been no Russian restoration. The present Russian regime appears alterable only by further revolution.

Aquarians are given to rebellion, and Uranians to extremes. S. Tompkins cites the Russian "resolve to press measures, ameliorative in themselves, to their extreme limit." Capricorn is gradualist, and this—except in special circumstances—has been the Western way. Saturn's sense of time prefers evolution; therefore *reform* (thus Reformation)—rather than revolution—is the Western watchword. By contrast, note the "revolutionary utopianism" practiced by "those who have not yet conquered, but who nevertheless proceed to map out the future for others," as Andrei Sinyavsky described the Russian type.

Fundamentally committed to the Capricornian values expressed in duty and responsibility, the Westerner will never make a very good Communist; Capricorn represents "the goal of individual selfhood" (Meyer and Wickenburg). The Russian feels in his Aquarian way that each should indeed give according to his ability and receive according to his need; the Russian will always be something of a communist. The Capricornian Westerner believes in private property because he feels that each person is responsible for his own actions and their results. The Russian believes in sharing, not as a mere economic program, but because he belongs to the Aquarian culture of brotherhood.

This Aquarian longing for brotherhoods and communities, for societies and causes, is expressed in what B. Pares calls the "loose and dreamy 'socialism' which is common practically to all Russians." Western Europe has always liked its class structures because Capricorn likes clear-cut organization. But Dostoevsky (in his *Author's Diary*) has noted, "We have no class interests, because strictly speaking we have no classes and because the Russian soul is wider than class differences, class interests, and class law." This "wideness" or breadth is Aquarian, whereas height and depth are Capricornian. Weidlé distinguishes between the "horizontal" culture of Russia and the "vertical" culture of the West.

Each astrological sign has its religious dimension. Jocelyn says of Aquarius that it is the "sign of the Son of Man...a man Christed with the help of the Angel in man, a man become all things to all men.... Awakened response to this Angel-Man sign deals with the individual, yet in the sense of the Christ-universal, hence it fosters friendship and brotherhood.... The idealism of God is the inner motive power of advanced Aquarians. They best express their ideals and make them a reality in terms of social life, for a love of human souls is the strongest quality of this sign of humanity." Berdyaev invokes "a type of society in which man will strive after wholeness and unity as opposed to the individualism of modern"—that is, Western—"history, and in which the significance of the religious principle will increase.... Russian creative religious thought has introduced the idea of God-humanity. As in Jesus Christ, the God-Man, there occurred an individual incarnation of God in man, so similarly in humanity there should occur a collective incarnation of God.... The idea of God-humanity as the essence of Christianity is but little developed in Western Christian thought; it is an original product of Russian Christian thought."

When we say of an individual person or of a culture that it is governed by or correlated with an astrological sign, we mean that this is its Sun sign. The Western culture is governed by Capricorn. The American sub-culture of the Western culture (while still under the overlordship of Capricorn) is itself ruled by Cancer; that is, Cancer is America's Sun sign (America was "born" on 4 July, 1776). America's Moon sign is Aquarius.

In a well-known reading, Edgar Cayce indicated potential relations between America and Russia. "In Russia there comes the hope of the world, not as that sometimes termed the communistic, the Bolshevistic; no. But freedom...in that each man will live for his fellow man! The principle has been born. It will take years for it to be crystallized, but out of Russia comes again the hope of the world. Guided by what? That friendship with the nation that hath even set on its present monetary unit, In God We Trust!"

Where the Sun of one entity and the Moon of another are in the same sign, there is a propensity for deep mutual understanding. Such understanding on the part of Americans may be called upon if and when, as Madame Blavatsky prophesied, "out of Russia will come the greatest civilization the world has ever seen."

III

Dating of the Russian Culture

The two major cultures presently within their Evolutionary epochs are the Western and the Russian. The Western is approaching the end of its tenth Evolutionary century, the Russian is now early in its second. The Russian Evolutionary epoch began in 1866, a date corresponding to AD 995 for the Western. The validity of this date will be demonstrated from several points of view.

At the beginning of its Evolutionary period the leading Western artistic activity was architecture. Capricorn is the cardinal earth sign; earth emphasizes structure and cardinal means dynamic. Therefore a dynamic, massive, and forceful architecture would logically be expected, and this is exactly what developed. Aquarius is the fixed air sign. The air signs deal in communication; the fixed signs can be attracted to ideas and ideals, also they like to "fix" things in the sense of establish and develop them. Thus where Gemini (mutable air) is given to the epistle and especially to conversation, Aquarius is more likely to prefer writing, and especially writing that is sustained and substantial. Where the Capricornian West turned to architecture and architectural sculpture, we should expect Aquarian Russia to produce a possibly speculative and long-winded literature, but in any case literature as her ideal activity. And this is exactly what Russia has done. The Russians "take literature perhaps more seriously than any other nation." A Russian author must "be a thinker also." Before the "supreme function of literature, the Russian writer stands awed and humbled" (Thomas Seltzer).

At the beginning of an Evolutionary development, the arts of form burst forth with an unprecedented strength, magnitude, and authority. There is not only a demonstration of creative energy, but it is pointed in the direction proper to the particular culture, and it exhibits a sustained power which reveals the beginning of an evolutionary process. When did this new Russian literature begin in force? In the West, around the year 1000, there was a furor of church-building which overwhelmed contemporaries. In Russia, centered in the 1860s, came what has been called the "literary fever of the times." Fevers of such height are not confined to a year or two: In the West there had been sporadic building over the previous half century or so; in Russia there were flurries of writing of high rank, also sporadic, beginning as early as the schooldays of Pushkin.

The inception of an Evolutionary epoch, however, requires works of absolute authority, works which exemplify the new expressive values and the new formal systems of the emerging culture. The three Russian writers of the period who attained absolute authority were Turgenev, Dostoevsky, and Tolstoy; and they were at least the equals of any contemporary Europeans. "Compared with the works of Dostoevsky and Tolstoy, the whole of Western literature in the second half of the century seems weary and stagnant" (Arnold Hauser). Not a few critics will place Dostoevsky in the company of Dante, Shakespeare, and Goethe. When Tolstoy died, Thomas Mann said Europe became "without a master." Hauser sees Tolstoy enjoying "the fame of Voltaire, the popularity of Rousseau, the authority of Goethe, and, more than that—he became a legendary figure, whose prestige was reminiscent of that of the old seers and prophets."

Unlike these two, Turgenev did not entirely embody the new Russian expression. It is true that he was preoccupied with the problems of the peasant (he was quoted as saying that all serfs are saints, all landlords tyrants); and that he was ahead of his time (S.R.

Tompkins). It is true that in *Fathers and Sons* (1862) he had succeeded "in giving a convincing portrait of the new strong man (this time a Russian) for which the age was clamouring" (Lavrin). It was Turgenev who (in the same work) introduced the word 'nihilist' into literature. And he "paved the way to the triumph of Russian literature as a European power" (Lavrin). Nevertheless, Turgenev did not embody the new social and ethical motivation; while profoundly devoted to emancipation of the serfs, he was "content to express through his works merely the observations of the artist" (Harcave). Finally, as a Russian, he was a Westernizer; more than that, he settled abroad, and died at Bougival.

This leaves—for the key figures—Dostoevsky and Tolstoy. Their eminence was recognized at once. Nietzsche said that there has been no European writer since Goethe to equal Dostoevsky, and also that he (Nietzsche) had learned psychology from no other writer. *War and Peace* was universally held nonpareil, and *Anna Karenina* (as Spengler observed) distances every rival. Of Russian authors these two qualify on all counts. Therefore the beginning of the Russian Evolutionary epoch ought to be revealed within the careers of Dostoevsky and Tolstoy.

Dostoevsky produced *Poor Folk* and *The Double* in the mid-forties, following with nine short tales in the late forties. Of *Poor Folk* Belinsky said that Dostoevsky began "as no author before him has ever begun"; but this was the beginning of the author's career, not of the breakthrough into the culture's Evolutionary. In 1854 Dostoevsky was released from prison and in 1859 from compulsory service in Siberia. There was, however, no material allusion to the Katorga until 1864, as is most significant. His journalism had begun by 1860. *The House of the Dead* began appearing in 1861. In 1863 he sketched the plan of *The Gambler*, and in the spring of 1864 *Letters from the Undergound* began to appear. *Crime and Punishment* was written in 1865 or 1866. In 1868 appeared *The Idiot* and in 1871-2 *The Possessed*. In 1873 *Journal of an Author* was privately printed. *A New Youth* of 1876 made a prelude to the climax: *The Brothers Karamazov* was completed late in 1880, just before the author's death in January 1881.

Where is the breakthrough to the Evolutionary? The Katorga experience was crucial, and not only to the author but to his culture, in whose experience it is a prime symbol. In *War and Peace* something comparable to the Katorga comes with Pierre's imprisonment and march in the snow. Dostoevsky's Katorga issued in 1864, the year of *Letters from the Undergound*, which Meier-Graefe held the first of the five principal novels and Lavrin a "key to many of his writings." Also it was in this work that Dostoevsky first rejected the "I" form of narration, previously a bad habit. (The "I" form suits the later, more self-conscious stage of a culture, and especially in an Arian or Geminian tradition; it does not suit the early or "medieval" phase of an Aquarian culture). Meier-Graefe said, "Together! That was his entire aim." A Russian proverb holds that "a body of men is one great man." The suppression of the "I" form further means that "the author's own reflections are suppressed, and the facts reveal themselves, relentless as in ancient tragedy" (Meier-Graefe).

Thus by 1864 Dostoevsky had almost attained the full force of his expression. But not quite. *Letters from the Underground* does not yet have the dimension of the epic Russian novel. It was in *Crime and Punishment* that "the picture, once a movable easel-painting, has become a fresco.... The dialog, Dostoevsky's born medium, achieves its purpose with the utmost economy. The words are chiselled and the dialog is full of symbols" (Meier-Graefe).

Compared with *Crime and Punishment*, *The Idiot* is still more profound; *The Possessed* goes in some ways further than *The Idiot* and the culminating work with the Aquarian "Brothers" in the title is the greatest of all. Nevertheless these stand as the four supreme works, four that are completely the author and completely Russia. Thus the breakthrough for Dostoevsky began in 1865-6.

Tolstoy's career started with *Childhood* in 1852, the *Cossacks* (written in 1854 but published in 1862), *Two Hussars* 1856, *Three Deaths* in 1859, *Kholstomer* in 1861, *War and Peace* in the mid-sixties, *Anna Karenina* in 1875, and others down to *The Living Corpse*, a play produced in 1911, the year after his death. There is no question as to which work achieves the breakthrough to total expression (Helen Muchnic called *War and Peace* "this Divine Comedy of the 19th Century"); the only question is of its dating. The writing and the publication of *War and Peace* have been given such varying spreads as 1862-9, 1865-8, or 1864-8. Sometimes the work is simply dated 1866.

Waliszewsky found that both Dostoevsky and Tolstoy repudiated Western civilization as "the *one necessary principle* which must rule the development of the national culture," and emphasized their "appeal to the faith of the popular masses as the indispensable complement of that development." He found in both Dostoevsky and Tolstoy a "new nation;" her people amounted to a new elect with a moral superiority based on humility and gentleness. Dostoevsky called this the "elect nation."

The identity of Russia as a culture distinct from Europe was first given exposition as a theory of history by Danilevsky. His book *Russia and Europe* was published in 1869 (it has not yet been translated into English). Leading thinkers of the preceding generation (Belinsky in the thirties and forties, Herzen and Chernyshevsky in the fifties and sixties) had aimed at reforming Russia along Western lines—looking to liberty and law, education and social reform. Danilevsky saw the profound separation, if not antagonism, of Russia and the West. These he saw as fundamentally different civilizations, each following its own law of growth and decay. In Danilevsky, "the universalism of the Slavophils has disappeared. He divides mankind on a cultural basis into exclusive historical types." To him, the question is "the formation of Russia into a peculiar cultural and historical type" (Berdyaev). And Danilevsky saw the future of Russia lying in opposition to the West.

Where the Westerner tends to be proud of his culture's developments toward freedom of religion (Protestantism, or separation of church and state), of philosophic and scientific thought, of political and legal forms, Danilevsky saw in such things only a "religious anarchy, a philosophical anarchy, or an all-embracing materialism, and a socio-political anarchy." Though giving the West credit for accomplishing domestic equality, he found the West not truly free at all, and saw in Russia on the other hand the love and capacity for freedom—an attitude which has persisted in the Russian mind to this day.

Danilevsky gave evidence of the Uranian totalitarianism of Russia in his curious but not incorrect prophecy: "Russia is the only state which never had (and in all probability never will have) a political revolution, i.e., a revolution having as its aim the limitation of the power of the ruler"; but he appears to have missed the Uranian extremism of Russia in his claim that "even an ordinary rebellion ...going beyond the limits of a regrettable misunderstanding, has become impossible in Russia so long as the moral character of the Russian people does not change." Danilevsky does not sound like a Western reformer, but more like the two great novelists, when he calls out to "the spirit of our society, suffering from spiritual decay and abasement." He sees in Russia "an inner discontent, a dissatisfaction with paganism, and...the unfettered search for truth." He speaks of the heritage of Hebrew and Byzantine traditions and indicates that Russia's destiny is "to be the chosen people." And he sees in the Russia of his day "a world still only at the beginning of its cultural-historical life."

Following 1866 came a line of distinguished writers continuing down to the present day. This writing has included history, poetry, belles-lettres, and stories, among other forms, but is generally strongest in the novel.

The other arts barely compare with literature. Russian architecture has emerged as distinctive from its Byzantine heritage, but is not on the level of a world art. Russia's painting must be rated even lower, and her sculpture hardly matters. In music, however, Russian genius has produced works of at least high quality and historical significance.

Russian national music had been founded by Glinka (1804-57), the contemporary of Pushkin, who played a comparable role in literature. But it was not until the "Mighty Band" developed folk song into a new realism that Russian music emerged into its Evolutionary activity. The Mighty Band included Balakirev, Rimsky-Korsakov, Mussorgsky and Borodin. And, although not appreciated by the public until much later, it was *The Stone Guest*, the opera Dargomyzhsky composed just before his death in 1868, that "became the new artistic testament' for the members of the 'mighty band' " (P. Miliukov). Mussorgsky began his first immortal opera, *Boris Godunov*, in 1869. Debussy was to speak of Mussorgsky's ability to "inhabit these magic landscapes so special to a child's mind," a quality like that to be found in some of Chagall's painting—both evincing the youthfulness of the emerging culture. Rimsky-Korsakov's first important work, the "musical picture" *Sadko*, appeared on schedule in 1866.

Another distinguishing feature of the emerging Russian landscape was the Intelligentsia. While the activity appeared earlier in the century, the word seems to date from the 1860s (Leonard Schapiro). In the age of Pushkin, the only culture had been in the hands of the liberal nobility, but by the sixties the democratization of literature and the formation of the new intelligentsia "was complete" (A. Hauser). Overall, in the "last third of the 19th century we can see a whole new life taking place in Russia, at least on the intellectual level that the *élite* had finally been able to climb on to." There was an "explosion of activity in all the arts, even those that Russia was to make no real contribution to." The intellectual life "began to revolve around the fundamental problem of Russian society—the social relationships that gave it its structure and momentum" (J. Carmichael). These social relationships are Aquarian, and it was in the 1860s that Russia began to show its Aquarian nature in full force.

As shown in Chapter I, the Evolutionary epoch is composed of twelve 99-year centuries, each governed by an astrological sign. The sequence begins with Capricorn and runs backwards to Aquarius so that the first Evolutionary century is Capricornian, the second Sagittarian. For the West this means that the 11th century (995-1094) was governed by Capricorn, the 12th (1094-1193) by Sagittarius.

For Russia, the first Evolutionary century began in 1866 and ended in 1965. It was a Capricornian century, marked by severity, discipline, drive, ruthlessness—qualities shared by such different personalities as Pobyedonostzev, Nicholas II, Lenin, and Stalin. The Russian century that began about 1965 reveals Sagittarian directions. The expansiveness of Sagittarius can become expansionist when applied to political policy. Thus the 12th century AD (the Western Sagittarian century) was almost exactly the period of the Crusades. Changes in Russian behavior dating from the 1960s seem to indicate the shift from a Capricornian constriction to a Sagittarian expansion. In the Cuban missile crisis of 1962, Russia pulled back. Since the fall of Khrushchev in 1964, however, infiltration and subversion in countries both within and outside the Communist block have increased. In the middle sixties Moscow armed Egypt and agitated the Six Days' War: The "cautious approach to foreign affairs" (Capricorn is cautious) "exploded with the blast of war in the Middle East" (James Foote) in 1967. In 1968 Russia invaded Czechoslovakia with an armed force in the neighborhood of 600,000 men, an action which Janko Lavrin calls not only insane but "aggressively expansionist." Meanwhile Moscow has enlarged its activity in the Middle East and in Cuba; Russia's "imperial expansion in the Middle East has been considerable" (Foote) but extends also to the Far East. The new expansionist tendency was voiced in 1974 by the Defense Minister, Andrei Grechko, in the words: "The historic function of the Soviet Armed Forces is not restricted to...defending the Motherland and other socialist states." Along with Sagittarian expansionist tendencies, however, we may logically expect—other things being equal—some further relaxation of the tight, hard-line policies so characteristic of Russia's Capricornian century from 1866-1965, since Sagittarius also has a relaxed side.

Certain other categories of evidence may be brought to bear on the problem of dating the beginning of Russia's Evolutionary epoch. Among these are the Inauguration systems, the Anticipatory systems, and the Overlaps.

A. Inaugurations

The twelve-century span of the Evolutionary epoch in each major culture is preceded by a germination period of ten centuries. The first inauguration, then, begins 990 years before the Evolutionary. Another period revealing a different kind of inauguration begins 640 years before the Evolutionary. During each of these spans certain directions emerge, but without any persistent evolution; their developments are sporadic, yet characteristic of the germinating culture.

1. The Ten-century Germininative.

Ten centuries before the beginning of a major culture's Evolutionary epoch, the people or peoples who will form the cast for this mighty drama make their first recognizable appearance on its geographical stage. These peoples may not compose the entire future cast, but they will manifest its core. For the Russian culture the core is the Slavic peoples, for the Western culture it is the Germanic peoples.

Germanic is used here not in the ethnocentric sense of the past century, but in its original sense. The historical Germanic peoples include Angles, Burgundians, Franks, Bavarians, Jutes, Lombards, Saxons, Helvetians, Scandinavians. These emerged or survived from the Teutonic tribes which in late Roman times were identifiable as the Burgundians (originally from Bornholm, migrating to the Main region and Gaul); the Gepidae (from the Vistula estuary); the Goths (after defeat by the Huns in 375, these split into the [east] Ostrogoths and the [west] Visigoths); the Lombards (at the birth of Christ these occupied the central Elbe valley, not moving to Italy until the 6th century); the Suebi or Semnones (moving from the Elbe in 113 to northern Portugal and northwestern Spain in the 6th century AD); the Vandals or Silingae, who in 407 invaded Gaul and Spain, where they settled in the central and southern regions (J. Schreiber).

These varied Germanic peoples thus formed the core of the Western ethnic structure, though the role of other peoples, and especially the Celts, is not to be overlooked. Ten centuries before 995 (the Evolutionary beginning of the West) is 5 AD (each century comprising 99 years). When did the Germans gell? "Their rise as a determining factor in the history of Europe came about the beginning of the Christian era" (*Columbia Encyclopedia*).

Ten centuries before the beginning of the Classical Evolutionary (1079 BC) takes us to 2069 BC. M.I. Finley sees Greek-speaking peoples as first migrating "into the Greek peninsula before the beginning of the second millennium BC, perhaps as early as 2200." A.R. Burn sees a period from about 1950 to 1550 when "the peoples of Greece spread out and mingled. By the end of this time Greek-speaking chiefs dominated from their castles almost every good plain...." Dating in this area is still conjectural, but if we interpolate a date intermediary between 2200 and 1950 we have 2075, suggestively close to the scheduled date of 2069.

The Levantine Evolutionary epoch began about 15 BC. Ten centuries back takes us to about 1005 BC. Around 1000 BC various Indo-European tribes, including the Scythians, Persians, and Medes, began to filter into Iran, one of the first and most important seed areas of the Levantine culture. Meanwhile in Israel a golden era began with David (c. 1012-972). He rallied the tribes about him and with a string of victories extended Israel's kingdom from Phoenicia to the Arabian desert, from the Orontes to the Gulf of Aqaba. Of particular significance was the capture of the impregnable Canaanite citadel of Jerusalem. Here David established the capital and made a sanctuary to house the Ark. "Lying midway between the tribes of north and south, Jerusalem attracted to itself the loyalty and devotion of all Israel, and soon became the focal center—national and religious—of a united people" (I. Epstein).

During the period 1078-935 Upper Mesopotamia was overrun by Arameans; the Aramean kingdom of Damascus dates from right around 1000. Somewhere around 1000 (the process was gradual) Aramaic replaced Babylonian as the language of the Near East. During the Persian period, Aramaic became the lingua franca of Western Asia (not to be displaced until the Moslem conquest); much of the religious literature of both Jews and Christians was in Aramaic. The change in language signifies the cultural shift in the Near Eastern areas from the old Babylonian civilization to the incipient Levantine.

For the ten-century Inauguration of the Russian people we look to the years around the scheduled date of 876 AD. Vernadsky notes "the 'calling of the Varangians from over the sea' which for centuries has been considered 'the beginning of Russian history'—according to tradition in 862, but actually about 856." This "calling", however, was more like a prelude, and we must look to fundamental events. The expedition to Constantinople in 865 was "the first announcement of the new Russia to civilized writers" (B. Pares). Still, only an announcement. The key event appears to have been the entry of Oleg into Kiev, where he set up as an independent ruler. Vernadsky dates this around 878 and says, "thus a new state, the so-called Kievan Russia, came into being." Pares dates the taking of Kiev at 882 and says, "This even may be regarded as the first foundation of the Russian empire." Harcave dates Rurik's death at 879, so that Oleg's ascendancy would have come about this time; Oleg proved to be "more ambitious than Rurik had been in expanding and strengthening his principality. He took over the city of Kiev and established there the central control of the many other cities and towns he brought under his rule.... Thereafter his Slavic and Varangian followers (all now being called *Russians*—from the Varangian designation *Rus*) profited by better-organized protection.... Thus was laid the foundation for Kievan Russia...." Dating is murky for this period (deriving from the Russian *Primary Chronicle* which for the 9th century is not entirely verifiable). Still, the various dates given for the founding of Kievan Russian and the name of Russia itself come within six years of the scheduled date.

2. The 640-year Inauguration.

The second Inauguration date is 640 years before the beginning of the Evolutionary. Where the 1000-year Germinative period is that of the "people" of the coming culture, the 640-year period is that of their "religion." This may take the form of mass conversions to what is going to be the principal faith; it may show the emergence of a religion in its characteristic form; it may amount to a native capture of control of the religion's administration.

The beginning of the Western Evolutionary was 995. Going back 640 years takes us to 355 AD. For the West, the religious experience was conversion. Of the history of the Goths, Thompson says that "the most momentous change among them was their conversion to Christianity." Ault notes that some Goths became converts as early as 250; "the great missionary to the Geths, however, the man who almost single-handed accomplished their conversion, was Ulfilas. He was born among them" around 310 and was consecrated bishop of the Goths at the age of thirty. Ulfilas had "great talents as an organizer as well as the special gifts of an evangelist. After seven years of labor among the Goths he was obliged to flee across the Danube into Roman territory...where he lived and worked more than thirty years longer, directing the missionary movement from this safe retreat. To forward the work of converting the Goths Uifilas translated the New Testament and parts of the Old Testament into the Gothic tongue" (Ault). The conversion of the entire Gothic nation soon followed. Langer gives the sending of Ulfilas to the Goths at c. 340-348 and his death at 381. The whole activity, then, would have occupied the period from about 340 to 380, nicely surrounding the scheduled date at 355.

The 640 years prior to the beginning of the Levantine Evolutionary epoch takes us back to around 655 BC. Deuteronomy, "or the oldest core of the book at any rate, probably dates from the somber period of the reign of Manasseh" (T.C. Vriezen); this means the years from c. 696-641 (I. Epstein). To epitomize Vriezen's analysis of the program of reform embodied in Deuteronomy: The sole aim must have been to rehabilitate religion and repair the spiritual life of the nation. As the elected people of Yahweh, Israel was brought under the law of Yahweh. The document was brought by its authors or their supporters to the temple, and deposited in the offerings-chest as a consecrated gift, in the hope that it would see the light of day and have its effect, as did indeed come to pass.

This amounted to a "Reformation which very thoroughly purified religious life." All objects devoted to alien gods were removed from the temple, and the priests who cared for these cults were dismissed. Likewise an end was made to child sacrifice and the sexual-agricultural rites. The Deuteronomic Reformation was a "grand attempt, by means of an all-embracing religious law sponsored by the state," to bring about cultic reform and the spiritual renewal of a nation. Deuteronomy "sets out to remake Israel (Judah), which it holds to be the chosen people of God, as a holy nation, consecrated to Yahweh, a nation which out of love fulfills the commandments of the one Lord...." Although for a time the law fell under official neglect, eventually Israel's "whole outlook on history came under the influence of the Deuteronomic viewpoint." The work and the viewpoint were later canonized in the Torah. With Deuteronomy, in fact, began the process of forming the canon of sacred books of the Old Testament. The Deuteronomic Reformation, in sum, "brief as its heyday may have been, did prove to be an enduring influence on the evolution of Israel's religion, the extent of which is incalculable" (Vriezen). It would be difficult to imagine a fuller example of the 640-year Inauguration of a culture's religious sense.

In Russia, the 640 religious beginning took the form of native control of the religion. Russia had been "officially" converted to the Greek Orthodox religion shortly before the year 1000. The 640 date for the Russian culture was 1226. From the conversion "until 1237 the appointed metropolitans were, with few exceptions, Greeks; and in the beginning, the bishops and priests were generally Greeks or Bulgarians" (Harcave). In other words, the Russian church was just a branch of the Greek, and did not belong to the Russians. Vernadsky notes that until the sack of Constantinople (1204) the Greeks played an important role in the Russian church and even in state politics (the two being more or less inseparable). "Byzantium sent to Kiev metropolitans who then headed the Russian church and constantly attempted to secure alliances with Russian princes by marriage with Byzantine princesses or aristocrats.... Byzantium attempted to employ the Russian princes in its own politics."

The change may also be seen in religious art. The 12th century icons are "so characteristically Byzantine that it is an open question whether they actually were painted in Russia and by Russians. In those of the 13th century it is comparatively easy to distinguish national traits of a formal nature" (Anisimov, quoted approvingly by Miliukov). The indication is of a date early in the 13th century. The dates given by Vernadsky (1204) and by Harcave (1237) encompass the scheduled date of 1226 for the Russian 640-year Inauguration.

B. Anticipations

There are two Anticipation systems. The first has one point of incidence, falling 110 years before the beginning of the Evolutionary epoch. The second is a system of quarter-century marks: These operate only during the three-quarters of a century preceding one of the twelve Evolutionary centuries.

1. The 110-year Anticipation

Closely surrounding the date which is 110 years prior to the beginning of a culture's Evolutionary epoch, certain developments may be detected, developments which sharply anticipate the culture's coming evolution and which characterize its inmost nature. These Anticipations are auspicious and specific.

The 110-year Anticipation date for the Levantine culture was due about 125 BC. Because the early years of the Levantine Evolutionary epoch were distinguished above all by the birth and ministry of Jesus and the emergence of the early Church, it is appropriate to look for premonitions of Christianity. The word "Essene," according to Edgar Cayce, means expectation: it is thus related to anticipation.

It seems clear that the Dead Sea Scrolls represent anticipations of Christianity (Geza Vermes, among others, has noted their parallels with the New Testament). And there is now sufficient evidence to identify the people of the Scrolls definitely with the Essenes (F.M. Cross); a majority of writers assume that the Qumranians were Essenes (M. Burrows). The questions then is: Did something occur at Qumran around 125 BC which would indicate an Anticipation?

Apparently about 135 BC a Qumran community center was established by a group of "pious, sectarian Jews, probably Essenes;" somewhere around 100 BC the center was greatly enlarged (J.C. Trever). If we allow (for the sake of argument) a few years for organization and construction, we may not unreasonably postulate a dedication date in the vicinity of 125 BC. With present evidence this must remain conjecture, and we cannot claim anything approaching the firmness of evidence available in the following two examples of the 110-year Anticipation date. Nevertheless the suggestiveness of that evidence which has been uncovered to date is too strong to be ignored.

For the Western culture, whose Evolutionary epoch began in 995, the Anticipation year was 885 AD. The Western culture is ruled by Capricorn. A dynastic tendency is typical of Capricorn; and all nations of the West, as Spengler observed, are of dynastic origin. Among Western dynastic traditions, the two most persistent have been the English and the French.

The founder of the royal house of England was Alfred, called the Great from his time to ours, and sometimes described as the most important figure of the 9th century. The dark period of his career, after 878, ended with the victory at Ethandune, followed by the modification of the Peace of Wedmore. By this new treaty Alfred "abandoned half his kingdom in order to make sure of the remainder, a decision which marks him as a statesman of high rank" (Ault). Here lay the beginning of Alfred's prophetic accomplishments, which include reform of administration and clergy, a code of laws, and major contributions in literature, learning, education, scholarship, and translations (Alfred himself was teacher, translator, and writer). These anticipate such generally Western and particularly English proclivities as literature, education, and law.

Alfred remains in the hearts of his people because he himself took heart when Anglo-Saxon civilization was on the brink of destruction. In addition he has been called the founder of the English navy, though this claim is somewhat exaggerated. So to literature, learning, and law should be added the anticipations of English moral courage and dogged military resourcefulness, of naval and administrative achievement, of daring yet discreet statecraft. So Alfred anticipated the English spirit—apart from the dynastic point that it was the descendants of Alfred who were the actual kings of England. The crucial event in all this was the peace of Alfred and Guthrum. While the treaty has been preserved, the date has not. Scholars estimate it as either 886 or 885.

In France there was also a time of troubles. The Norse were threatening Paris itself; in 884 "it took a bribe of 14,000 pounds of silver to buy off one of these Norse armies" (Ault). At just the time of Alfred's victory (which diverted more Norse to Gaul), came the turning point. "A very large expedition pushed up the Seine in 885. It is estimated that this raid was participated in by 40,000 men in more than 300 boats. They occupied Rouen and then continued on to Paris. For eleven months they undertook the siege of Paris. The defense of the city on this occasion is perhaps the most famous event of the century.... Count Odo maintained a stout and in the end a successful resistance" (*ibid.*). So far we have merely a stunning victory by entrenched courage resulting in a strong reversal of military fortunes, comparable to Alfred's. But the key fact for the anticipation is that "the fame won by Count Odo in his defense of Paris laid the foundation for the prestige of his family, which was eventually to succeed the Carolingians as the royal house of France" (Ault). This house was the Capetian, and it was to become the greatest royal house of Europe. Odo's significance remains anticipatory, for the House of Capet did not actually start in his time. Between the empire of Charlemagne and the new dynasties of Europe lay another kind of polity. When the Frank Empire of Charlemagne fell to pieces, Europe "lost its political unity forever. A new Europe came into being, feudal in genius and character, feudal in government and institutions, feudal in social structure, feudal in its economy—a Europe in which for a long time kings reigned, but did not govern, a Europe in which political power was in the hands of great lay nobles and the bishops" (J.W. Thompson).

The end of the Frankish empire may be timed with the deposition of Charles the Fat in 887; his last official acts took place in 885 or 886.

While the Carolingian Empire was now dissolved, the Carolingian line continued. The last Carolingian was Louis V (986-7), killed accidentally at the age of 19. The royal title was bestowed on Count Hugh Capet, duke of the Franks. "Thus ended the Carolingians of the west, and thus began the famous house of Capet, which, directly or through collateral heirs, was destined to rule over France for nearly a thousand years" (Ault). Hugh's "anticipator" was Odo, and the date of his historical emergence was 885, just 110 years before 995.

It had been an anticipation only. During the course of the ensuing hundred or so years the crown passed from the Carolingians to the Capetians and back again, and "during all that time the ruin of the central power became more and more pronounced" (René Sédillot). The Capetians came to stay in 987, when Hugh was anointed King by the Archbishop of Reims. With the coming of the Capetians in force, "everything changed, and was to change still more. A re-establishment of authority began which would grow progressively stronger" (*ibid.*). This was accompanied by marked improvements in the national economy, in literature and the arts. The Evolutionary epoch had begun in France.

The anticipation of the Western Evolutionary is especially striking in the area of dynastic creations, with their Capricornian instinct to form (the Baroque, which was to the West what the Classical period had been to the Greeks, has been described as a state system resting in dynastic relations). But the anticipations did not appear in dynasties alone. The Evolutionary outburst of ambitious architecture also had anticipations. The abbey church of Corvey on the Weser was consecrated in 885. Corvey is given special notice by scholars. Jean Hubert writes that the westwork, "a mighty 'hand of peace' reaching heavenwards over the monastery and the surrounding countryside, remains the finest symbol of that yearning for the heights which the architects of the 9th century so keenly felt," and which, it should be emphasized, is the keynote of the coming Romanesque spire and Gothic vault. Conant finds the original east end more important than the westwork. "Here indubitably we have the germ of the scheme of apse, ambulatory, and radiating chapels which is one of the finest contributions of the Middle Ages to religious architecture," and which, it might be added, is the core of the Romanesque plan from the beginning of the Evolutionary.

The 110-year date for Russia is 1756. For dynastic or architectural anticipations we need not look in early Russia. Being an Aquarian civilization Russia has given and will give rather to such areas as literature and science, and to theories and programs involving these. The idea of a university is particularly appealing to the Aquarian, both for its "universality" and for its programs of study. In 1748 a university (of only a few students) was created in connection with the Academy of Sciences in Moscow. From this embryo emerged the University of Moscow, which opened its doors in 1755.

This university is now named after one of its founders—and one of the most remarkable Russians of the 18th century—Lomonosov (1711-65). Typically Aquarian, Lomonosov's work was fruitful both for science and for letters. His *Letter on the Use of Glass* was dated 1752, while he had been involved in "extremely intensive" laboratory work from 1747 on (Menshutkin). As early as 1739 his *Ode on the Capture of Khotin* marked "the first production in a pure Russian language." Menshutkin called him the real founder of the university, which was an "elaborately conceived project."

In the same year—1755—appeared another elaborately conceived project, entailing "long and painstaking work;" Lomonosov's *Russian Grammar*. This was to be the first effective Russian grammar (previous attempts having amounted only to grammars of Church Slavonic); indeed it was the only one in Russian until 1831. Kroeber calls Lomonosov the "first positive landmark" in Russian literature, saying that he helped create the literary language of Russia out of the Moscow dialect. Kroeber singles out the publication of 1755, calling it the standard grammar of the language and noting that it "fixed its prosody." Bernard Pares identifies the beginning of modern Russian literature in "the person of Lomonosov...also the first notable poet of the new Russia;" and D.S. Mirsky terms Lomonosov in one place the "legislator and the actual founder of the literary language of modern Russia"; and in another "the real founder of modern Russian literature and of modern Russian culture." This man, held the actual founder both of the literary language of Russia and of her first university, was as Pushkin said "himself a university." Both foundings took place in 1755, within a year of the Anticipation date.

2. The Quarter Century Marks

During the century preceding the beginning of each of the Evolutionary centuries there occur three major breakthroughs anticipating the style of the coming century. These occur at the one-quarter, one-half, and three-quarter marks of the anticipating century. The span of each breakthrough is several years, up to a maximum of seven, though usually with a concentration more closely around three or four years. At the outside, the anticipations may begin 4-3 years before the quarter-century mark, and continue until 3-4 years following it.

These quarter-century breakthroughs remain only moments—that is, they do not mark the beginning of a new stage but rather they represent a bust of anticipatory activity, to be followed by the natural course of the century's proper evolution. Their activity is sporadic, whereas the style they anticipate will enjoy its own continuous evolution when its time arrives. These quarter-century marks represent probings of coming possibilities, probings which, by virtue of hindsight, we call anticipations. They are sporadic but not irregular, for the regularity of their beat is pronounced and meaningful. The three quarter marks are followed by the beginning mark of the new century, so that actually there are four marks in all, thereby composing a rhythm in 4:4 time. It signifies the intensity of breakthroughs following a regular beat, like marching steps.

Since it is the Evolutionary centuries only that are anticipated by quarter systems, in the West the quarter marks first appear during the 10th century: in the years surrounding the dates 921, 946, and 970. The seven years surrounding 921 are c. 918-25. One of the prime expressions of early Romanesque (that is, 11th century) architecture is the radiating plan, whch appears in force at the end of the 10th century. It is anticipated in the ambulatories of Chartres, begun 918, and of S. Pierre-le-Vif at Sens, begun about 920. S. Martin at Tours was dedicated in 918; it was the rebuilding of this church, after a fire in 997, which probably initiated the truly Romanesque radiating plan.

The seven years surrounding 946 are c. 942-9. At this time reappeared the theme of the radiating plan. Conant refers to interesting work in the ambience of Cluny. The priory church of Charlieu (founded 872) appears to have been rebuilt "about seventy years later as a vaulted building with an ambulatory arcade." Seventy years after 872 brings us to 942. An early building at the cathedral of Clermont-Ferrand was dedicated in 946 and reveals the first use of an east end "in the form of an ambulatory with radiating chapels," according to Zarnecki, while Conant calls this "an early stage in the development of the ambulatory and radiating chapels."

The seven years surrounding 970 are 966-73. The church of S. Cyriacus at Gernrode was begun in 963 and probably completed after 972 (H. Saalman). It shows an alternation of supports, that is, of piers and columns, which is highly prophetic in that, when this principle became combined with other features (such as the ambulatory) later at Hildesheim, the entire early Romanesque system was set forth. The Gero Crucifix of around 970 is unprecedented in its expression of the agony of Christ, which was to become a specifically Western subject. Since 970 is the last anticipation point before the Western Evolutionary, it may be significant that Panofsky dated the Ottonian Renaissance from around 970, and that Carroll Quigley marked the end of the Western gestation at just that date.

Among the most striking developments of the 12th century is the appearance of a highly inventive monumental sculpture. This is anticipated in the quarter marks of the 11th century, at the years around 1020, around 1044, and around 1069. The Hildesheim Doors were, according to the inscription, cast in 1015. From 1019-20 (again by inscription) date the Roussillon slabs, variously considered the earliest testimony to the sculptural revival, and the beginning of the sculptural development leading to S. Sernin and Moissac (Conant). Consecrated in 1022 was the monastery church of S. Pedro de Roda, of which Georges Gaillard noted the precosity of the beautiful capitals, adding that such sculptures are of "much interest for their precosity, but were sporadic and had scarcely any continuation in that region," herewith providing an apt description of the function of the quarter-century anticipation.

The 1045 mark picks up the architectural development. Pevsner notes the importance of Jumièges (around 1040, or in the 1040s) as initiating what will be fulfilled at Winchester, Ely, and Durham (that is, in the High Romanesque of the 12th century). Zarnecki stresses the importance of Durham as "the high point in the development of

Romanesque architecture. It is a worthy successor to Jumièges" (Durham was begun in 1093 and sounds the fourth note of the beat). Edouardo Arslan sees the second half of the 11th century as the time when the architecture of cross vaults "was finally born.... Perhaps as early as the middle of the century there was already the vogue at Milan for simple non-ribbed cross-vaults and domical cross-vaults, of which there were echoes at the end of the century" (citing S. Michele of Belocco with an "almost perfectly barrel-vaulted roof supported by arches or interior buttresses").

With the quarter mark around 1070 we return to the sculptural development. This does not mean that the marks signify now one art, then another, for indeed all major forms of the period may find expression at an anticipation mark. It means rather that the evidence from the period is so slim and so controversial that we must find what we can. Of the capitals at S. Benoit sur Loire, generally dated c. 1070, Zarnecki holds that the future development of "the best Romanesque sculpture went along this path of close unity with the architectural member to which it is applied." Paul Deschamps finds figures "more freely detached from the mass, a more accentuated relief, and an abler distribution of design elements" in these same capitals. Throughout the 11th century, it was Spain that actually led Europe "not only in the art of the figure capital but also in major figure sculpture" (Pevsner). Gaillard finds the birth of Spanish Romanesque sculpture in Leon, at the church of S. Isidro, finished in 1067. With the certainty of their early date and the originality of their forms, the sculpture of the capitals here (he writes) "can be considered the point of departure" of an influence that was to permeate all Spanish Romanesque art.

The 12th century marks reveal anticipations of 13th century style, namely Gothic. It is true that "early Gothic" is dated from the 1140s, but this does not represent the beginning of a continuous development, rather it shows the sporadic steps of the anticipation process, for Romanesque style continued to dominate the century. The anticipation marks in the 12th century are clustered around 1119, 1144, and 1168. The chief features of Gothic architecture are the pointed arch, the rib vault, and the flying buttress, while the underlying characteristics are unity as against differentiation and continuity versus distinction.

For anticipations around 1119 we have evidence at S. Ambrogio and at Moissac. Zarnecki finds the entire interior of S. Ambrogio (Milan) covered with rib vaulting, "presumably soon after 1117." Frankl writes that the introduction of the pointed arch in the diagonals "must be recognized as the completion of the first phase in the development of the rib-vault." The earliest example is "to be found in the porch at Moissac, built around 1120."

The year of consecration of the choir at S. Denis was 1144. Whoever designed the choir of S. Denis, writes Pevsner, invented the Gothic style, for it was the first time that the earlier innovations were combined into a system. Nevertheless, this system was applied only to a choir, not to an entire building, and it was followed only sporadically until the rebuilding of Chartres (from 1194). Surely the choir of S. Denis was revolutionary and a work of genius, but the force of the anticipation mark is seen in the fact that S. Denis was not alone. Frankl calls Le Mans (from 1145) the first building since the porch of Moissac in which ribs are deliberately built in the form of pointed arches, and also notes that S. Martin near Etamps belongs to the transition: the transverse arches are pointed, while the ribs are distorted. "The choir was begun in 1140, at the same time as the choir of S. Denis."

Anticipations of Gothic style around 1168 are evident in several buildings in France. The quadripartite vaults at Noyon date from around 1170 (Frankl), and the building is newly enlivened by a triforium (Pevsner). At Laon (designed around 1170) appear spatial relationships more subtle and ramified than any to be found in all the earlier styles (J.I. Sewall). At Laon the regular row of round piers partly does away with the Romanesque emphasis on square subordinate bays (Frankl), so that the halting at every major support is avoided (Pevsner); this regular row of identical piers later became a specifically Gothic motif (Frankl). Others consider Laon as possibly the first great building to break completely with the Romanesque. Paris Cathedral is, as it were, a development of Laon in that the openings are slimmer, the shafts no longer differentiated, and the spatial rhythms of the ground plan are smoother (Pevsner).

The quarter-century marks of the 13th century anticipate the late Gothic style of the 14th century (as against the High Gothic of the 13th). Late Gothic on the continent is approximately equivalent to

Decorated in England, with its double-curved ogee arch, star vault, and profuse enrichment (Pierre de Montreuil). The late Gothic in general stresses the decorative as against the structural, even the two-dimensional as against the three-dimensional. Frankl considers the chapter house at Wells (from 1293) the first of the late Gothic, noting that virtually all the arches there are identical and that we do not inquire into their function or their structural significance: "Their effect is one of texture."

The anticipation dates of the 13th century cluster around 1218, 1243, and 1267. Amiens was apparently begun immediately after the fire of 1218 (Sewall). Much of the cathedral may be taken as one of the most classic examples of High Gothic; yet in the triforium is to be found a double curve "which was later, as the ogee arch, to reign supreme as a two-dimensional figure in tracery" (Frankl). Reims provides another classic example of High Gothic style. But a "new stage of development began when the architects of the rose window in the west facade" (probably around 1243) and that of the Sainte Chapelle in Paris (in its original form, begun about 1243) decided to transplant the tracery of the usual oblong windows into circular ones. "This might be called akyrism" or a "misinterpretation, or a deliberate change in interpretation.... We can understand from the general development of the Gothic style why tracery lost its structural character and took on a purely textural one" (Frankl).

In 1243 was begun the Sainte Chapelle: "one tall room with—except for a low dado-zone—walls entirely of glass" (Pevsner), an astonishing prophecy of late Gothic. Begun about 1243 was S. Catherine at Barcelona, which has been called the first example of a wide nave with no aisles (thereby creating a new unity of overall space prophetic of the late Gothic). Pevsner sees a beginning of the late Gothic in the Angel Choir at Lincoln, begun in 1256, and with good reasons. Nevertheless it seems true, as Zarnecki maintains, that the Angel Choir repeats many decorative elements inspired by Westminster, which was begun in 1245. In general, the "sumptuous surface decoration of Westminster Abbey was symptomatic of things to come in the development of English Gothic" (Zarnecki). The case here is instructive, reminding us that the anticipation marks are not the only points in the anticipating century when prophetic steps may be taken; they are, however, the points when the major breakthroughs are made. Thus the Angel Choir may be the more beautiful, but the credit for the breakthrough remains with Westminster.

The third quarter mark of 13th century anticipations came around 1267. The church of S. Urbain de Troyes is generally dated from 1261-c. 1277, but some date it more closely at 1264-5. Grodecki notes the immense windows replacing the clerestory, the greater spatial unity and growing refinement of decoration, calling the result "a real innovation." Pevsner cites this "amazing church" in which the structural members have been given an "unprecedented brittleness and slenderness," and notes that the system of Saint Chapelle has been transferred to a major church (brittleness and slenderness are 14th century traits).

During the 14th century the quarter marks anticipate the 15th, which was the first century of the Renaissance. Thus we look for anticipations of Renaissance style in the years surrounding the dates 1317, 1341, and 1366. One of the most prominent inventions of the Renaissance was perspective, as we know it in the West. In 1317 Simone Martini painted the *S. Louis of Toulouse Crowning Robert of Anjou*. The predella scenes of this altarpiece contain what have been called the boldest compositions in perspective up until that time. Furthermore, the predella seems to show the first example of the perspective grouping of several scenes around a clearly defined central axis; the new relationship between narrative and observer is "unequivocally defined"; there is a uniform and parallel recession which replaces Duccio's "tentative advance" toward focusing receding lines on a single point (John White). In the main scene, it may be noted that the portrait figure is almost the same size as the saint, anticipating the Renaissance importance both of the portrait itself and of the living presence.

Also dated 1317 is a French manuscript illuminating the *Legend of S. Denis*. The scene is freshly observed, showing painted reflections in the water (for the first time) and differing from earlier manuscripts in that the main action here is not separated "from these genre scenes. At this point the artist's conception began to be equivalent to a painter's approach to his panel as a total surface." Cuttler adds: "However, progress was not made evenly. The full-page miniature, here only in germ, was yet to come"—so that the phenomenon may properly be considered an anticipation.

The year 1342 could be called the year of the Lorenzetti. Both Pietro's *Birth of the Virgin* and Ambrogio's *Presentation in the Temple* show a naturalistic description and perspective that anticipate the Renaissance proper (*Oxford Companion*). Pietro's picture marks a significant step in the direction of illusionism, according to F. Hartt, who adds that the gold background is largely eliminated and the architectural setting identified with the curved shape of the frame. It is a "pioneer attempt" to build up consistent interior space and represents an "enormous step" in the direction of the "unified perspective space of the Renaissance." Furthermore in this work the picture becomes a stage—directly anticipating the Renaissance stage created by Claus Sluter in the early nineties.

In the years around 1366 a new stage in the Western portrait emerged. The panel portrait of John the Good is dated between 1360 and 1364 by Panofsky, and amounts to what Cuttler calls the first preserved portrait in the modern sense, that is, the objective portrayal of an individual: not a donor in religious setting nor a monarch in court, but an image focused on the subject's distinct personality—all this anticipates the Renaissance, and differs from other contemporary portraiture.

During the 15th century the quarter marks anticipate aspects of 16th century style, generally called High Renaissance. The marks are located around the dates 1416, 1440, and 1465. Janson dates Donatello's *S. George* at c. 1415-17. Herein the "statement of form as the dynamic counterpoint of space anticipated a theme which was to become dominant in the art of the High Renaissance" (Luisa Becherucci). The seven years surrounding the mark at 1440 run from Uccello's *Hawkwood* (1436 ff.) to Donatello's *Gattamelata* (1443 ff.). These two figures epitomize the theme of the heroic conqueror, the ideal portrait, unifying rhythms, grandeur, and force of will—all of them qualities that anticipate the Leonine 16th century.

The seven years surrounding 1465 apparently include Alberti's remarkable buildings in Mantua, S. Sebastiano (begun 1460 but developed later) and S. Andrea (designed 1470). These two buildings "herald a new and less archeological attitude to antiquity. They reach forward from the Early to the High Renaissance" (Fleming and Honour). In northern painting the Louvain Altarpiece (1464-7) of Dirk Bouts is unusual in its time and anticipates High Renaissance style in that it is frontal, formal, symmetrical, and concentrated (Hartt) as well as showing rigorous regularity, rational one-point perspective (unusual in northern art), and severe geometrical order (Cuttler).

The 16th century marks anticipate the Baroque style of the 17th century; they cluster around the dates 1515, 1540, 1564. Titian's *Assunta* was begun in 1516 and has often been called the first Baroque picture: The movement is upwards, in diagonals and zigzags, the composition is as much fused as it is segregated, and the handling is painterly. At the same time, in the cupola mosaic of the Chigi Chapel, Raphael had shown God overhead in a Baroque view (designed 1515), and in the cartoon *The Healing of the Lame Man* (1515-16) he created twisting columns anticipating those of Rubens and Bernini, along with Baroque thrust and chiaroscuro.

For the quarter mark around 1540 we have Titian's three large pictures in the Salute. The overhead views are as Baroque in concept as those of Rubens, though they remain 16th century in linear style. That Titian's *Assunta* did not lead directly to the pictures in the Salute is plain when we consult his monumental *Presentation of the Virgin* of 1534-8 which is conceived entirely in Renaissance planes. On the same mark around 1540 are Sansovino's Library and Loggietta in Venice, both begun in 1537. Here is an anticipation of Baroque city planning. The Library not only connected with his other work in the area, but made the Piazzetta "an impressive approach, almost a triumphant gateway, towards S. Mark's and the Clocktower, and additionally a preparation for the huge Piazza opening unexpectedly" (M. Levey), all of which are Baroque desiderata.

In Rome, Michelangelo began to paint his *Last Judgment* in the Sistine Chapel in 1536; it was unveiled in 1541. The painting anticipates Baroque continuity in its spatial organization, Baroque emotiveness in its color and expression. As opposed to earlier paintings by Michelangelo, the entire composition moves (H. Hibbard); it dissolves the wall (F. Hartt), while engaging in a great circular motion, and it creates a "fluid pulsation" which is new (Hartt). That this is an anticipation (not an initiation) is evident if we examine Michelangelo's subsequent frescoes in the Pauline Chapel (Vatican) of 1542-5: Compared with the *Last Judgment,* these are more rigid and more Mannerist.

Begun in 1539 was Michelangelo's Conservatori Palace on the Capitoline. Of the period, Wölfflin observed that the "most determined innovator was Michelangelo, in whose Capitoline palaces the two stories are boldly held together with a single order of giant pilasters"—an anticipation of Baroque subordination and continuity. Michelangelo anticipated the Baroque; he did not inaugurate it, for it was not until the 17th century that architects were able "to appreciate and began to emulate his dynamic control of mass and space" (Fleming and Honour).

The third quarter mark came in the years around 1564. Michelangelo's designs for the Porta Pia occupied the years from 1561 until his death in 1564; the work "anticipated the principles of Baroque town planning" (Fleming and Honour). To precisely the same years can probably be attributed Michelangelo's work on the exterior of S. Peter's, the "first exterior of the Renaissance to be created as a unified piece of architectural sculpture rather than as a congress of architectural units" (H. Hibbard). Unity is basic to Baroque style; and unity "was Michelangelo's contribution to S. Peter's" (J. Ackerman). In these same years appeared the first early Baroque churches. In S. Caterina dei Funari (1564) "the new spirit is present, though still discreet and tentative" (Wölfflin). It has a narrowed upper story and volutes anticipating the Gesù, often considered the first Baroque building and itself begun (at least in plan) in 1568.

Barocci's *Deposition* (Perugia) was begun in 1566. Already at this time the painter "showed a feeling for space and atmosphere, for color and light, for naturalistic form, and for religious sentiment that contrasts markedly with the flat and dry formalistic conceptions of his Mannerist contemporaries"—making him "clearly the forerunner of such great Baroque artists as Giovanni Lanfranco, Pietro da Cortona, and Bernini" (D. Posner). In 1565 Bruegel painted his *Seasons* or "Months", pictures in which for the first time nature is seen as unified with man, rather than a background, and in which man is caught up in and subordinated to the flow and process of nature—all anticipating 17th century naturalism.

The 17th century quarter marks anticipated the style of the 18th century, known as Late Baroque or Rococo. The marks are at about 1614, 1639, and 1663. In 1616 Domenichino began his painting *The Punishment of Midas* (London), in which Midas decides for Pan in contest with Apollo. The subject is significant in itself, for in the 18th century Pan and Venus were to become favored over the weightier gods Apollo and Hercules. In this Domenichino picture the whole effect is light, amusing, witty, and charming—in 18th century vein—quite unlike his *Last Communion of S. Jerome* of two years before. In the Midas picture, Rococo lightness also appears in figures and landscape, tone and color. There are mere touches of chiaroscuro (as in Tiepolo); the border is highly decorative and the effect is like wallpaper, another 18th century favorite.

In 1639 Borromini began the interior of S. Carlino. The effect is "exquisite" (G. Bazin), depending partly on the fact that, unlike Bernini, Borromini did not like rich color but preferred the pure tones of white stucco, and the combination of white and gold, which were to be 18th century predilections. In general Borromini was more important for Austrian and South German (that is, 18th century) architecture than for Italian. But it does not mean that all his work was anticipatory of the coming century. After the S. Carlino interior, on the anticipation mark, he designed (1653-7) S. Agnese, which is more constrained and controlled, more monumental and less vertical, in a word more of its own time. But while still under the influence of the anticipation rhythm he had designed (1639-41) the Palazzo Falconieri, for whose river facade he planned an open, U-shaped court enclosed by walls "subtly handled to produce a delicate play of light and shade and decorated with a restrained elegance that anticipated not only the 18th century but neo-classicism as well" (P. Portoghesi).

The third quarter mark came in the years around 1663. Here Borromini returned to S. Carlino, now adding the facade (1665-7), whose reverse undulation creates an 18th century-like continuity of flow. Borromini inaugurated a "new departure. Whatever their innovations, Benini, Cortona, Rainaldi" and the rest never challenged the old tradition. But Borromini broke "with this tradition and erected fantastic structures" (Wittkover)—that is, fantastic in the chimerical sense of the 18th century.

The quarter marks during the 18th century anticipated the 19th, which was the first modern century, so that what was anticipated was modern style. The dates center around 1713, 1737, and 1762. Vico approached his New Science through "a new theory of knowledge, announced in his publications of 1709 and 1710" (*Encyclopedia Britannica*). His metaphysical essay "On the Ancient Wisdom of the Italians" was published in 1710, following the inaugural lecture published in 1709. Such writings have reminded historians more often of the historical method of the 19th century than of Vico's contemporaries such as Gravina. By this time Vico was "far in advance of any of his contemporaries in his understanding that every stage of social progress is an organic whole" (H.P. Adams).

In 1712 Addison wrote (in the *Spectator*), "I would rather look upon a tree in all its luxuriance and diffusion of boughs and branches than when it is cut and trimmed into a mathematical figure"—an anticipation of 19th century Romanticism, as is the beginning of natural gardening around this time (in 1713 Pope followed Addison with "Nature unadorned"). Watteau's *Embarkation from Cythera* (1717 or before) anticipated the Romantic; his *Signboard of Gersaint* (1719) was pure 18th century.

Published in 1738, Hume's *Treatise on Human Nature* broke the connection between reason and the empirical world, anticipating modern empiricism. In 1739 Thomas Gray (later the author of the *Elegy*) took a tour of the continent; after crossing the Alps, he wrote: "Not a precipice, not a torrent, not a cliff, but is pregnant with religion and poetry." Kenneth Clark observes that it never occurred to previous crossers of the Alps to admire the scenery, adding that Gray's reaction anticipates Byron, Turner, and Ruskin.

The mark around 1762 is revealed in two works published in 1765. Piranesi's *Parere sull'architettura* advocated a "free and imaginative use of Roman models for the creation of a new architectural style" (Fleming and Honour). Peyre's *Oeuvres d'architecture* presents "megalomaniac designs" (Pevsner) for a palace, a cathedral, etc.— that is, anticipating designs like those of Boullée in the 1780s and 1790s, which belong to modern architecture proper.

Rousseau's *Emile* of 1762, with its concept of the "noble savage" and its glorification of the child, anticipated the nature experience so profoundly characteristic of the 19th century, for example in Wordsworth and the natural man. A similar anticipation may be found in Richard Wilson's painting *Solitude*, also of 1762, an unusual work for this classical landscape artist. Here a pair of monks take their "lonely places in a landscape made all the more melancholy by the presence of weeping willows" (R. Rosenblum). Thus the Wilson picture, like the Rousseau book, also anticipated 19th century Romanticism.

The 19th century quarter marks anticipated 20th century style. They fell around 1812, 1836, and 1861. About 1811, Constable, "for some mysterious reason...suddenly found a means of expressing his emotions in paint, and he did the oil sketches of the Stour which were something new in European art" (K. Clark). That this "expressionism" anticipated the 20th century kind is clear if we consult a picture like *Lock and Cottages on the Stour* (1811 or 1812, in the Victoria and Albert): From this to Soutine is but a step. Here there is a dark vehemence, almost violence, as well as a dash and freedom which anticipate aspects of Munch and Van Gogh. In such works Constable developed an expressionist power and urgency unlike the natural life acceptance that marked the usual tenor of his art. The year 1814 saw Goya's *Executions of the Third of May*, a monumental anticipation of abstraction and expressionism.

Turner painted at Petworth from 1830 to 1837. His famous painting *Interior at Petworth* in the Tate appears to date toward the later part of this span. The picture (there are also a few similar scenes, so that it does not stand entirely alone) was very popular in the 1950s, in the heyday of Abstract Expressionism. Kenneth Clark calls it "surely the most liberated picture of the 19th century." And indeed it leaps far beyond most 19th century styles so that, were it not for the debris of observed reality, we might take it for a mid-20th century work. Also abstract and expressionist are certain sepia drawings of Constable, full of unwonted violence and contrast. Usually these are attributed to the years 1830-36.

The third quarter mark in the 19th century was due in 1861. Manet's earlier work belonged pretty much with Realism, his later work with Impressionism. But in 1862 he painted the *Déjeuner sur l'herbe*, and in 1863 the *Olympia*. The two are based on various Renaissance models, are artificial in flavor, and represent a deliberately posed studio art. Almost all the best 19th century painting was nature painting in the sense of being based in life experience; the most characteristic 20th century work has been studio painting—art based on art. It is presumably for this reason that many critics begin modern painting with Manet, but in fact pictures such as these represent only a moment which falls at the third anticipation mark. The rest of the century—that is, until around 1886—returned to an art based on life.

3. *The Quarter Marks in Russia*

Of the three quarter marks of an anticipating century, the most impressive tends to be the middle one, the half-century mark (S. Denis for early Gothic, Michelangelo and Titian for early Baroque). Russia's first Evolutionary century began about 1866; the half century mark fell around 1816. A variety of anticipations appeared at this time.

One was the emergence of a Russian poetry which led the other Russian arts of the time, and which was capable of competing with Western poetry. The prime mover was Pushkin, whose poetry was also to have a powerful effect on Russian music (Lang). Pushkin began to write in his teens, around 1815. That this was an anticipation (rather than the beginning of a continuous development) is evident from the fact that poetry, the first of Russia's great literary arts, was quickly supplanted by other literary forms. The short story, for example, gained in importance, but by the beginning of the Evolutionary epoch it was the novel—that is the Russian novel, which has little to do with the European—that became the major vehicle of Russian literary genius.

Earlier in the century Russian prose showed potential but remained in need of being cleared for action. It was the lot of Karamzin to free Russian prose through his development of history, letters, and the novel itself. His crucial historical work, the *History of the Russian State*, eventually reached eleven volumes. It was begun in 1803, but the telling date in its publication appears to have been 1818, when the first eight volumes appeared. Vernadsky locates the first edition as appearing in 1816, calling it "a great event in the spiritual life of Russia." The saying was current that Karamzin had discovered ancient Russia as Columbus had discovered America. S.R. Tompkins calls it a landmark in Russian literature, and concludes that Russian historiography "took an immense step forward with Karamzin. Cizevskij warns that Karamzin "did not take part directly in the literary controversy over language and style reform. These matters were not decided until after 1810, when the younger generation formed the 'Karamzin School.' Significantly, literary societies were formed, and for the first time in Russia they became involved in literary disputes"—an Aquarian predilection.

Another Aquarian development anticipated the Russian reform movements of the later 19th century. The "Society of Salvation" or "Southern Society" was formed in 1817. Its aim was to achieve a constitutional form of government (Kornilov), and included Muravyev, who favored an English type of constitution; N. Turgenev, who was strong on emancipation; and, among others, Pestel, who advocated conspiracy to overthrow the autocracy, the abolition of all class distinctions, and a division of the land to be half-communal, half-private enterprise (Pestel later turned out to be a ratter). This was no idiosyncratic collection of individuals: Alexander himself during these years was quite open in his views (he knew of the Society, even though the public did not), and in 1818 he gave a remarkably liberal speech to the Polish Diet. All this remained an anticipation—and not the beginning of a steady development—since by 1820 Alexander's policies had become reactionary in many ways, and under his successor Nicholas there came the repression that was to last until the 1860s.

The first breakthrough anticipating the Russian Evolutionary epoch came three quarters of a century before 1866, that is, around 1791 or 1792. In 1790 Radishchev published a book which is one of the "landmarks in Russian social literature. Under the unassuming title *A Journey from Petersburg to Moscow* he relates plain scenes from official, and especially from peasant, life, of which some are such as to make the blood boil. The book is instinct with a noble altruism" (Pares). For this publication Radischev "was actually sentenced to death, though this was commuted to exile in Siberia. In 1791 Novikov's bookstore was searched; he himself was seized and conveyed with unusual secrecy to the state prison" (*ibid.*). Novikov was a critical thinker; Radishchev's book has been credited with depicting the peasant as a human being for the first time in Russian literature. It was to have an enormous impact. Also at this time we again meet Karamzin, who had been a student in Moscow. In 1789 "he left Moscow to take a trip to Europe that was to affect the cultural history of Russia" (Cizevskij). This trip produced *Letters of a Russian Traveller, 1789-90*. The book was published in 1792.

One quarter of a century before the Evolutionary came the third and last anticipation. The dating is about 1841. According to Vernadsky, while there were other writers of distinction, it was Pushkin, Lermontov, and Gogol who "laid the corner stones of the foundation upon which all subsequent Russian literature arose." So far as the anticipations are involved, Pushkin (for his early poetic invention) belongs to the half-century mark, Lermontov and Gogol to the one-quarter mark before the Evolutionary.

While Lermontov first became famous with his poem on Pushkin's death, in 1837, the collection of his best poems was published in 1840. The same year saw his key work, *A Hero of Our Time*. Pares is not alone in finding Pushkin and Lermontov the two greatest poets of Russian literature; he notes that Lermontov's "scorn was not merely, like that of Pushkin, for the banality and servility of his own social world, but for the baseness of life itself in Russia during this period." So Lermontov moves closer than Pushkin to a direct anticipation of the sixties. In artistic form, he is the specific anticipator of Dostoevsky: As Lavrin points out, Lermontov was the first Russian poet to turn the bulk of his work into self-confession.

The supreme figure of the one-quarter anticipation, however, was Gogol. His extraordinary career culminated in *Dead Souls*, which was begun in 1836 but published in 1842, and *The Overcoat* of 1842. No less than Dostoevsky said, "We have all come out of Gogol's greatcoat." With previous writers, Russian literature had been expressive mainly of a given class or a way of life. With Gogol, claims Lavrin, literature "made a decisive attempt to become a moral and social force in life." The attempt was not yet successful, but it was "decisive" enough to constitute a major anticipation of the achievement of Tolstoy, Dostoevsky, and the greatest of their successors. With the coming of the Evolutionary epoch, Russian literature attained, almost at a stroke, the highest level of effectiveness and acceptance. No tsar had such a burial as Dostoevsky.

Such moral force had not been possible before the 1860s. Even "Gogol himself, as soon as he turned from describing and tried to preach some lesson, lost his footing and fell into an obscurity of mysticism. So perished in isolation the great Russian authors, because they were alien to all their surroundings, and a critical thinking public had yet to be created" (Pares). As late as the thirties,

Belinsky answered the question "Do we possess a literature?" with the answer "No, we have nothing but a book-trade!" Pushkin's work had been "charged with foreign elements" (Lavrin) and, while Gogol nearly created the Russian novel, still with him there remained a gap between the artist and the man, whereas it was the full realization of the one in the other that was to distinguish Dostoevsky. Another gap with Gogol lay between inspiration and form. The national art, writes Waliszewski, attained "its sovereign expression by the fusion which Gogol failed to realize, of the artist's inspiration and the artist's conscious endeavor, in the novels of Turgenev." (*Fathers and Sons* was published in 1862, *Smoke* in 1867, embracing 1866, the inception of the Evolutionary epoch.)

This national art required the stages from Karamzin to Turgenev in order to develop its full working form. The Russian was a type of novel new in world literature. Compared with the European novel (a development of the later Western culture), it is less matter-of-fact, more epical. And it contrasts with the poetry which occupied comparable periods in Greek or European literature. "When we speak of Russian literature we mean the novel. Unlike other literatures, where poetry occupies the most prominent place, in Russia it is prose. For various reasons, the Russian genius expressed itself much better in prose. The majority of Russian writers considered poetry as entertaining literature—but Russian literature as a whole is not entertaining" (I. Spector).

It is not entertaining because entertainment is never more than subsidiary in the early literature of a major culture, a literature characteristically religious or mythic. The Russian myth deals with the elevation of mankind through perfection of the social condition. Russian writers are almost inevitably involved with political situations and social issues. "It is a rare work among the novels and plays of the second half of the 19th century that escapes some discussion of these social problems; no other modern literature of international stature has responded to the impact of social and political events so strongly" (T. Lindstrom).

Russian realism is neither merely aesthetic nor merely programmatic, else it would be no more than propaganda. It is far deeper than these, so deep that Count Keyserling could see in Dostoevsky's works an influence unparalleled since Luther. And it aims far higher than the late Western kind of realism, so that Gorky could say, "I want literature to rise above reality and to look down on reality from above, because literature has a far greater purpose than merely to reflect reality. It is not enough to depict already existing things—we must also bear in mind the things we desire and the things which are possible of achievement." Thus the transcendental quality of the early Evolutionary, as in the Romanesque-Gothic cathedral. These are some of the main conditions of the Russian Evolutionary, which Gogol "anticipates" at the last quarter-century mark.

C. Overlaps

The third system is the Overlap, of which there are two kinds. One begins four centuries before the Evolutionary epoch and ends four centuries after it. The other begins two centuries before the Evolutionary and ends two centuries after.

Unlike the Anticipations, the Overlaps denote periods of more or less continuous development. Unlike the Evolutionary period, however, the overlap periods do not reveal a highly directed, sequential development, evolving strictly and regularly within. Overlap periods show general tendencies, but not the sense of inner purpose and the keen regularity of the Evolutionary, whose works can be dated to within a very few years by style alone.

1. The Four-century Overlap.

The four centuries preceding the Evolutionary are the period when the culture first begins to recognize itself as such, to be aware of its new sense of destiny. At the same time appear the first distinctive art forms, those which will prove uniquely characteristic of the new culture, and therefore of its self-identity.

Four centuries before 995 takes us to 599 in the West. "Supposing it were absolutely necessary to set a precise date for the beginning of that slow revival which paved the way for the Carolingian renaissance, the year 590 would probably be the most acceptable. In about 590 Columban, accompanied by a dozen Irish monks, founded an establishment on the continent.... In 590 Gregory...ascended the throne of St Peter, shed fresh luster on the Papacy and embarked on the conversion of the Anglo-Saxons. It was this collaboration between Rome and the regions situated at the furthest limits of the Roman world which was to provide the decisive impulse" (Philippe Wolff).

The year 590 is actually a little early, since Columban only began his mission to Europe in that year (he lived until 615), and since Gregory's papacy covered the years 590-604. The first monk to become pope, Gregory has been also described as the first of the medieval prelates. Giving charter to the monks, he made alliance between the Benedictines and the papacy, at the expense of the bishops. In 596 he sent Augustine (of Canterbury) to Britain. He laid the base for German conversion, and campaigned against paganism in Gaul, Italy, and Sicily.

It was Gregory "who dictated to the Eastern Empire a settlement with the Lombards, confirming them in their lands. Thus early did a pope become the dominant political figure in the West" (Ault). Gregory was "the important exponent of the doctrine of divided powers; the emperor was God's vicar in things temporal, the pope in things spiritual" (*Columbia Encyclopedia*). He transformed the patriarch of Rome "into the papal system that endured through the Middle Ages" (*Webster's Biographical Dictionary*), and established the origins of papal absolutism. On top of this, "he laid the foundations of a new empire for Rome in the place of her old empire which now lay in ruins—a new Roman Empire, established by missionary zeal and not by military force, which was eventually to conquer new worlds whose soil the legions had never trodden and whose very existence had never been suspected by the Scipios and Caesars" (Toynbee). So it was in Gregory's time that there emerged the dynamic political-clerical entity characteristic of the Capricornian West for a thousand years to come.

At the same four-century overlap date may be observed the emergence of the first really new and indigenous art forms of the West. In music, a bowed string (the Celtic crwth) was attested to by 609 AD; its essence was the "simultaneous sound of one string bringing out the melody against the harmony of the drone strings" (Alfred Einstein), making it a key to polyphony, the music of the West. The Greeks had had "no bowed instrument and despised the many-stringed harp of the Egyptians" (Einstein). Western music does not "represent a type of music culture, as though there were other representatives of the same type; it is *sui generis*. Its achievements and its fruits are unique in the history of the world; it has no counterpart" (Walter Wiora).

Specifically, by "about 600 AD...the church had, in its plain song, found a superbly expressive type of music exactly fitted to the spirit of its ritual.... The roots of this musical style were Jewish, and to a less extent Greco-Roman; but by the 7th century this style had moved far beyond its origins"; it amounted to a "glorious and original" achievement (F.B. Artz). From Gregory's school of music came the Gregorian Chant; he worked to perfect the ritual of the church and established its liturgical music. And from the 7th century—probably very early, though remains are scanty—come the first new pictorial styles of the West. These appear primarily in metalwork and in manuscript illumination. Interlacing bands "as an ornamental device occur in Roman and Early Christian art," notes H.W. Janson, "but their combination with the animal style" is a new invention, and apparently of just this time. The Hiberno-Saxon or Anglo-Irish manuscript illuminations are unprecedented both in style and in quality. The Cathach of S. Columba may date from the late 6th century. The Book of Durrow and the Lindisfarne Gospels belong to the 7th century, and the Book of Kells to the 8th. H.W. Janson describes the period 600-800 as the golden age of Ireland; Carl Nordenfalk refers to Celtic and Anglo-Saxon painting as belonging to the period 600-800.

What is striking about these Anglo-Irish manuscripts is their absolute originality and the fact that they are the first Western paintings of absolute quality. Their special significance in the present context, however, is that they represent the salient beginnings of Western pictorial style. The Capricornian instincts of the West are revealed in the development of spatial dynamics and the beat of time. The interlocking patterns of these manuscript illuminations create an intense spatial dynamics not to be found at all in, say, Islamic arabesques, and only incipiently in the older Celtic art forms. At the same time, the manuscripts of the 7th and 8th centuries show clocklike vibrations, swirls that wind and unwind like the inner movements of a Swiss watch; these are the first examples of the Western dynamics of time, which by the Gothic age were to be expressed in clock-towers and bells interminable.

On the Continent, the architecture of the time has been lost or buried. The only building above ground in France that still shows architectural elements from this period is the baptistry of S. Jean at Poitiers; of this Jean Hubert notes, "Perhaps it is here that we should look for the distant origin of this taste for ornate facades which was so much alive in the nearby valley of the Loire from the end of the 10th century onwards." In England the architectural evidence is clearer, and Saalman has concluded that the importance of England for medieval developments "lies in the architectural production following the Benedictine mission of St Augustine...in 596."

Roberto Salvini has drawn attention to the "huge volume of figurative and more frequently ornamental sculpture of the 7th to the 11th centuries in all the western provinces of the former Roman Empire. It is to this sculpture...that we intend to reserve the title 'pre-Romanesque', in the same way that the term 'pre-Romance' is used for the dialects which during these same centuries evolved in Italy, Gaul, and Hispania, and from which later the Romance languages were to be born in parallel with Romanesque art." The first reference to the Arthurian legend came apparently around 600 AD.

Four centuries before the beginning of the classical Evolutionary takes us back to 1475 BC. From somewhere in the vicinity of 1500 may be dated the earliest distinctive Mycenaean remains, such as funeral masks and the Vaphio Cups. By the second half of the 15th century, Greek vases can be easily differentiated from Cretan (the principle of self-recognition). Also at about this time appeared the *tholos*, or round tomb. "Nothing prepares us for such tombs. There is no architectural forerunner, either in Greece or anywhere else" (M.I. Finley).

Four centuries after the Classical Evolutionary takes us to 506 AD. The last architecture that could be called Roman, as opposed to Early Christian, is to be found in an occasional basilica of the fourth or fifth centuries, the last sculpture an occasional sarcophagus. But in literature something substantially Classical persisted to the end. While Kroeber is right in observing that "what was left of philosophy upon its absorption into Christianity fell on evil days," still, even so late as the beginning of the sixth century when civilization was crumbling, "the work of Boethius and Cassiodorus passed on a summary of ancient knowledge to the medieval world" (Cary and Scullard). Langer calls Boethius the "last classical philosopher." Gibbon called him the "last of the Romans whom Cato or Tully could have acknowledged for his countryman." Boethius' last work, *The Consolation of Philosophy*, was written on the eve of his execution in 524.

The precedent Overlap—the one preceding the Evolutionary—is distinguished by the first appearance of integrated works and systems: Celtic manuscripts, Mycenaean tombs, the Gregorian sense of organization. The succedent Overlap ends in disintegration. Already "in the fifth century the Roman system contained a division within itself, which was likely to prove fatal—the division between culture without function and function without culture" (C.D. Burns). The Roman world, Burns concludes, "might have survived, even in the West, the new crisis of the fifth century. But it did not." In the great Christian basilicas of Rome, "the Romans of the fifth century gathered and prayed, while the old social system fell into ruins." The Roman mind of the fifth century became *déraciné*, and even by the middle of the century the belief had become dominant that an end of all things was at hand.

It was not the power of the barbarians that was the crucial factor in the deposition (in 476) of the last Roman emperor. This event attended the disintegration of the "moral authority" of the emperor (Burns), and of the "ideal of the Empire" (Norman F. Cantor). In the course of the fifth century, the "system had become useless to the majority of its subjects" (Burns). It had simply spent itself in accordance with historical process, and we may compare Philippe Wolff's analysis of the emergence of Irish culture around 600 AD, which he calls "one of those facts before which the inadequacy of all historical explanations becomes rapidly obvious."

The four-century Overlap at the conclusion of the Levantine Evolutionary epoch takes us to about 1570. By this time the political power of Persians and Jews, of Byzantium and Arab Islam, had long declined. One major cultural manifestation, however, remained: Persian poetry. While no longer an Evolutionary form, this was no mere aftermath, nor latter-day manifestation. Persian poetry goes back to Pehlevi times (3rd to 7th century) if not before, but the great Persian literature that has survived dates from around 900. Persian poetry proper continues down to around 1530, while Persian poetry in India runs from the middle of the 16th to the beginning of the 17th century (Kroeber).

Persian painting is slighter than the poetry, but is not without relevance. Here a truly Persian style did not emerge until the end of the 14th century. While production continued until the early 18th century, the last century or more was merely derivative. Riza-i-Abbasi is accounted the last great painter of Persia (M.S. Dimand), being followed by imitators in quantity but without originality. Riza appears to have lived and worked in the mid- and late 16th century (D.T. Rice).

Four centuries before the beginning of the Russian Evolutionary takes us to around 1470. It was in the reign of Ivan III (1462-1505) that Russia was finally put together and that her destiny took form. The Russia of Kiev had been supplanted by that of the Golden Horde. But from Ivan's day on, it was to be the Russia of Moscow. The subsequent accomplishments of Ivan the Terrible were invariably consummations of things set in motion by his father and above all his grandfather (Ivan III), who was called The Great not on account of his personality (which was uninspiring) nor of any unusual heroism (which is not in evidence) but because of the developments that emerged during his cautious reign.

The official date for the end of the threat of the Golden Horde is usually given as 1481 (Vernadsky gives 1480) with the defeat and despatch of Ahmed. But in fact the depredations had decreased since the 1450s. The critical turning point probably came in 1472, when Ahmed was on the Russian border and "after a brave resistance took the little town of Alexin; but a Russian army estimated at 180,000 men barred his way" (Pares). Hence forward Ivan was able to take a position of open challenge, leading to the ultimate triumph.

Internal developments were of comparable significance. It fell to Ivan III "not only to accelerate the growth of Muscovy but also to invest it with new and important goals" (Harcave). His predecessors had considered themselves princes more or less equal to other Russian princes. But Ivan believed that the title "Grand Duke of Vladimir and all Rus" (won by Ivan I) was more than a symbol: to him it was the legal basis for his claim to being head of the Russian state. Ivan "succeeded in annexing almost all the hitherto independent cities and principalities of northern Russia" (Vernadsky). The key was Novgorod. The absorption of its enormous territory by Moscow "was achieved by different stages between 1465 and 1488. In the time of

Andrew of Vladimir a small Novgorod army could rout an immense force of Volga Russia. These conditions were now reversed" (Pares). There was no single crucial campaign in this struggle, during which Ivan held the advantage by his grip on the hinterland and food supplies, and on his allies within Novgorod.

If there is a turning point it would seem to come as follows: In 1470 Novgorod makes a treaty passing her under the sovereignty of Kasimir, who is to defend Novgorod against Moscow; Novgorod "reclaims its old supremacy over Pskov.... Ivan denounces Novgorod.... In May, 1471, Ivan with well-thought-out dispositions, advances towards Novgorod; not a drop of rain falls this summer, and all the roads are practicable.... Tver and Pskov support Ivan.... Kasimir does nothing.... A large Novgorod levy stands on the Shelon; Ivan's army crosses the stream and with one charge routs it.... A treaty is concluded; Novgorod is the patrimony of Ivan, but the men of Novgorod are free...the Archbishop has to be consecrated in Moscow" (Pares). There is more to the Novgorod story, but the developments of 1470-72 appear to settle the issue.

Meanwhile, in 1472, "before finishing with Novgorod, Ivan had already made himself master of the vast region of Perm near the Urals" (*ibid.*). Yaroslavl had been acquired by voluntary submission in 1463; the long struggle with Tver was concluded with annexation in 1485. The consolidation of Russia under Moscow thus centered around 1470. But this was not merely a consolidation of power. Under the influence of Mongolian ideas, "the Russian state developed on the basis of universal service. All classes of society were made a definite part of the state organization. Taken together, these ideas amount to a peculiar system of state socialism. The political theory developed into a finished plan," says Vernadsky, "in the Moscow Kingdom and the Russian Empire"—a Russian destiny indeed.

In the area of religion appeared another destiny. In 1453 the last emperor of Constantinople had fallen with his city. "His niece Zoe became a ward of the Pope. Ivan III was a widower. The political extinction of Constantinople seemed to Latin minds to offer an opportunity for the reunion of the churches.... The hand of Zoe was now offered to Ivan.... In 1472 Ivan married Zoe, who took the name of Sophia.... The effect of this marriage was exactly the opposite to what the Pope had contemplated. Ivan took up the role of successor of the Greek emperors, the natural champion of the Orthodox Church" (Pares). Remembering that the four-century Overlap signifies the self-recognition of a culture's destiny, we may note C.N. Parkinson's observation that "from 1472, when Ivan III...married the niece of the last emperor of Constantinople...the Russians had been pursuing their imperial destiny as the 'third Rome.'"

Hence was made manifest the call that "the Third Rome, Moscow, stands, and a fourth there will not be." This call was reflected not only in Ivan's choice of Zoe, but also in the new use of the term "tsar", an appeal to succession from the Roman caesars. In the 15th century Grand Princes began tracing family descents back to Roman emperors and while Ivan the Terrible was the first to be crowned "Tsar of Russia", it was his grandfather who was the first to call himself Tsar.

The Graeco-Roman frescos of the 13th and 14th centuries gradually disappeared; they were replaced by a rapidly increasing number of icons on wooden panels. The "pictorial style of Byzantine icon painting yielded more and more to the graphic manner, with its straight lines and sharp contours in drawing, and acquired a flat character" (P. Miliukov). This is not unlike the drastic drawing which emerged in the first authoritative painting of the West: in the Anglo-Irish manuscripts.

The 15th century was "the time when purely Russian forms of roof construction were introduced into the Moscow style" (*ibid.*). Early in the 16th century the Muscovites tired of the dome, and reproduced in stone and brick the pyramid-shaped steeple from the wood tradition; this was quickly mastered, and by the end of the century had supplanted the domed church of Byzantine origin. By the middle of the 16th century, "the principal elements of an original Russian architectural style were definitely established" (*ibid.*). During the 16th century an independent attitude in music also was manifest.

From this time may be dated the subordination of church to state, the tying of the peasant to the land, and the eclipse of the middle class. In the judgment of Ian Grey, Ivan "expanded his realm and unified his people." According to Karamzin, Ivan was "the Great Gatherer of the Russian land." With this unity came the sense of a new mission, a Russian mission. The four-century Overlap entails the dawning of the new culture's sense of destiny, and it has been said that from Ivan came a new sense of Fate.

2. The Two-century Overlap

The second Overlap begins two centuries before the Evolutionary. At this point—for the first time—we can say: there is a Greece; there is a Europe. In the West, the two-century date was 797 AD. Charlemagne was crowned in Rome on Christmas Day of 800. So effective was the new hegemony that "Europe" is widely held to have begun at that time (some astrologers give Europe's birthday as 25 December 800, with Sun in Capricorn and Aries rising; the Sun sign is the same as that of the entire Western culture).

Along with western Germany (Saxony, Bavaria, Carinthia), Charlemagne's empire included Italy down to Monte Cassino, as well as what are now France and the Low Countries. It was the core of the first Europe in the context of the Western culture. From the surviving Palatine Chapel at Aachen, Pevsner dates "the beginning of Western developments" in architecture.

The two-century Overlap reveals a new period of integrated culture, with works of art in many fields, not just a few suggestive types as in the four-century one. The Carolingian cultural "renaissance" was tied in with a new state administration. Charlemagne "set out to reform political and ecclesiastical administration, communications and the calendar, art and literature, and—as a basis for all this—script and language" (Panofsky). Nevertheless, while "the Carolingian *renovatio* pervaded the whole of the empire and left no sphere of civilization untouched," still "it was limited in that it reclaimed lost territory rather than attempting to conquer new lands. It did not transcend a monastic and administrative *Herrenschicht* directly or indirectly connected with the crown; its artistic activities did not include major sculpture in stone" (*ibid.*)—so that there can be no confusion here with the great developments of the 11th century.

Yet this is the moment of emergence of truly ambitious monuments of architecture. Centula (S. Riquier) is dated shortly after 790, the Palace and Palatine Chapel at Aachen from c. 790-805, St Germigny-des-Prés from 806, the S. Gall monastery plan from around 820. These are major monuments and seminal. They do not represent the beginning of an unbroken evolutionary chain, since during the period from 850 or 870 to 970 or 980 there was no progress at all. But they are considerable works and of an authoritative Western stamp.

The Classical two-century Overlap began just after 1300 BC. From this time is dated the misnamed Treasury of Atreus, the last, the most ambitious, and by far the finest of the *tholos* tombs. Here, as in the Palatine Chapel, we see the beginning of something clearly characterizing the coming style of the Evolutionary period. The Treasury of Atreus is "at once powerful and refined. It is inspired by the same spirit that later produced the Parthenon" (*Oxford Companion*).

Overall, around 1300, occurs a "dramatic shift from concentration on impressive burial-chambers to the erection of a number of palace-fortresses" (Finley). The Lion Gate at Mycenae still survives, as well as fortress remains like those to be found at Tiryns, Thebes, and the Athenian acropolis. Such as these "now looked more like medieval fortress-towns than like the open, agglutinative Cretan complexes" (Finley). It is like the difference between the Carolingian and the Merovingian, which was still heavily influenced by late Roman or contemporary Byzantine forms. As with the Treasure of Atreus, the anticipation of coming Evolutionary styles is unmistakable. No one, writes Donald Strong, can look "at the ground plan of the palace of Tiryns, with its ordered succession of courtyards and entrances leading to the megaron, without thinking of classical planning. The megaron form, itself, is connected with that of the later Greek temple."

Above all, this is the time of which we can first say: There is a Greece. "This is essentially the age to which Greek legend looks back; legend preserved partly in Homer's epics, partly in later authors who drew extensively on epics now lost. The 'map' is essentially the same" (A.R. Burn). Around 1300 the Arcadians settled in the central Peloponnesus. The Mycenaean Greeks were known as Achaeans. "It is in the archives of the Hittite capital," says Burn, "that we find our first contemporary reference to Mycenaean Greece. For Greece, with its 'High King' at Mycenae, is almost certainly to be recognized in a kingdom, apparently in the west and connected with the sea"—a kingdom whose name, that is, probably corresponds with Achaea (Finley points out that the evidence is not conclusive, but is accepted by most scholars). The date is very close to 1300.

The succedent two-century Overlap lasted until AD 308. Here we find the last of the truly monumental and comprehensive Roman buildings. The Constantinian Baths, the Porta Nigra, and the Aula

Palatina at Trier all date from around or just after 300. Diocletian's Palace at Split (covering eight acres) was built about 300. These do not represent a stylistic progression from the Evolutionary, which had ended soon after 100 AD. The Arch of Constantine (315) had to borrow its sculpture and decoration from a variety of earlier buildings. Roman building of the later second to early fourth centuries tends to be overinflated and variable in execution. The architects of the period of Maxentius and Constantine showed "a technical ability scarcely inferior to that of Agrippa's or Hadrian's architects.... Yet their work achieved its effect by mere bigness or by the floridity of its decorations, rather than by its good proportions and elegance of details" (Cary & Scullard). This was an aesthetic condition that obtained throughout the two centuries of the succeedent overlap. Early in the third century the Baths of Caracalla show an elevation which is "not unified; its multiplicity of roofs cannot have presented a coherent, logical building"; its design "tries to group as compactly as possible the units for different functions forcing them into a rigid oblong" (Hanfmann). Comparable developments are seen in sarcophagi sculpture. "Toward the end of the third century and during the first decades of the fourth, the disconnected pictorial elements are collected into a new compositional order" (H.P. L'Orange); this new order is no longer organic but merely mechanical.

As the preliminary Overlap revealed for the first time the existence of a "Greece," so the concluding Overlap ends with the disappearance of a "Rome." This was revealed in two notable developments.

(1). For as long as Romans could remember, the sanctity of the Roman state depended on acknowledgement of its tutelary gods, with which other gods might not compete. Suddenly the entire polity was given over to a new and foreign religion, one which had until very recently been proscribed. It was not the Edict of Milan in 313 (tolerating Christianity throughout the Empire), however, which marked this change. Neither was it the "In Hoc Signo" of 312, nor yet the conversion of Constantine himself (who was baptized only on his deathbed). For the change came slightly earlier. The edicts and persecutions of Diocletian and Maximianus had continued down to 309. Then there was an abrupt turnabout in the fortunes of Christianity, and by 311 "Galerius, mortally ill, issued an edict granting freedom of worship to all members of the Christian faith" (M. Grant). At the same time or even before this, Maxentius, the ruler at Rome (306-12), "although himself a devoted adherent of patriotic cults and the banisher of two Christian bishops, restored to the church its property that had been confiscated during the persecutions" (*ibid.*).

(2). The end of Rome as the locus of the Classical empire is likewise seen in the reorganization of the Imperial structure and in the removal of its capital from Rome to Constantinople. Since the reorganization of the Empire is attributable both to Diocletian and Constantine, a mid-point may be placed somewhere around 300. The dedication of Constantinople as the new capital did not take place until 330; but for some time before this the emperors had been spending less and less time in Rome—even to the point of setting up de facto centers of administration elsewhere—so that the official siting of the new capital must be taken as the formal conclusion of a longer process. Construction had been begun in 325, and this was only after the choice of the new site, which was geographically superior to that of Nicomedia, which had for some time satisfied the need of an eastern capital (D.R. Dudley). The end of Rome as an organization and a central location may then be dated to the years surrounding AD 300.

The two-century Overlap following the conclusion of the Levantine Evolutionary epoch was scheduled to end around 1370. At this time we observe the last of originality, monumentality, and structural impressiveness in Islamic architecture. At Granada, the Alhambra was built during the middle part of the 14th century; at Cairo the Mosque of Sultan Hasan was built 1356-63, the Mosque of Sultan Barquq 1384. Such buildings were still truly monumental. After them, although details and decoration might continue to be refined, the structural elements became attenuated; although technical skill might continue in evidence, there was a tendency to repair and embellish existing structures. The Mosque of Ahmed I, in Istanbul (early 17th century) is derivative from Hagia Sophia; the Taj Mahal (mid-17th century), while from all accounts authentically beautiful, lacks any sense of weight or mass.

The end of Islam as a cultural power was marked by the ascendancy of the Ottoman Turks. The Ottoman empire was to endure until 1922, but its forte was politics, and its politics chiefly military; even its bureaucracy was a farce, and the Ottomans "all along had nothing beside their magnificent military organization" (Runciman). The Ottoman takeover was gradual, but certain key points are telling. In 1345 the Ottomans first crossed into Europe; in 1354 they took Gallipoli and spread rapidly over Thrace (W. Langer). In 1359 they took Angora (Ankara) and in 1362 Adrianople, which after 1402 became the capital of the empire. Thus their dominions extended from central Anatolia into Europe. The key reign appears to have been that of Murad I, from about 1361 until 1389; during this time the Ottoman State became the leading power in Anatolia and the Balkans. Around this time originated the Janissaries, the elite corps of the Ottoman army, which was to gain enormous power, including that of making and unmaking sultans. In the year 1371, Murad's suzerainty was recognized by the rulers of Bulgaria, Macedonia, and the Byzantine Empire.

For the Russian culture, the precedent two-century Overlap began in 1668. Here was a critical time in the development of the Russian state. Since 1648 the Cossacks had sustained rebellion against Poland, which was at war with Sweden part of the time, while the rebels received aid from Moscow. Forced to ask "for an armistice at last, in 1667, the Poles signed an agreement with the Russians" acknowledging Russian "retention of that part of the Ukraine lying east of the Dnieper and to Russian occupation of Kiev for two years"—Kiev was to be returned but this did not happen. "The acquisition of the eastern Ukraine and Kiev...was to have far-reaching consequences for Russia. It was the first successful step toward the acquisition of the whole of the Ukraine. It placed Russia on the border of the Ottoman Empire" (Harcave)—much as Charlemagne had carried his border to the Moors and Saracens. To Vernadsky, "the union with Ukraine was a very important event in the political history of Russia. It made the Moscow tsar the nominal tsar of all Russia and, moreover, gave Moscow a decisive superiority over Poland. Poland could not agree to the loss of the Ukraine without war." When this ended in 1667 the issue was resolved; "Moscow abandoned its claims to Lithuania, but retained Smolensk and acquired the left bank of the Dnieper as well as the city of Kiev."

According to Pares, "this treaty marked an epoch in the relations between Russia and Poland.... From this time onwards it was the policy of Russia rather to support Poland, of whom she was no longer afraid." That is, from this time may be dated the ascendency of Russia and the descendancy of Poland. But it was the formation of the core area of the Russian culture into a state that was the signal event (just as Charlemagne had formed a state of the core area of Europe). This was indicated not only by the acquisition of the Ukraine and of the area of Smolensk and Kiev, but by the conversion of the tsar of Moscow into "the nominal tsar of all Russia."

The political developments were attended by a new sense that now there is a Russia, just as around 800 the new European consciousness had emerged. "During this period there lived in Russia a notable Croatian scholar, Yury Krizhanich, a man with a mission of uniting the Slavs, who on coming to Russia in 1659 declared 'I have come to the Tsar of my race, and to my own people.' He rendered great services to Russian culture, especially by his studies in language, which is the one great bond between all Slavonic peoples; and he urged" on the Orthodox Russian "more character and more self-reliance so that he could stand his own ground" (Pares). In the same period the practice of levying foreign troops gave way to that of securing Western military instructors to train Russian troops.

Again in this period, the "foreigner who came into Russia had, as a matter of course, to be treated far better than there was any need to treat a home-bred clerk or officer. He had to have a higher salary, European conditions of personal freedom, and a guarantee of free exit. This of itself provoked an instinctive patriotic revulsion." And Pares finds here already the "antithesis of Europe and Russia, of the Westernizers who wish to bring in wholesale what is so obviously better, and the Slavophiles who fear to lose their souls in wholesale imitation of the foreigner." Here was the beginning of that Slavophile cultural consciousness which was to lead to Danilevsky's *Russia and Europe*. The Overlap was the two centuries in between.

We have examined the extraordinary outburst of creative activities in Russia during the 1860s, activities in themselves sufficient to suggest the inception of Russia's Evolutionary epoch. Further evidence supplied by the Inaugurations, the Anticipations, and the Overlaps enable us now to confirm the beginning of the Russian Evolutionary schedule at 1866.

D. The Meaning of Numbers

With certain exceptions—such as the 640-year Inauguration or the 110-year Anticipation—all the configurations so far investigated are built upon the harmonic "century" of 99 years. This 99 reduces to eighteen and then to Nine, the number of Pluto, denoting the definitive. The keyword for Nine, according to Lloyd Cope, is "completion". Each 99-year century, then, is a complete and self-defining unit.

The overall span of the major culture is forty centuries. Forty reduces to Four, the number of Saturn. Saturn governs time, especially time as dynamic structure. The overall time span of the major culture, then, is represented by Father Time himself. But Saturn is also the planet of limitation. The forty-century span represents the outer limits of a major culture. Before the forty centuries begin there exist nothing but unlocated intimations of what is to come; after they end, there remains nothing but echoes.

The first inauguration period begins ten centuries before the Evolutionary epoch (the period on which all others are keyed). The ten-century Inauguration represents the new people or peoples, on whom the incipient culture is based. Ten in graphic form (10) can mean marriage (Cirlot); and the family is the foundation of a people. Ten can be composed of several additions, but the primary composition is One plus Nine. One is the number of the Sun, signifying creative power; Nine is that of Pluto, meaning the sex and regeneration that produce a new people. Furthermore, Ten reduces to One, here meaning activation or germination. The term germinal means the earliest stage of development or activity.

The second inauguration period is 640 years. The number 640 also reduces to One (six plus four equals ten which becomes One) and likewise represents the principles of inception and of taking into its own (One: the Sun). But the 640 is composed of a Six and a Four which count in themselves. Four is the number of Saturn, representing foundation and organization. Six is the number of Jupiter, representing philosophy and religion, notably in the sense of faith and religious doctrine. The 640 Inauguration is distinguished by the establishment of the religious consciousness of the incipient culture, by the inauguration of religious institutions and doctrine, by the implanting and the implementation of the new religion.

The 110-year Anticipation embodies the number Eleven—an auspicious number (like Seven), and one that corresponds to Neptune. This anticipation is distinguished by developments prophesying certain characteristics of the coming culture, characteristics which will appear fully developed in the Evolutionary epoch (which it anticipates). For example, the Levantine 110 mark anticipates religious developments; the Western, dynastic structures; the Russian, literature and science. Neptune signifies ideals and spiritual vision, imagination and precognition, dreams and prophecy. Thus certain special qualities of the new culture are auspiciously (Eleven) previewed (Neptune) in the 110-year Anticipation.

The quarter-century Anticipation gives us a fraction; this is significant in that the common denominator (of 1/4, 2/4, and 3/4) is Four, which is Saturn's number and denotes time especially in the sense of rhythmic beat. The interval between each of these anticipations is 1/4 century—that is, 25%. Twenty-five reduces to Seven. Among the varied meanings of Seven is its role as a lucky number. In this it is like Eleven: Both are auspicious (Eleven especially in the sense of an omen or prophecy when favorable). That Seven and Eleven are "lucky" is reflected in the imagery of dice games (which go back at least to the Babylonians and Egyptians). The sense of good auspice is essential to both the 110-year and quarter-century Anticipations. Unlike the Inaugurations and the Overlaps, which are periods (though without the regularity of directed development seen in the Evolutionary epoch), the Anticipations are breakthroughs whose new vision may or may not be followed up. They are points marked by events of good auspice.

The four-century Overlap is governed by Saturn, which in this connection stands for solid foundation, orderly arrangement, tangible achievement, fundamentals, building, and discipline. The four-century Overlap shows the first appearance of disciplined works (e.g. the Anglo-Irish manuscripts) and integrated systems (e.g. the Muscovite monarchy). Saturn also designates limitation or limits. The four-century Overlaps—precedent and succedent—define the most clearly self-limited period (outside the Evolutionary itself) of the major culture. Thus the Greco-Roman culture appears as an integrated whole from Mycenaean times until the deposition of the last Roman emperor of the West (476) or the termination of Latin literature around 500.

The two-century Overlap presents the number Two, governed by the Moon. According to Lloyd Cope the number Two signifies union, receptivity, cooperation, absorption. The two-century Overlap marks the inception of an integrated culture—not merely some integrated systems, as in the four-century Overlap—and of creative works in unified areas, all of which require cooperation and absorption. The Moon also has to do with the home, especially in the inward sense. With the precedent two-century Overlap, there first appears the sense of identity of a home-land (Charlemagne's Europe), and with the succedent Overlap this dissolves (the removal of the classical capital from Rome to Constantinople).

The Evolutionary epoch constitutes the basic time system of the major culture: All other chronological breakdowns are measured against it. If we measure the two-century overlap against the twelve-century Evolutionary period, we find a 1:6 ratio. Six is the number of Jupiter; but it appears now in a different role from that in the 640 anticipation. Jupiter is the planet of expansion. The first great expansion of the West began with the Vikings at the end of the 8th century. The expansiveness of Roman architecture continued down to Diocletian's palace at Spalato (c. 300), the Basilica Nova in Rome (began by Maxentius, finished c. 313 by Constantine), and the great structures in Trier around 300. Despite the lack of originality in these late works, a certain amount of experimentation was still in evidence. But shortly after 300 the Jupiterian expansiveness was over: Later monuments of Roman architecture are few and meager by comparison.

Taking the entire forty-century span of a major culture, we find three major epochs: the Germinative epoch of ten centuries, the Evolutionary epoch of twelve centuries, and the Redundant epoch of eighteen centuries. The symbolic significance of the Germinative's ten centuries has been discussed, in terms of the Inauguration.

The Evolutionary epoch is characterized by rhythmic orders of evolution. It is the only epoch, for example, to which apply the quarter-century marks of Anticipation. This epoch is highly ordered within itself, being composed of two six-century halves, three four-century epicycles, and six two-century periods (Romanesque, Gothic, Renaissance, Baroque, and so on). Furthermore it is the only epoch to which the astrological signs apply: one to each of the Evolutionary centuries. Twelve is the number of cosmic order, as signified by the Twelve Tribes of Israel or the Twelve Apostles, which also correspond to the zodiacal signs.

The eighteen centuries of the Redundant epoch reduce to the number Nine. Nine is the number of completion and fulfillment and may stand for a complete cycle of growth (Javane and Bunker) or for the completion of a cycle, as is its force here. The Redundant is the epoch that perpetuates and transmits what was inaugurated in the first ten centuries and systematically developed in the next twelve. The force of a culture's Redundant epoch is a potential force. It can create minor civilizations of its own (such as China's T'ang or Sung periods) if there is no intrusion of another major culture. If there is, then this Redundant force may appear in the form of "renaissances", that is, minor yet significant rebirths within the context of another major culture, such as the Classical renaissances in Byzantium and later in Western Europe. Regeneration belongs to Pluto, the planet corresponding to the number Nine.

Number has long been recognized as lying at the base of the physical sciences. It is time to recognize the importance of number for the historical sciences. Like the study of order in the structure of atom and galaxy, the study of harmonics in history can only increase our sense of wonder. Not wonder at the ingenuity of our schemes or at the power of science, for these are simply crude tools used toward glimpsing the cosmic creative order. But wonder at the beauty and clarity, the simplicity and force, the intelligence and purpose that underlie historical process, whose configurations we have only recently begun to discern.

IV

The Astrological Month

The precession of the equinoxes produces a sequence of astrological periods usually called the Months of the Great Year. Unlike the major cultures, which belong to certain areas only, the astrological Month affects life throughout the globe. And unlike the dating of structures within the major culture, which is regular and precise to within a year or so, the dating of the Months and of the Great Year is susceptible of certain variations.

These variations are caused by astronomical factors which do not concern us here. But the range may be seen in a sample of estimates of the duration of the Great Year. Among ancient sources, the Great Pyramid gives 25,827½, Plato gives 25,920. Among modern investigators, Vera Reid gives "approximately 25,800"; Charles Jayne and Max Heindel both give 25,868; Dane Rudhyar 25,900. Jayne's figure is an estimate for the present; he gives ranges for the Precession from 25,413.6 to 25,976 years. Where astronomers and astrologers cannot agree, the task of the historian is to find a serviceable solution. This is attained by empirical testing of the twelve sub-ages of each Month.

The Astrological Month   175

The sub-ages turn out to be 179 years in length, so that the Month comes out very close to 2150 years, and the Precession approximately 25,800.

It should be emphasized that these figures are approximations of astronomical phenomena: They are not categorical figures such as are often to be found within the structure of a major culture. Not being categorical, they are not exact nor can they be symbolic in themselves. But the essential periods which they outline are of considerable interest, both in regard to the tendencies of world history, and through comparison with the structural composition of the major cultures.

It is from the major cultures that we see the rationale for the astrological Month and its sub-ages. A cycle of the major cultures begins with Aquarius (e.g., the Russian) and ends with Capricorn (e.g. the Western). The twelve centuries of the Evolutionary epoch of a major culture begin with Capricorn and run backward to Aquarius. While the most internally logical of zodiacs begins with cardinal fire and ends with mutable water, this is by no means the only zodiac that has meaning nor the only one that has been used. Of the old Jewish zodiacs, some go clockwise (though most go counterclockwise, as do ours today); at least one starts with Cancer (with some others the starting sign is uncertain); and there are certain Mithraic zodiacs that begin with Aquarius and end with Capricorn.

The principle of a large cycle moving in one direction with sub-ages moving in the other has already been seen in the major cultures and their Evolutionary centuries. This principle is the key to the sub-ages of the astrological Month. For while the cycle of Months of the Great Year runs backwards from Aquarius to Pisces, the cycle of twelve sub-ages within each Month runs forward from Pisces to Aquarius. It is from the character and terminals of the sub-ages that we are able to identify the structure of the astrological Month and to identify its own terminals. This enables us to locate the beginning of the Age of Aquarius, a topic of more than topical interest.

It is natural that an astronomical period of around 2150 years will have termini neither so clear nor so regular as the termini of a categorical period such as an Evolutionary century of 99 years. Nevertheless we can establish a calendar for the astrological month which is accurate to within a few years. The dates given are therefore meant as (a) the closest that demonstration provides, and (b) approximate rather than categorical.

From the evidence (which will be given) we conclude that the Age of Aquarius, or the Aquarian Month, began about 1962. The main support for this date comes from the structure of the sub-ages, but a brief indication of the appropriateness of this approximate date may be entertained. For one thing, it was in the 1960s that there emerged a consciousness of the very question of the precessional Months and especially of the import of the new Age of Aquarius. Among specific and responsible studies are the books of Vera Reid and Dane Rudhyar (addressed largely to these problems) both published in 1969. And in 1967 appeared the musical show *Hair* with its symptomatic song "Aquarius".

In political and social spheres the Aquarian principle is likely to be manifested in large public movements, especially those involving the ideas of equality, brotherhood, and reform. Uranian phenomena such as unrest and protest are also likely to appear. A few examples must suffice. In 1960 the Greensboro (N.C.) "sit-ins" set the stage for desegregation. In 1964 President Johnson outlined his "war on poverty"; and the poll tax was made unconstitutional by the 24th Amendment. The year 1965 saw the civil rights demonstration and enforcement at Selma, Alabama, and President Johnson outlined his program for the Great Society. The year 1966 saw the founding of N.O.W., the Supreme Court decision in Miranda versus Arizona (the right to counsel and to remain silent), and the election of the first black U.S. Senator (Brooke).

In Africa, the years from 1957 to 1967 saw a shift from white-controlled to black-controlled governments in most countries (government by and for the people). In China, 1965-8 saw the Great Proletarian Cultural Revolution, which was not cultural at all but an attempt to introduce collective leadership into the dictatorship. In 1962 Japan, one of the most disciplined and voluntarily regimented of societies, saw a protest march by 6,000 students, and in 1965 student disorders began in Korea, disorders which were to become chronic.

In other areas, Aquarius is manifested in space-age ideas, technologies, and explorations. While much of the 20th century has been involved in a growing consciousness of outer space, and while technology has its own timetables, nevertheless the cluster of activities around the 1960s appears too strong to be treated as casual. Briefly: The Soviet Sputnik was launched in 1957 (first man-made satellite); 1958 saw establishment of U.S. National Aeronautics and Space Administration (NASA) and U.S. Pioneer went 70,000 miles into space and returned; 1961—Gagarin the first man to orbit the earth, Shepard the first American in space; 1962—Glenn the first American to orbit the earth; U.S. *Telstar* the first communications satellite; U.S. launched unmanned craft for Venus; 1963—the United Nations declaration of principles to govern the exploration and use of outer space; 1964—U.S. craft relays photographs of Mars; 1965—the first commercial communications satellite which would prove very important in international communication; the first Russian and the first American walk in space; the French launch their first satellite; the U.S. executes the first space rendezvous; 1966—Soviets make first unmanned landing on moon; U.S. launches first weather reporting satellite and achieves first successful docking in space; 1967—U.N.-sponsored Treaty on the Exploration and Use of Outer Space is signed; Russians land a first capsule on Venus; 1968—U.S. orbits the moon with a manned craft; 1969—Americans walk on the moon.

Such a cluster of record-breaking accomplishments in space seems too concentrated, as well as too unprecedented to signify merely another stage in world technological development. All these events are Aquarian or Uranian in character (e.g., they are "breakthroughs"), and they belong to a dozen years or so surrounding the scheduled year of 1962.

Some small part, at least, of the difficulties people have had in identifying the beginning of the Aquarian Month lies in the fact the last sub-age of the Piscean Month is an Aquarian period (the last sub-age of any Month is an Aquarian period). For two centuries now world history has exhibited certain Aquarian tendencies, but those from the 1780s to the 1960s belong to the old Aquarian sub-age, whereas those since the 1960s belong to the new Aquarian Month. Indications as to the new Aquarian Month have been given; a discussion of the Aquarian sub-age, however, will be left to the end of the analysis of the twelve sub-ages of the Piscean Month, for these sub-ages make most sense when taken in order.

The following periods will be given as lasting 179 years (the closest approximation we can make), except for the first and second periods, which are longer. This is done in order to bring the Piscean Month closer to 2150 years (itself the most serviceable approximation), and also to provide a more rounded date for the beginning of so vast an age as is an astrological Month.

The Piscean Period, 190 - 10 BC

In this first period of the Piscean Month we are confronted with the incidence of a Piscean period within a Piscean age. The qualities of the one must be distinguished from those of the other. Those belonging to the entire age—lasting for over two millennia—are not only more enduring but deeper and more pervasive. Belonging to the entire age are such features as baptism by water, religious fanaticism and renunciation, self-pity and self-undoing, an underlying emotional turbulence, and symbols like the fish or the ship at sea. Features like these may be found from the second century BC until our own time. As against these, certain more transient features can be identified with the Piscean sub-age belonging to the first two centuries BC.

Pisces is a water sign, and this period seems to show an unusual taste for the flow, power, and supply of water. The Romans, around 100 BC, were the first to use waterpower to mill flour and in 16 BC a vertical waterwheel was described by a Roman engineer. Also around 100 BC the Chinese developed the navigational compass and reached India for the first time. In 81 BC the Japanese began a vast shipbuilding program in an effort to provide more seafood. The two supreme political crises of the period were related to water: Caesar crossed the Rubicon in 49 BC, and the battle of Actium (31 BC) was a sea battle. Rome built her first high-level aqueduct in 144 BC. A culmination of this species (though not a conclusion) was the Pont du Gard at Nimes, probably from 19 BC. Sewage disposal by water flow also became highly developed by the Romans during this period. While the largest Roman "Baths" were to come later they were actually multi-purpose emporiums; the Bath as a structure for bathing had its main beginnings in known works such as the Stabian Baths of the second century and the Forum Baths of the first century, both at Pompeii (there were four public baths at Pompeii, placed at main intersections).

The Punic Wars do not belong to this period, but the final destruction of Carthage (a deliberate and unnecessary program) does: Cato's motto began in 150, and Carthage was destroyed in 146. Fanaticism and dissolution are both Piscean traits. The second and first centuries BC were also the period of the three great Servile Wars of Rome—that is, the great slave rebellions, of whose leaders Spartacus is the best known. Pisces means to serve or suffer.

Pisces also can mean indulgence, and it is noteworthy that in this period the Romans, who were still strongly imbued with republican virtues, nevertheless began to introduce Eastern indulgences, notably in a taste for luxury and for cuisine (the adjective "Lucullan" dates from the first century BC).

This Piscean period also appears to have been marked by more or less secret societies, most famous being the Essenes (who believed in purification through baptism). The Essenes originated in the second century BC and culminated in the training of John the Baptist, Mary, and Jesus. Secrecy and mystery, as well as cleanliness and redemption, are Piscean proclivities.

The Aries Period, 10 BC - 172 AD

Aries is the cardinal fire sign: active and eruptive. The first century AD saw the burning of Rome (in 64) and the eruption of Vesuvius after sixteen years of violent earthquakes. It was the period of gladiatorial combat, an egregiously Arian practice which was to be abolished by Constantine—the Colosseum was dedicated in 80 AD. It was also a period of violent martyrdoms, of which those of Jesus, James, and Paul merely head the list. But these were not Christian (i.e. Eastern) martyrs only, for there were many Stoic (i.e. Western) ones as well.

While most of the periods of the Piscean Month have been warlike, this Arian period (ruled by Mars) seems particularly so. The time from Tiberius to Domitian was called by Tacitus "The Terror." The Jewish Wars ranged from 67—leading to the destruction of the Temple and the Masada—to 135, ending in the sack of Jerusalem. In 167 began the first full-scale barbarian attack on Rome.

But Aries does not mean war and destruction only. It is also the sign of new activities, of initiating projects, and of independence. In 9 AD the battle of the Teutoburger Wald established the independence of the Teutonic tribes (and the Rhine as the boundary between Latin and German lands). Among new cities and communities, London was founded in 43, Cologne in 50, while Paris (a fishing village taken by Caesar in 52) began to develop into a city. With the ministries of Jesus and Paul one of the world's great religious—and militant—movements was initiated.

The Taurus Period, 172 - 351

Taurus is the money sign. In 193 the Roman Imperium was literally sold, for the first time, to the highest bidder. During the third and fourth centuries the Empire was dominated by rich landowners, who as senators were exempt from taxes (they worked outside the Senate, which was without political power); smaller landowners were charged with providing recruits for the legions. Taurus rules land and property, of which money is the symbol of value.

Taurus is the most fixed of the "fixed" signs. It was under Diocletian that the economy was fixed: Not only prices and wages but even professions were strictly controlled. All this was furthered by Constantine, who likewise "fixed" external peace, internal unity, and a new coinage, along with which came material prosperity (a Taurean desideratum). Taurean stability is seen not only in the Constantinian settlement in the West but also in the East: In 320 began the Gupta Dynasty, which unified India after long divisions. In Persia, Ardashir (226-240) established a strongly centralized nation.

The Gemini Period, 351 - 530

Gemini is the most dual of the signs, being symbolized by the Twins. This period is distinguished by dualities. In 395 the Roman Empire split into its Eastern and Western halves (Constantinople and Milan). The split was thought to be temporary but proved not; the Western empire ended in 476 at Ravenna. Though the split between the Eastern and Western churches had a long history and was not final until the ninth century, it actually began in the fifth century (schism of

484 - 519). And the Far East showed a comparable tendency: between 317 and 589 China was divided into North and South.

Amongst the theological controversies of the period it is probably significant that the Nestorians sharply divided the role of Jesus Christ into two natures (truly man and truly God), and that Augustine sharply opposed the actual and the ideal in Christianity. But the main significance of the theological controversies of the period seems to lie in the fact that they were controversies and that they tended to invoke abstruse distinctions (the Arians and the Monophysites as well as the Nestorians and others)—abstruseness and distinctions being highly palatable to the Geminian with his mercurian and intellectual bent.

The Cancer Period, 530 - 709

Cancer is the family sign. Feudalism is a family business when considered as containment on the land, as vassalage, family "feuds", mutual loyalties, and protection by the older or stronger in exchange for service by the younger or weaker. In its later flowering, feudalism involved chivalry and courtly codes which signify the Libra period (1067-1246). But feudalism was Cancerian in its family-like, protective origins. The beginnings of feudalism in the West can be traced to the seventh century, and were interrupted by Charlemagne's centralizing and anti-feudal tendencies of the Leonine period.

Cancer is cardinal water; cardinal means directed action. In the seventh century the Byzantines invented or developed "Greek fire," which was used with critical importance in sea battles and in defense of Constantinople. "Greek fire" amounted to jets of liquid fire which are said to have burned in water. It sounds Cancerian, as does certainly the concept of a canal, which also involves directed water. In 605 the Chinese Grand Canal, an astonishing enterprise, was completed; in 610 it was extended to Hangchow.

Most striking of all Cancerian traits during this period is what Rudhyar has called the search for the homeland. Cancer can mean houses or lands, basing or removal. The search for the home is a matter of mass consciousness; it raises the question whether to stay in or to leave the birthplace. Assimilation is its aim.

The sixth and seventh centuries marked the end of the nomadic restlessness of the preceding Geminian Period. Now came the final movements of the Western peoples and their establishment in new homes. In 563 Columba started a monastery on Iona and began to convert the Picts; in the ensuing century and a half four Scottish kingdoms were established. In 568 the Lombard Kingdom was founded. In 584 Mercia (the new Anglo-Saxon kingdom) was founded. In 687 Venice elected her first Doge and began her rise to power; also in 687 was achieved the unification of Austrasia (the eastern Frankish lands, or Germany) and Neustria (the western, or France). The seventh century saw the beginning of English nationality, and the emergence of French and German language differences. And in the seventh century the Bulgarian empire was founded by people settling in districts south of the Danube, while the Slavs settled in the Balkans.

In the Far East, Japan adopted Nara as its permanent capital (the capital belongs to Cancer): previously a new capital had gone with each new ruler. But the most impressive Cancerian developments came in the Near East, with Byzantium and Islam. Under Justinian (527-65) Byzantium gave up its experimenting in Italy, Africa, France (the old Roman imperial territories) and found its proper home. Church membership became confined to the boundaries of the Byzantine Empire. Justinian's reign coincided with the birth of a distinctive Byzantine culture, and the emergence of a distinctive way of life. During this period Byzantium survived enormous external pressures in great part because of her vast economic resources, which were based on land, commerce, and high-quality industry—Cancerian matters.

During the same period, Islam settled what was to be its essential homeland. By 642 Egypt was conquered, and Persia in the following year. 708-11 saw the pacification of North Africa, and 708-15 of the Sind and part of the Punjab. In 711 the Moors began their settlement of Iberia—but this was to be the the end. In 717-18 the seige of Constantinople failed, and in 732 the Moors were turned back from France to Spain. Later Islamic conquests (notably from the 10th century on) were to be attained under Turkish leadership, but this means another people.

The Leo Period, 709 - 888

Leo bespeaks power, central concentration, dominance. In the West, the concentration of power that was to mark the Carolingian dynasty may be dated from Pepin's election as king in 752; the Donation of Pepin in 756 established the Papal States and marked the beginning of the temporal power of the papacy. As for the Carolingian empire, not since the ancient Roman dominion had there been a centralized, constructive power covering the larger part of Europe—nor has there been an enduring one since. The character of the Carolingian court and culture was Leonine: the monumentality of its architecture; the splendor of other arts; the generous patronage of literature, theology, education; the quality of crafts; the power of administration. "Only Carolingian emperors had dominion in Western Europe; German Holy Roman emperors never did" (Rushton Coulborn).

Carolingian power correlated closely with the Leonine period. Pepin became Mayor of the Palace in 741; by 751 he had deposed the last of the Merovingian kings. Charles the Great continued the Frankish (and Leonine) policy of expansion and consolidation until all Europe from Brittany to Rome was included in the empire (not included were Spain beyond the Spanish March, Britain, and Scandinavia). He continued the process of centralization, systematized the army, and inaugurated military service. By the 10th century, the Carolingians were suffering declining power; in the meantime they had enjoyed an impressively Leonine imperium.

Leonine too were the early years of the Abbasid Caliphate, at least from its founding in 750 down to the Carmathian revolt which began in 891. Despite rebellions and losses, the Abbasid dynasty was marked by a social strength and creative power evocative of Leo. Baghdad was founded in 762. Al-Mahdi (775-85) fortified major centers, founded towns and schools, and encouraged the arts. Harun al-Rashid (785-809) made of Baghdad the center of Arabic culture, exchanged gifts with Charlemagne, and began diplomatic relations with T'ang China; his splendor became legendary in the *Arabian Nights*. An even more glorious reign may have been that of Mamun the Great (813-33), during which the arts and sciences were generously endowed, observatories and libraries were established, translations were made from Greek and Persian, Syriac and Sanskrit, and a generous religious attitude prevailed. Al-Mu'tasim (833-42) transferred the capital to Samarra, and formed a standing military corps. Mu'tamind (870-92) transferred the court to Baghdad and established power over the Turkish guard. Thus concluded the Moslem period of Leonine centrality and luminosity, creativity and splendor, power and glory.

In China, the Leonine period was occupied by the greater part of the T'ang dynasty (618-907). "Emerging slowly from the post-Han chaos, the new imperial dynasty guided China through the most brilliant and refined age any civilization had ever known" (de Riencourt). T'ang evokes Leo in many respects. The general reputation of T'ang art is one of extrovert character, of vivid beauty and gorgeous splendor. Laurence Sickman refers to the "monumental, solid grandeur" of the T'ang manner. And elsewhere he notes that the "ponderous majesty of an emperor, the frail emaciation of an ascetic, the poise and well-groomed refinement of a court beauty, no less than the spirit of a high-bred horse, were challenging subjects which the T'ang artist attacked with confidence. Their art is lucid, balanced, and at once elegant and solid." Everything in this description, except the frail emaciation of the ascetic, smacks of Leo.

T'ang had begun in the 7th century (before the Leonine period) but it was not until the 8th century that painting compositions became filled with architecture, figures, and landscape suitable to the broad expanse of wall and the grander scale that was evolving. The great names in T'ang painting were those of the court painters; the court in this sense is Leonine with its monarchical connection, and these painters were not servile but were particularly gifted individuals distinguished by creative genius. Also there was a premium on Leonine fame, which included the most famous name in all Chinese art, Wu Tao-tzu.

The fire signs are inclined to sports and warfare. In Sung (which occupied the Virgo and Libra periods), the soldier "lost all esteem" while the "philosopher and the man of letters were reputed to be the real leaders"; in this later period "academic life and the examination system reached their peak" and the emperors were occupied in particular with the maintenance of peace. But the T'ang dynasty was one "of a warlike complexion" (William Cohn), as were the Abbasid Caliphate and the Carolingian empire.

The Nelson Gallery-Atkins Museum, Kansas City, Mo.

Plate VII
"A Solitary Temple amid Clearing Peaks," attributed to Li Ch'eng, 919-967, Sung Dynasty.

The Virgo Period, 888 - 1067

In China this period covers the time of the Five Dynasties (906-60) and the early part of Northern Sung (960-1127). The Five Dynasties followed the breakup of T'ang, together marking an era of Virgoan fragmentation. For "in reality, not only the five dynasties after which the period is named, but a much larger number succeeded each other on the throne. Governors and generals not infrequently proclaimed themselves masters of their provinces and founded independent states" (Cohn).

Meanwhile the 10th century was "also the century of the giants of landscape painting" (Sickman), indeed to such an extent that the landscapists "of the period of the *Five Dynasties* are cited in all Chinese writings on art as pioneers" (Cohn). In a word, if we think of Chinese landscape we think of Sung, and Sung landscape both originated and excelled in the 10th century. There is probably a correlation here with Virgo. For landscape is an "earth" subject, and is especially pronounced in cultures or periods governed by an earth sign—the landscape art of the Capricornian West in general, or of its Taurean 19th century in particular. In 10th century China, we may assume something of the earth sign Virgo was expressed.

Plate VII   Moreover, the character of this landscape art was Virgoan in what has been described as its "tangled masses of leafless, dormant trees, and lonely temples reached by tortuous and narrow paths" (Sickman). A small landscape painting of the last quarter of the 10th century (signed by Yen Wen-kuei) "may be taken as characteristic of the grand manner of early Northern Sung. A basic mountain shape of precipitous sides and weather-rounded top crowned by dense vegetation is repeated" in what amounts to "an infinity of varied shapes, minor ridges, deep gorges, and winding mountain paths.... All the surfaces are closely textured with small ink dabs and washes running the entire tonal gamut. Waterfalls appear as thin white lines against black gorges. Details are explicit and descriptive, as with the small traveller on a donkey" and so on. "If such a development was the contribution of the later 10th century, then by the early 11th, landscape was well on its way to becoming a vehicle for intimate, personal expression" (Sickman). Terms cited above such as dense vegetation, infinity of varied shapes, minor, closely textured, small, thin lines, intimate—all suggest Virgo more than any other sign.

In the West, the unity and monumentality of Carolingian times was followed in the Virgo period by the political fragmentation and cultural differentiation which marked the 10th and 11th centuries. The East Frankish line of the Carolingians came to an end with the death of Louis the Child in 911. The weakening of the royal power "left the way open for the emergence of the Stem duchies" (W. Langer). Stem means tribal; the result was an "independent development under semi-royal dukes" for the most part. It represented a disruption of German unity which was to last a long time. In 919 began the Saxon, or Ottonian House.

Meanwhile the Western Franks chose differing directions. In 888 Odo, count of Paris, was elected king by one faction; another chose Charles the Simple, who died in 923, "the last Carolingian with any real authority in France" (Langer). In 899 Alfred the Great died after a 28-year reign, in which he had accomplished much that has a Leonine ring: he forced the Danes to withdraw, "consolidated England round his kingdom, ...compiled the best laws of earlier kings, and encouraged learning by bringing famous scholars to Wessex" (James Trager).

In 911 Charles III granted Rollo (Hrolf the Ganger) a larger part of what was to be Normandy. The colony was recruited "with fresh settlers from Scandinavia for the best part of a century, and was able to retain a strong local individuality" (Langer), so furthering the Virgoan fragmentation. Even within itself, from this time until the accession of William the Conqueror "Norman history is fragmentary" (Langer).

In the arts it was much the same. In place of the term Carolingian, which covered the whole central part of Europe, we must now make reference to the traditions of the various provinces, or of the Ottonian areas. It was not until the later 11th century that we can speak of Romanesque in the sense of a Western-wide style.

During the Virgo period in the Levant, a new fragmentation appeared in the establishment of the Ziyarids (in Tabaristan, Jurjan, Hamadhan) as independent sovereigns during the years 928-1024. With the rise of the Buwayhids (923-1025) came the division of Persia and Iraq, which dominions then fell piecemeal through divisions among their rulers. Meanwhile in Syria and Mesopotamia four Arab dynasties and one Kurdish one held sway (Langer). Even the astonishing Seljuks were unable to consolidate an enduring empire; they entered Baghdad in 1055 and broke the Byzantine power in 1071, but by 1092 a civil war broke out between the Sultan and his brother, and separate branches of the Seljuk family gained virtual independence in differing parts of the empire.

The Libra Period, 1067 - 1246

The Crusades began in 1095 when Pope Urban proclaimed a crusade to defeat the infidel and to liberate the Holy Land. Liberation is a Libran ideal, indeed Libra means free. These journeys in the name of freedom (for all their ulterior purposes) continued down through the seventh Crusade (1248-54), which failed, and the eighth, which was cut short by the death of Saint Louis (a ninth Crusade was abortive).

A related Libran activity of the period was the rise of the knightly brotherhoods (brotherhood in the sense of a particular society is Libran). The Knights Templars (Knights of the Temple of Solomon) originated about 1118 in a band united for the protection of pilgrims. The Knights Hospitalers (Order of the Hospital of St. John of Jerusalem) emerged around 1120 to care for pilgrims in the Holy Land. The Teutonic Knights were founded 1190-91, modelled on the first two. Later such orders turned to power, conquest, even piracy, but in the early days they appear to have been inspired by Libran ideals.

Provencal troubadour poetry flourished from c. 1100 to c. 1230. Its main theme was a somewhat mannered courtly love, and it was "overwhelmingly lyrical" (Kroeber).

In China, the Libran period was occupied in large part by the Southern Sung dynasty (1127-1279). Libra likes to classify people and things—not in the minute, detailed, or labyrinthine way of Virgo, but in the way of dividing into classes, distinguishing as to types, sorting out and clarifying. Libra likes to determine clear relationships and functional proportions, using a philosophical logic to establish categorical or abstract groupings. In this sense the Classical Greeks were arch-Librans: Their drama was based on types, their thought on categories; their artists were classified not by the materials used but by the ideas conceived. To classify by subject is to distinguish by idea, to compose by ideal categories. During the Libran period in China, the extensive collection assembled by the emperor Hui-tsung (c. 1101-25) was arranged not chronologically but by subject.

The classical has been invoked in another sense by William Cohn, who noted that it was in the 13th century that the "classic era of Chinese landscape painting set in. Although the imagery was limited, there seems to have been no limit to the range of vision. To say much with little means was the highest aim." All this is Libran, and again sounds like the classical Greek: self-limitation, but with vision; much to say, but with economy of means.

When the Southern Sung dynasty began, there was a party strong at court which favored a vigorous opposition to the Tartars and recovery of the lost provinces of the Yellow River Valley and the north. The policy "advocated by this party, which was conservative and Confucian, was countered by a clique advocating compromise and conciliation. The latter won" and the Southern Sung settled down "to enjoy what was left them in the productive and beautiful lands of central and southern China. No city of the East could be better suited as the capital of a dynasty whose emperors were almost without exception devoted to cultivation of the spirit. Hang-chou on the banks of the beautiful Western Lake...was still the most beautiful city of China when Marco Polo visited it after its fall to the Mongols" (Sickman). The vigorous, conservative, and Confucian party represents the recurrent Chinese values which accord with Leo's rulership of the entire civilization. But that which was new during this period was clearly Libran: the taste for compromise and conciliation, the enjoyment of a modest or contained area, the selection of a beautiful site, the cultivation of the spirit, especially in the aesthetic sense.

The Libran spirit in China produced a highly classical institution: the Academy of Painting. "Academy" had been the name of a "district in the north-west of Athens in which there were several temples, a gymnasium, and" a park in which Plato conversed with pupils and taught his philosophy. "As time went on the people of Athens got used to calling the community of Plato's followers Academy too" (N. Pevsner). It was all very classical and Libran. Comparable values were expressed in China when, under the emperor Kao-tsung, the Academy of Painting was re-instituted, and "a large number of the painters who had practiced their art in the old days of Hui-tsung's Academy were reunited at Hang-chou so that, with a slight interruption, the tradition was continuous"—or, to sum up the situation: The "most active Imperial support of contemporary painting was the establishment of the Painting Academy" which played "so important a role during the 12th and 13th centuries" (Sickman).

This Academy was itself distinguished by qualities of precision, elegance, and high technical standards—which, when taken together, are Libran qualities. In the work of the Academy's painters, the distress and misery of mankind were consistently avoided as subjects for the artist, perhaps because they offended the sense of propriety—as is Libran. Also there was "a kind of ideal figure painting during the Southern Sung" that depicted "the activities of scholars at leisure" (*ibid.*)—the ideal, the figure as such, and leisure all are Libran. The typical landscape art of the period, except when immediately following the "old masters", was more spare and less detailed than during the previous (Virgo) period.

Of Sung pottery it has been observed that, "against the motifs and color contrasts of the preceding period, the form was now covered by a glaze of a single color, which was sufficient by itself, and decoration was reduced to delicate engraving" (Madeleine Paul-David). Simplicity, self-sufficiency, reduction, delicacy—all are Libran.

Southern Sung style has been described as extremely sophisticated (a Libran quality). At this time there is found the expression of an androgynous love transcending sexuality, as well as of the idea of "the pure distilled spirit of humanity" (Honour and Fleming): Both these qualities are Libran as well as reminiscent of Classical Greek culture. Overall, the art of Sung tends to be characterized as peaceful, brilliant, subtle, delicate, contemplative, refined. It would not be easy to compose a context of more purely Libran qualities.

The Scorpio Period, 1246 - 1425

There had been other plagues before, some terrible enough, but none so devastating as this one. It was called the Black Death (in reference to the darkened color of an expired victim). Black is a Scorpionic color, death a Scorpionic experience. Between 1347 and 1350, at the very heart of the Scorpio period, this plague spread from Constantinople to Ireland, destroying anywhere between one-quarter and three-quarters of the population (destruction itself is Scorpionic). It was a disaster unparalleled, and it spanned East and West.

While the Black Death connected Europe with the Middle East, the

Golden Horde connected Russia with the Far East. The entire Mongol and Tartar experience had a Scorpionic flavor, which was epitomized in the Golden Horde. A horde means a huge crowd bent on destruction, and the practice of the Horde was deliberate cruelty (also a Scorpionic bent), applied internally as well. De Riencourt refers to the "destructive fury and ferocity of the Mongols," whom William Cohn calls a people "of whose cruelty and rage for destruction the sources tell us again and again."

The period of power for the Horde ran from the early 13th to the mid-15th century,—that is, more or less contemporary with the Scorpio period. By 1227 Genghis Khan had conquered one of the largest land empires ever known (from Korea to the Crimea). In Russia it was from about the mid-13th century that the Horde attained its "highest development both in respect to international politics and to internal order" (Vernadsky). Yet in little more than a century the power of the Khans began to deteriorate. The resistance by the Horde's subjects and enemies was not impressive: rather it was a matter of internal strife and indecision. A great victory by the Russians in 1380 remained indecisive, for the Horde's authority continued. By the early 15th century, however, the Horde was torn by internal dissension. In 1405 it appeared before Moscow, stayed a month without attacking, and accepted a large sum to withdraw—at a time when troubles at home compelled the leader's return anyway. In the thirties and forties, Russia herself was torn by internal contests, but it is "striking that the Tartars could get so little profit out of this desperate struggle.... The Tartars secured only temporary or partial successes and in 1451, when they appeared before Moscow, they were beaten off at all points and disappeared in a single night, leaving all their heavy luggage behind them" (Bernard Pares). The Tartar kingdoms of Kazan and Crimea broke off from the Horde, which was now crumbling fast.

In China, a painter such as Ni Tsan (1301-74) would reject the Libran delicacy and lyricism of Sung style, in favor of "austere detachment and understatement without any atmospheric effects or displays of virtuosity" (Honour and Fleming); a 17th century Chinese painter found in such art a cold purity that overawes. Austerity, awesomeness, cold purity, and a disdain for ingratiating effects are all Scorpionic.

The Sagittarius Period, 1425 - 1604

Almost identical with these dates is the period of the great Western voyages of discovery (Sagittarius rules distant travel). From 1418 onward Henry the Navigator sent out, "almost annually, expeditions carefully prepared and ably conducted" (Langer). By 1433 the Portuguese doubled Cape Bojador; by 1445 Dinis Dias rounded Cape Verde; in 1487 Bartolomeu Dias rounded the Cape of Good Hope. The year 1497 saw the voyage of Vasco de Gama, 1500 that of Pedro Cabral, 1492-1502 those of Columbus, 1497 that of John Cabot, 1499 and 1501 those of Vespucci. Magellan's circumnavigation of the globe was accomplished 1519-22. In 1517 the Portuguese reached Canton and in 1542 they entered Japan (where they were followed by Francis Xavier: By 1600 there were 200,000 Christians in Japan, and more in India). In 1578 Francis Drake became the first Englishman to cross the Pacific. In 1606 Tahiti and the New Hebrides were discovered and, about the same time, Australia. But in 1610, Henry Hudson, having navigated his River and found his Bay, was cast adrift by mutineers, never to be seen again. The great Sagittarian distances had been covered, and the rest was a matter of filling in.

Meanwhile in Russia, Ivan the Great was crowned in 1462. Things flow freely and with abundance for the Sagittarian. Ivan was "one of those rich heirs of history who are able to use freely the resources left to them, and find that instead of exhausting them they have vastly increased them" (Pares). Examples include the relatively easy absorption of Novgorod with its immense territory, or the way in which Moscow acquired what was left of the principality of Yaroslavl through the voluntary submission of all its princes.

Expansiveness itself is a Sagittarian trait. The growth of Moscow (the heart of the Russian culture) during this period was phenomenal. Basil the Sightless prepared the absorption of Novgorod; in the second half of the 15th century Ivan the Great "succeeded in annexing almost all the hitherto independent cities and principalities of northern Russia" (Vernadsky). From a small area around Moscow city, Muscovy reached, by the late 16th century, to the Urals and the Caspian and, by the mid 17th century, beyond Archangel in the north, past the Urals in the east, past Pskov and Smolensk in the west, and south to Rostov and the Caspian sea. It was an expansion comparable only to that achieved by Western exploration and colonization during the same period.

In Chinese art, the Sagittarian period is entirely covered by the Ming dynasty (1368-1644). Compared to the economical style of Sung (Libran period), that of Ming has been characterized as opulent and vigorous, with rushing effects and a bold originality (Honor and Fleming); it was an art with growing Baroque tendencies (William Cohn). Baroque suggests extravagance, energy, and an extroverted comprehensiveness which, along with a rushing vigor and opulence, are Sagittarian qualities.

The Capricorn Period, 1604 - 1783

The Puritan is the very type of the Capricornian figure. The term Puritan was known already in the later 16th century, but it was not until the early 17th century that the Puritan stepped forth upon the world stage. In 1604 the Puritans sought to impose their program upon the state church (Hampton Court Conference), though they were disappointed by James I. In 1606 a branch of Puritan separatists called Pilgrims began to function; in 1607 they removed to the Netherlands. By 1620 they were able to proclaim a "Holy Commonwealth" in New England wherein, by 1640, thirty-three churches had been formed. And in England the period 1620-50 represented the height of power of the Puritan Revolution.

The end of the Puritan ascendancy did not mean the end of Capricornian tendencies, however, for they continued to be expressed in the practice and theory of disciplined government and authoritarian policy by Cromwell and Hobbes, Richelieu, Mazarin, and Colbert. Indeed government either by rigorous administration or by an authoritarian aristocracy was to obtain in all European countries, even Holland and England, until the 1770s and 1780s, when the climate changed to such an extent that people of all kinds in many countries were to welcome the American and the French revolutions.

Meanwhile, Puritanism was not confined to the northern countries. French Puritanism was established at Port-Royal after the death of Jansen in 1638; Port-Royal counted brilliant members from the Netherlands as well as France. Capricornian virtues are exemplified in the paintings of Philippe de Champaigne in the 17th century but are hardly less impressive in Chardin (d. 1779). Comparably, the Capricornian aspect of Spanish culture as exemplified in Ribera or Zurbaran (17th century) continued to appear in Melendez through the mid 18th century, only to be put aside by Goya. Throughout the entire period, social standing and prestige held Capricornian sway throughout Europe.

In Russia, a Capricornian development is visible from the early years of the Romanov dynasty (established 1613), when crystallization became as pronounced as in Europe. Capricornian severity and restriction came to a head in the treatment of the serfs. There had been a time limit of five years during which a fugitive peasant could be sought. In 1637 certain gentry obtained a ten-year limit; in 1642 this was extended to all gentry, and in 1646 the time limit itself was abolished. It had been "the one last hope of legal escape for the peasant" (Pares); thenceforward ownership was fixed by government registers and serfdom became hereditary (both serfdom and heredity are Capricornian).

Along with this went general restrictions of freedom, and a new state discipline with a high degree of central organization. "While the mass of the Russian people sank into serfdom, all the terms of liberty born in the last period likewise disappeared. The government, always strengthening the grip of the center, was everywhere opposed to local initiative." From its beginning the dynasty entered into a new process, "that of militarizing the internal government of Russia" (Pares). This internal militarization amounted to a severe Capricornian discipline.

Such a state of affairs obtained throughout most of the 18th century. In 1768 a commission entertaining the question of revising the serfdom laws was dissolved. Even the right of private property was extremely limited; for example, the owner of land had no right to fell oak—which was wanted for ships which were also government property—under threat of death. Only in the second half of the 18th century "were protests heard against this interference, and in 1782 Catherine II rescinded the limitations" (Vernadsky); this applied only to the nobility, but it represented the telling breakthrough.

The next phase was the extension of property rights to other classes of society; in 1801 the right to own land was granted to individuals of all classes except serfs. Such a recognition of rights was "evidence of the fact that new groups in Russian society were acquiring full civil status" (Vernadsky). Further evidence of more liberated and enlightened attitudes lies in the foundation of learned societies such as the Free Economic Society (1765), the Friendly Society of Learning (1782), the Society of Russian History and Antiquity (1805), the Society of Experimental Science (1805). With such interests, Russia, like the West, responded to the spirit of the new Aquarian period.

The Aquarius Period, 1783 - 1962

Following these promising beginnings in Russia came more solid expressions of the Aquarian period. By 1814 Alexander could say publicly to Lafayette, "With God's help, serfdom will be abolished in my reign." In 1817 the Society of Salvation was founded; it was kept secret from the public but was "well known to the Emperor, who was familiar with many of its members and even read memoirs which they wrote" (Pares). One or the dominating interests of the Society was emancipation of the serfs. Despite some reactionary turns, the groundwork was laid for the final Emancipation of 1861

In 1825 came the Decembrist Revolt, which was practically the first palace revolution that had anything like a political program. Although it was unsuccessful—mainly because Russia was not yet ready for its ideas—nevertheless it amounted "to the first act in the Russian Revolution" (Pares).

Aquarius, with its Uranian connection, rules revolution and upheaval, especially in the name of freedom and equality. In Europe such upheavals began in the 1780s. The American Revolution of 1776 was not wholly an Aquarian one. While it held to the self-evident truth that all men are created equal and have inalienable rights, its immediate aim was not actually to rebel against constituted authority but to restore the situation of relative independence which had obtained before the 1760s. Colonial America before the Stamp Act had enjoyed more freedom than any other people of the 18th century. The Declaration of Independence anticipated the coming Aquarian period; but the War for Independence was, at least in its origins, an attempt to restore a Capricornian status quo.

The Aquarian period began to show itself in force in the 1780s. In 1781 Uranus was discovered. The discovery of planets has its own history as a function of technology, but in this case the discovery is symptomatic of a new and revolutionary period, for it was the first planet discovered in recorded history, and its discovery was to revolutionize astronomy.

A brief résumé of Aquarian or Uranian developments during the 1780s may read as follows. In 1780 serfdom was abolished in Bohemia and Hungary, while manhood suffrage was proposed in England (by a duke). In 1781 Pestalozzi expounded his educational theory. The year 1782 saw the Irish Declaration of Rights. In 1783 the Besançcon Parlement demanded the calling of the French States-General; civil marriage and divorce were established in the Austrian Empire; the Montgolfiers launched their balloon. In 1784 came Jefferson's land ordinance (which was to be the basis for the Land Ordinance of 1787); Denmark abolished serfdom, and established a free press and educational reforms. In 1785 Campe pioneered educational reforms in Germany; James Madison's religious freedom act rescinded religious tests in Virginia.

The year 1786 saw the publication of Burns's poems (a man's a man for all that), the Shays Rebellion, and the Annapolis Convention which deliberated a Congress (to coin exclusive money; but the idea of a Congress was Aquarian, and bore fruit in the following years). In 1787 the United States Constitution was signed (it was a tight constitution but its aim was "to promote the general Welfare"); the Paris Parlement demanded the summoning of the States-General; the Edict of Versailles gave religious freedom and legal status to French Protestants. In 1788 the Paris Parlement presented a list of grievances; Louis XVI decided to summon the States-General for May 1789 (which transpired). In June 1789 the Tennis Court Oath was sworn; in July came revolution in Paris and the Declaration of the Rights of Man; in October, revolution followed in the Austrian Netherlands. If the American Revolution was not yet Aquarian, the French Revolution and those that followed emphatically were. Aquarius is the sign of friends and friendship, of wishes and programs, of freedom and hope: Liberty, Equality, Fraternity!

Electricity is associated with Aquarius. The entire second half of the 18th century was filled with electrical experiments, from the Leyden jar of 1746 to Franklin's *Experiments and Observations on*

Electricity of 1751-4 and Priestly's *History of Electricity* of 1767. By the end of the century, Galvani had postulated the existence of animal electricity (1791) with which Volta disagreed (in an essay of 1800), leading him to construct the voltaic pile, the "forerunner of the modern battery and the first source of a continuous electric current" (Langer). By 1821 the electric dynamo was developed, and in the following decade the electric motor and generator. The center of this period of electrical discovery and application lies in the 1780s.

The Aquarian period—the last sub-age of the Piscean Month—came to an end around 1962. At this time the Aquarian Month began with its first sub-age, the Piscean period. Much of the confusion about the appearance of both Piscean and Aquarian qualities in the 20th century must be attributed to this gratuitous conjunction of ages and sub-ages. We need to sort them out. The deeper and more pervasive qualities belong to the age, or astrological Month of around 2150 years. The more topical factors can be attributed to the sub-age or period lasting about 179 years.

A few symptoms of the present Piscean period in the new Aquarian age may be worth noting. Drugs, especially of a psychedelic nature, are Piscean. The emergence of a drug culture is associated with the 1960s. What we are looking for with drugs, as with other criteria, is not their availability or employment, but their appearance strongly in the mass consciousness. In 1958 Syanon was founded (to rehabilitate alcoholics and drug addicts); in 1964 methadone was found to help heroine addicts; 1965—Leary's *Psychedelic Reader*; 1967—the Beatles' "Lucy in the Sky with Diamonds"; 1968—Castaneda's *The Teachings of Don Juan*; in 1969, Woodstock drew 300,000, replete with drugs; during the whole period came new laws seeking to control drugs which previously were ignored, used without issue, or not well known.

With its penchant for cleanliness and redemption, Pisces can be very much concerned with poisons and their control. The year 1960 saw the cranberry scandal; in 1962 Rachel Carson's *The Silent Spring* warned of pesticides, and Diet-Rite Cola was the first sugar-free soft drink; 1970—the Poison Prevention Packaging Act; 1972—the Water Pollution Act; throughout the period Cyclamates, DDT, and other controversial products—not to mention industrial and atomic wastes—have been high in the public mind, in many countries.

Oil (vast seas of Piscean liquids) has played a world-wide role. In 1959, Eisenhower imposed quotas on U.S. oil imports to stimulate domestic production; 1967—the Torrey Canyon oil spill, the biggest of an increasisng number (in the age of the supertanker); 1960s—discovery of oil fields underseas (Piscean); OPEC emerges as a world power.

The killing of fish by pollution on an ever larger scale during this period connects the Piscean poison with the Piscean fish. But fish and fishing, especially internationally, have become public issues. For example: In 1964, Danish fishermen discovered major feeding grounds of salmon off Greenland, and fished them to the serious detriment of growing crops elsewhere; in 1967 came the Fisherman's Protective Act; in 1969 there was a massive fish kill on the Rhine; and, throughout the period, there was an increased concern with fish as food.

During this period there has also emerged a Piscean concern with prisons and their reform. Crime and punishment are Scorpionic concerns, but prison—in the sense of serve or suffer—and prison reform—in the sense of compassion—belong to Pisces. The list of prison riots is too long and too familiar to repeat; but under reforms we may note that in 1972 the U.S. Supreme Court found the death penalty unconstitutional as being cruel and unusual punishment; to this there has been some backlash, but the issue here is only that such things are currently of issue.

For the student of history a particular need is to distinguish clearly the ages (or Months) from the sub-ages (or periods) during our century when they twice overlap. That is, we must distinguish the Aquarian sub-age of the Piscean Age from the immediately succeeding Aquarian Age itself; and we must distinguish the Piscean sub-age of the new Aquarian Age from the more penetrating and persistent Piscean qualities which obtained throughout the entire preceding Month of more than two thousand years.

One last consideration. An astrological cusp is the area of transition from one period to another. Usually this is considered to amount to one degree of a sign, that is, 1/30 of the type of period in question, so that the cusp of an astrological Month (of 2150-2160 years) would be about 72 years. Therefore the cusp between the Piscean and Aquarian Months would consist of the 72 years surrounding the theoretical date of 1962. This means a transition period running from about 1926 to 1998. Lindbergh flew the Atlantic (conquest of, or by the air) in 1927. The year 1998 (or one of the two or three succeeding years) is given by many prophets, new and ancient, as a date of cosmic import. Such significance, however, lies beyond the scope of the present inquiry, and we must be content to observe the coinciding of these dates.

SELECTED BIBLIOGRAPHY

Adam, Major C.G.M. *Occult Astrology*. London, 1971.
Adams, Henry P. *The Life and Writings of Giambattista Vico*. New York, 1970.
Artz, Frederick B. *From the Renaissance to Romanticism*. Chicago, 1962.
Ault, Warren O. *Europe in the Middle Ages*. Boston, 1937.
Bagby, Philip. *Culture and History*. Berkeley, 1959.
Bazin, Germain. *The Baroque*. New York, 1968.
Berdyaev, Nicholas. *The Origin of Russian Communism*. Ann Arbor, 1960.
─────── *The Russian Idea*. Boston, 1962.
Blunt, Anthony. *Art and Architecture in France: 1500-1700*. London, 1953.
Brion, Marcel. *Art of the Romantic Era*. New York, 1966.
Bukofzer, Manfred F. *Music in the Baroque Era*. New York, 1947.
Burckhardt, Jacob. *The Civilization of the Renaissance in Italy*. New York, 1961.
Burn, A.R. *The Pelican History of Greece*. Baltimore, 1966.
Burns, Cecil D. *The First Europe*. New York, 1948.
Burrows, Millar. *The Dead Sea Scrolls*. New York, 1955.

Carcopino, Jerome. *Daily Life in Ancient Rome.* New Haven, 1964.
Carmichael, Joel. *A Cultural History of Russia.* New York, 1968.
Carpenter, Rhys. *The Esthetic Basis of Greek Art.* Bloomington, Ind., 1959.
———— *Greek Sculpture.* Chicago, 1960.
Carpenter, William S. *Foundations of Modern Jurisprudence.* New York, 1958.
Carter, Charles E.O. *The Principles of Astrology.* Wheaton, Ill., 1972.
Cary, Max, and Scullard, H.H. *A History of Rome down to the Reign of Constantine.* New York, 1975.
Chase, G.H., and Post, C.R. *A History of Sculpture.* New York, 1925.
Cirlot, J.E. *A Dictionary of Symbols.* New York, 1962.
Clark, Kenneth. *Civilization.* New York, 1969.
———— *Landscape into Art.* New York, 1979.
———— *Leonardo da Vinci.* Baltimore, 1971.
———— *The Nude.* Garden City, New York, 1956.
———— *The Romantic Rebellion.* New York, 1973.
Cohn, William. *Chinese Painting.* London, 1950
Conant, Kenneth J. *Carolingian and Romanesque Architecture.* London, 1959.
Cope, Lloyd. *Your Stars are Numbered.* Garden City, N.Y., 1971.
Coulborn, Rushton. *Feudalism in History.* Hamden, Conn., 1965
Cross, Frank M. *Qumran and the History of the Biblical Text.* Cambridge, Mass., 1975.
Cutter, Charles D. *Northern Painting.* New York, 1968.
Danilevsky, Nikolai. *Russia and Europe.* See Kohn, Hans.
Delacroix, Eugène. *Journal.* Translated by Walter Pach. New York, 1948.
Deschamps, Paul. *French Sculpture of the Romanesque Period.* New York, 1930.
DeVore, Nicholas. *Encyclopedia of Astrology.* New York, 1947.
Dimand, M.S. *A Handbook of Muhammadan Art.* New York, 1958.
Disselhoff, Hans D. *The Art of Ancient America.* New York, 1961.

Dudley, Donald R. *The Civilization of Rome.* New York, 1962.
Dvorak, Max. *Idealism and Naturalism in Gothic Art.* Notre Dame, 1967.
Einstein, Alfred. *A Short History of Music.* New York, 1954.
Encyclopedia of World Art. 15 v. New York, 1959-68.
Epstein, Isidore. *Judaism.* Baltimore, 1970.
Ferguson, Wallace K. *Renaissance Studies.* New York, 1963.
Ferrero, Guglielmo. *Ancient Rome and Modern America.* New York, 1914.
Finley, M.I. *The Ancient Greeks.* New York, 1964.
———— *Early Greece.* New York, 1970.
Fleming, John; Honour, Hugh; and Pevsner, Nikolaus. *The Penguin Dictionary of Architecture.* Baltimore, 1976.
Focillon, Henri. *The Art of the West in the Middle Ages.* 2 v. New York, 1969.
Frankl, Paul. *Gothic Architecture.* Baltimore, 1962.
———— *Principles of Architectural History,* Cambridge, Mass., 1968.
Friedell, Egon. *A Cultural History of the Modern Age.* 3v. New York, 1930-32
Friedländer, Max J. *Landscape, Portrait, Still-Life.* New York. 1963.
———— *On Art and Connoisseurship.* Boston, 1942.
Garraty, John A., and Gay, Peter, editors. *The Columbia History of the World.* New York, 1972.
Goldwater, Robert. *Symbolism.* London, 1979.
Grant, Michael. *The World of Rome.* New York, 1960.
Grodecki, Louis. *Gothic Architecture.* New York, 1977.
Hagen, Oscar. *Art Epochs and Their Leaders.* New York, 1927.
Hall, Manly P. *Astrological Keywords.* Los Angeles, 1966.
Hamilton, George Heard. *19th and 20th Century Art.* New York, 1970.
Hanfmann, George M.A. *Roman Art.* New York, 1975.
Harcave, Sidney S. *Russia, a History.* Philadelphia, 1968.
Hartt, Frederick. *History of Italian Renaissance Art.* New York, 1979.
Hauser, Arnold. *The Social History of Art.* 2 v. London, 1951.

Hayes, Carlton, J.H. *A Political and Cultural History of Modern Europe.* 2 v. New York, 1932-6.
Held, Julius S., and Posner, Donald. *17th and 18th Century Art.* New York, 1979.
Hibbard, Howard. *Michelangelo.* New York, 1974.
Hodin, J.P. *The Dilemma of Being Modern.* New York, 1959.
Hone, Margaret E. *The Modern Textbook of Astrology.* London, 1951.
Honour, Hugh, and Fleming, John. *The Visual Arts.* Englewood Cliffs, N.J., 1981.
Houston, Mary G. *Medieval Costume in England and France.* London, 1939.
Hubert, Jean. *The Carolingian Renaissance.* London, 1970.
Hucker, Charles O. *China's Imperial Past.* Stanford, 1975.
Huizinga, Johan. *The Waning of the Middle Ages.* New York, 1954.
Hunnisett, R.F. *The Medieval Coroner.* Cambridge, England. 1962.
Janson, H.W. *History of Art.* New York, 1970.
Javanne, Faith, and Bunker, Dusty. *Numerology and the Divine Triangle.* Rockport, Mass., 1979.
Jocelyn, John. *Meditations on the Signs of the Zodiac.* Blauvelt, N.Y., 1970.
Kalnein, W.G. and Levey, M. *Art and Architecture of the Eighteenth Century in France.* Harmondsworth, 1972.
Kidson, Peter. *The Medieval World.* London, 1967.
Kitto, H.D.F. *The Greeks.* Baltimore, 1957.
Kluckhohn, Clyde. *Mirror for Man.* New York, 1960.
Kohn, Hans, ed. *The Mind of Modern Russia.* New York, 1955.
Kroeber, A.L. *Configurations of Culture Growth.* Berkeley, 1969.
Lang, Paul Henry. *Music in Western Civilization.* New York, 1941.
Langer, William L. *An Encyclopedia of World History.* Boston, 1972.
Lavrin, Janko. *An Introduction to the Russian Novel.* London, 1942.
Levey, Michael. *High Renaissance.* Baltimore, 1975.

_____ *Rococo to Revolution.* New York, 1966.
Licht, Fred. *Goya: the Origins of the Modern Temper in Art.* New York, 1979.
Lindstrom, Theis. *A Concise History of Russian Literature.* New York, 1966.
Linné, Sigvald. *Treasures of Mexican Art.* Stockholm, 1956.
Lopez, Robert S. *The Birth of Europe.* New York, 1967.
Lowry, Bates. *Renaissance Architecture.* New York, 1965.
Lucie-Smith, Edward. *A Concise History of French Painting.* New York, 1971.
Mackay, Ernest J.H. *Early Indus Civilizations.* London, 1948.
Mahler, Jane Gaston. See Upjohn, *et al.*
Marshall, John H. *Mohenjo-daro and the Indus Civilization.* 3 v. London, 1931.
Martin, John Rupert. *Baroque.* New York, 1971.
Martindale, Andrew. *The Rise of the Artist.* London, 1972.
McClain, Ernest G. *The Myth of Invariance.* New York, 1976.
Meier-Graefe, Julius. *Dostoevsky.* New York, 1928.
Melko, Matthew. *The Nature of Civilizations.* Boston, 1969.
Menschutkin, Boris. *Russia's Lomonosov.* Princeton, 1952.
Meyer, Michael R. *A Handbook for the Humanistic Astrologer.* Garden City, N.Y., 1974.
Miliukov, Paul. *Outlines of Russian Culture.* 3 v. New York, 1960.
Muchnic, Helen. *An Introduction to Russian Literature.* Garden City, N.Y., 1947.
Muller, Herbert J. *The Loom of History.* New York, 1958.
Needham, Joseph. "The Elixir Concept and Chemical Medicine in East and West." *The Comparative Civilizations Bulletin,* V, No. 4.
Novotny, Fritz. "The Reaction against Impressionism." In *Studies in Western Art,* IV. Princeton, 1963.
The Oxford Companion to Art. Oxford, 1970.
Pagan, Isabelle M. *From Pioneer to Poet.* London, 1969.
Panofsky, Erwin. *Early Netherlandish Painting.* 2 v. New York, 1971.
_____ *Renaissance and Renascences in Western Art.* New York, 1969.

_____ *Scholasticism and Gothic Architecture.* New York, 1968.
Pares, Bernard. *A History of Russia.* New York, 1948.
Parker, Else. *Astrology and its Practical Application.* Amsterdam, n.d.
Parkinson, C.N. *East and West.* Boston, 1963.
Pevsner, Nikolaus. *Academies of Art.* New York, 1973.
_____ *An Outline of European Architecture.* Baltimore, 1963.
Piggott, Stuart. *Prehistoric India to 1000 B.C.* Baltimore, 1950.
Pollitt, J.J. *Art and Experience in Classical Greece.* London, 1972.
Quigley, Carroll. *The Evolution of Civilizations.* New York, 1961.
Randall, Henry J. *The Creative Centuries.* London, 1945.
Read, Herbert. *The Meaning of Art.* Baltimore, 1963.
Reid, Vera M. *Towards Aquarius.* New York, 1969.
Rice, David Talbot. *Byzantine Art.* Baltimore, 1954.
_____ *Islamic Art.* New York, 1965.
Riencourt, Amaury de. *The Soul of China.* New York, 1958.
_____ *The Soul of India.* New York, 1960.
Robinson, Lytle. *Edgar Cayce's Story of the Origin and Destiny of Man.* New York, 1972.
Rosenberg, Jakob; Slive, Seymour; and ter Kuile, E.H. *Dutch Art and Architecture.* Baltimore, 1972.
Rosenberg, Jakob. *Great Draughtsmen from Pisanello to Picasso.* Cambridge, Mass., 1959.
Rosenblum, Robert. *Modern Painting and the Northern Romantic Tradition.* New York, 1975.
_____ *Transformation in Late Eighteenth Century Art.* Princeton, 1967.
Rostovtzeff, M. *Rome.* Oxford, 1960.
Rowland, Benjamin. *The Art and Architecture of India.* London, 1953.
Rudhyar, Dane. *The Astrology of Personality.* Garden City, N.Y., 1970.
_____ *Birth Patterns for a New Humanity.* Servire-Wassenaar, Netherlands, 1969.
Runciman, S. *Byzantine Style and Civilization.* Harmondsworth, 1975.

Saalman, Howard. *Medieval Architecture*, New York, 1962.
Sachs, Curt. *The Commonwealth of Art*. New York, 1946.
―――― *World History of the Dance*. New York, 1963.
Salvini, Roberto. *Medieval Sculpture*. New York, 1967.
Schäfer, H. *Principles of Egyptian Art*. Oxford, 1974.
Schreiber, Hermann. *Teuton and Slav*. New York, 1965.
Schuré, Edouard. *From Sphinx to Christ*. Blauvelt, N.Y., 1970.
Sédillot, René. *An Outline of French History*. New York, 1952.
Seltzer, Thomas. *Best Russian Short Stories*. New York, 1917.
Sewall, John I. *A History of Western Art*. New York, 1953.
Sickman, Laurence, and Soper, Alexander. *The Art and Architecture of China*. Baltimore, 1956.
Spector, Ivar. *An Introduction to Russian History and Culture*. Princeton, 1969.
Spengler, Oswald. *The Decline of the West*. 2 v. New York, 1929.
Stoddard, Theodore L. *The Rising Tide of Color*. New York, 1920.
Stokes, Adrian. *The Quattro Centro*. New York, 1968.
Strong, Donald. *Roman Art*. Harmondsworth, 1976.
Swann, Peter C. *Art of China, Korea, and Japan*. New York, 1963.
Thompson, James Westfall. *The Middle Ages*. 2 v. New York, 1931.
Tietze, Hans. *Tintoretto*. London, 1948.
Tompkins, Stuart Ramsay. *The Russian Mind*. Norman, Okl., 1953.
Toynbee, Arnold. *Civilization on Trial*. New York, 1959.
Trager, James, ed. *The People's Chronology*. New York, 1979.
Trever, John C. *The Dead Sea Scrolls*. Grand Rapids, 1977.
Turner, Richard. *The Vision of Landscape in Renaissance Italy*. Princeton, 1966.
Upjohn, Everard M.; Wingert, Paul S.; and Mahler, Jane Gaston. *History of World Art*. New York, 1949.
Venturi, Lionello. *Four Steps toward Modern Art*. New York, 1965.
Vermès, Géza. *The Dead Sea Scrolls: Qumran in Perspective*. Cleveland, 1978.
Vernadsky, George. *A History of Russia*. New York, 1944.
Vriezen, Theodore C. *The Religion of Ancient Israel*. Philadelphia, 1967.

Walissewski, K. *A History of Russian Literature*. New York, 1915.
Walsh, J.J. *The Thirteenth, Greatest of Centuries*. New York, 1924.
Watson, William. *Style in the Arts of China*. Baltimore, 1974.
Weidlé, Wladimir. *Russia: Absent and Present*. New York, 1961.
Wells, H.G. *The Outline of History*. New York, 1931.
Wescott, Roger W. "The Enumeration of Civilizations." *History and Theory*, IX, No. 1.
Whinney, Margaret. *Early Flemish Painting*. New York, 1968.
White, John. *The Birth and Rebirth of Pictorial Space*. London, 1967.
Wiora, Walter. *The Four Ages of Music*. New York, 1965.
Wittkower, Rudolph. *Architectural Principles in the Age of Humanism*. New York, 1965.
Wolff, Philippe. *The Cultural Awakening*. New York, 1968.
Wölfflin, Heinrich. *Classic Art*. New York, 1953.
―――― *Renaissance and Baroque*. Ithaca, N.Y., 1968.
Zarnecki, George. *Art of the Medieval World*. Englewood Cliffs, N.J., 1975.

Index

Abelard, 31-2
Absolutism, 43-4
Addison, 49, 150
Air sign: *see* Signs, zodiacal
Alchemy, 99
Alfred the Great, 136-7, 187
Aquarius in Russian culture, 118-22; dance, 119; descriptive qualities, 119-22; literature, 119-20; revolution, 120-1
Aries in African culture, 62-4; art, 62; dance, 63; descriptive qualities, 63
Astrological Month, *see* Periods

Baptism, 96
Baroque, 17-19, 146-8
Blake, William, 23
Boethius, 159-60
Burns, Robert, 23, 51, 196
Byzantine, 60-1, 67, 98, 100, 102, 163, 181-2

Cancer in Egyptian culture, 69-73; architecture, 72; art, 71-3; descriptive qualities, 73
Capricorn in Western culture, 106-18; architecture, 109, 113, 116; art, 110, 118; descriptive qualities, 107, 114-18; music, 108, 117-18; science, 110-14
Cardinal sign, *see* Signs, zodiacal
Carolingian, 137-8, 164, 183, 187
Cayce, Edgar: on Scorpio, 97; on Russia, 122
Centuries by astrological sign: 11th, Capricorn, 29-31; 12th, Sagittarius, 31-3; 13th, Scorpio, 33-6; 14th, Libra, 36-8; 15th, Virgo, 38-40; 16th, Leo, 41-4; 17th, Cancer, 44-7; 18th, Gemini, 47-51; 19th, Taurus, 51-4; 20th, Aries, 54-6
Cézanne, 26, 115
Christianity, 96, 159, 166, 181
Constable, John, 151

Constantine, 166, 179
Coroners (in 13th century), 35
Crusades, 11, 32, 79, 188
Cubism, 26, 54
Cusp, astrological, 29, 198-9

David, Jacques-Louis, 21-3, 51
Degas, 26
Delacroix, 51, 84, 92
Deuteronomic reformation, 133-4
Dickens, Charles, 51-3
Dostoevsky, 121, 124-7
Dürer, 17, 38, 41-2, 113

Earth sign, *see* Signs, zodiacal
Enlightenment, 50
Essenes, 135-6, 179
Evolutionary epochs, 2, 9, 124, 129, 135; African, 58; Ancient American, 61; Babylonian, 58, 66; Chinese, 59; Classical, 2, 59, 79, 131, 159; Egyptian, 58, 66; Indian, 59; Indus Valley, 58; Levantine, 60, 131, 133, 135, 160, 167; Russian, 123, 129, 152-3; Western, 9, 61, 106, 123, 133
Expressionism, 25, 54-5
Eyck, Jan van, 39

Fire sign, *see* Signs, zodiacal
Fixed sign, *see* Signs, zodiacal

Gemini in Babylonian culture, 66-8; architecture, 67; art, 67-8; descriptive qualities, 68
Germinative epoch, 1, 3, 172; Classical, 131; Levantine, 131; Russian, 132; Western, 130-1
Gogh, Vincent van, 24-5, 51
Gogol, 154-5
Golden Horde, 161, 191

Gothic, 11, 142-3; Early, 11, 142; High, 11-12, 143-4; Late, 12, 143-4
Goya, 21-2, 51
Gregory I, Pope, 157-8
Gregory VII, Pope, 30-31

Hadrian, 80
Hellenistic style, 80

Impressionism, 23-5, 151
Inca, 103
Inquisition, 33
Islam, 96-7, 99, 167
Ivan the Great, 161-2, 192
Ivan the Terrible, 161, 163

Judaism, 96-7
Jupiter, 31, 70, 103, 170, 172
Justinian, 182

Karamzin, 152-3, 155

Leo in Chinese culture, 73-6; architecture, 75; art, 75; descriptive qualities, 74-5
Leonardo da Vinci, 16-17, 39-42
Libra in Classical culture, 79-94; architecture, 79-80, 83-4, 89, 93; art, 80-1, 88, 92-4; descriptive qualities, 85, 90-1
Lomonosov, 139

Major culture (definition), 1, 61
Manet, 151
Mars, 54-5, 70
Materialism, 52-3
Maya, 102-3, 105-6
Mercury, 40, 70
Michelangelo, 14, 40, 42, 146-8
Monet, 23, 26
Moon, 45-6, 70, 88, 172

Index

Mutable sign, see Signs, zodiacal

Nietzsche, 55, 125
Novgorod, 161-2
Numbers, 70, 72, 74, 88-9, 103, 108, 170-3

Periods of Astrological Month: Aquarius, 195-9; Aries, 179-80; Cancer, 181-2; Capricorn, 193-5; Leo, 183-4; Libra, 188-90; Pisces, 178-9; Sagittarius, 192-3; Scorpio, 190-1; Taurus, 180-1; Virgo, 186-8
Peru, 103, 105-6
Pluto, 70, 170, 173
Puritans, 193
Pushkin, 124, 139, 152, 154-5
Pyramids (Egyptian and Ancient American), 104-5

Radischev, 153
Raphael, xiv, 41-2
Realism, 51-2; Russian, 155
Redundant epoch, 2-5, 172-3
Rembrandt, 45, 113, 117
Renaissance, xiv, 13-15, 145; Early, 12, 15; High, 15-17, 146
Revolution, 120-1, 127-8, 195-6
Rococo, 19-20, 148-9
Romanesque, 10, 142-3; Early, 140-1; High, 11, 141
Romanticism, 51, 150-1

Sagittarius in Ancient American culture, 102-6; architecture, 104-6; art, 104, 106; descriptive qualities, 104-6
Saturn, 29, 31, 70, 108, 115, 170-1
Scorpio in Levantine culture, 95-102; architecture, 100-1; art, 96, 98; descriptive qualities, 98-9; religion, 96-8
Seurat, 23, 26
Signs, zodiacal: air, 50, 67, 83-4, 89, 94, 118, 123; cardinal, 31, 84, 107, 181; earth, 94, 107, 123; fire, 54, 103, 179; fixed, 107, 180; mutable, 49, 107; water, 67, 69, 83, 95-6, 119
Sluter, Claus, 13-15
Spengler, xiv, 3, 97, 115, 125
Sun, 42, 70, 74-5, 122, 164, 170
Surrealism, 25, 55
Symbolism, 25

Taurus in Indus Valley culture, 64-6; art, 64, 66; descriptive qualities, 64-5
Tintoretto, 18, 41
Titian, 41-2, 147
Tolstoy, 124-7
Trajan, 80
Turgenev, 124-5, 155
Turner, 151

Ulfilas, Bishop, 133
Uranus, 70, 119, 195-6

Velasquez, 45-6
Venus, 36, 70, 88
Vikings (Northmen), 79, 172
Virgo in Indian culture, 76-9; architecture, 78; art, 77-8; descriptive qualities, 78

Water sign, see Signs, zodiacal
William the Conqueror, 29-30

Zodiac: see Signs, zodiacal
Zoroastrian, 96, 98